Communications
in Computer and Information Science 1680

More information about this series at https://link.springer.com/bookseries/7899

Chunhua Su · Kouichi Sakurai (Eds.)

Science of Cyber Security - SciSec 2022 Workshops

AI-CryptoSec, TA-BC-NFT, and MathSci-Qsafe 2022
Matsue, Japan, August 10–12, 2022
Revised Selected Papers

 Springer

Editors
Chunhua Su (ID)
University of Aizu
Aizuwakamatsu, Fukushima, Japan

Kouichi Sakurai
Kyushu University
Fukuoka, Fukuoka, Japan

ISSN 1865-0929   ISSN 1865-0937 (electronic)
Communications in Computer and Information Science
ISBN 978-981-19-7768-8   ISBN 978-981-19-7769-5 (eBook)
https://doi.org/10.1007/978-981-19-7769-5

This Springer imprint is published by the registered company Springer Nature Singapore Pte Ltd.
The registered company address is: 152 Beach Road, #21-01/04 Gateway East, Singapore 189721, Singapore

Preface

This volume contains the papers presented at three parallel workshops in the 4th International Conference on Science of Cyber Security (SciSec 2022), which was held during August 10–12, 2022, in Matsue, Shimane. There were 30 submissions, 11 of them recommended by the main SciSec 2022 Program Committee. Each submission was reviewed by at least two, and on average 2.3, workshop Program Committee members in a single-blind review process. The committees decided to accept 15 papers and three posters.

The workshops also included two invited talks: Hiroaki Maeshima's "Dataset-based robustness against adversarial examples" and Shingo Fujimoto's "The smart contract-based token economy in the NFT era". We would like to thank Kunibiki Messe for being our sponsor.

August 2022

Chunhua Su
Kouichi Sakurai
Guenevere Chen
Weizhi Meng
Akira Otsuka

Organization

AI Crypto and Security Workshop (AI-CryptoSec)

General Chair

Akira Otsuka   Institute of Information Security, Japan

Program Co-chairs

Weizhi Meng   Technical University of Denmark, Denmark
Chunhua Su   University of Aizu, Japan

Technical Program Committee

Alessandro Brighente   University of Padua, Italy
Konstantinos Chalkias   Meta, USA
Dieter Gollmann   Hamburg University of Technology, Germany
Georgios Kambourakis   University of the Aegean, Greece
Mario Larangeira   Tokyo Institute of Technology/IOHK, Japan
Wenjuan Li   The Hong Kong Polytechnic University, China
Jiqiang Lu   Beihang University, China
Javier Parra Arnau   Universitat Politecnica de Catalunya, Spain
Claudio Juan   Universitat Zurich, Switzerland
Kouichi Sakurai   Kyushu University, Japan
Andreas Veneris   University of Toronto, Canada

Theory and Application of Blockchain and NFT Workshop (TA-BC-NFT)

General Chair

Kouichi Sakurai   Kyushu University, Japan

Program Co-chairs

Akira Otsuka   Institute of Information Security, Japan
Guenevere Chen   University of Texas at San Antonio, USA

Technical Program Committee

Habtamu Abie   Norwegian Computing Center, Norway
Noseong Park   George Mason University, USA

Chunhua Su	University of Aizu, Japan
Jia Xu	Nanjing University of Posts and Telecommunications, China
Xiaofan Yang	Chongqing University, China
Jeong Hyun Yi	Soongsil University, South Korea
James Zheng	Macquarie University, Australia

Mathematical Science of Quantum Safety and its Application Workshop (MathSci-Qsafe)

General Chair

Yasuyuki Kachi	University of Aizu, Japan

Program Co-chairs

Kouichi Sakurai	Kyushu University, Japan
Chunhua Su	University of Aizu, Japan

Technical Program Committee

Alessandro Brighente	University of Padua, Italy
Konstantinos Chalkias	Meta, USA
Dieter Gollmann	Hamburg University of Technology, Germany
Hao Wang	Shandong Normal University, China
Qianhong Wu	Beihang University, China
Peng Xu	Huazhong University of Science and Technology, China
Sherman Chow	Chinese University of Hong Kong, China

Additional Reviewers

Jin, Shuyuan	Tian, Youliang
Li, Peng	Wang, Weizheng
Lian, Zhuotao	Wang, Ziyue
Qiu, Chen	Ye, Guang
Shorna, Sabira Khanam	

Contents

Mathematical Science of Quantum Safety and its Application Workshop (MathSci-Qsafe)

Posters

AI Crypto and Security Workshop (AI-CryptoSec)

Image Data Recoverability Against Data Collaboration and Its Countermeasure

Takaya Yamazoe, Hiromi Yamashiro$^{(\boxtimes)}$, Kazumasa Omote, Akira Imakura, and Tetsuya Sakurai

University of Tsukuba, 1-1-1, Tennodai, Tsukuba, Ibaraki 305-8577, Japan
s2220544@s.tsukuba.ac.jp

Abstract. The development machine learning and related techniques has accelerated the use of data in a variety of fields, including medicine, finance, and advertising. Because the amount of data is increasing extremely rapidly, it is often necessary to integrate data from multiple organizations for analysis. Accordingly, distributed data analysis methods that enable data analysis while protecting the privacy of the data are being prioritized. A method called data collaboration, in which data is dimensionally reduced and shared as an intermediate representation, has been proposed as a non-model-sharing learning method. In this paper, we propose an attack model based on a generative adversarial network (GAN) to evaluate the security of this new framework. We also propose a method to improve the security of data collaboration. In addition, we experimentally evaluated the risk of reconstructing the original data from the intermediate representation and determine the effect of privacy protection using an attack model.

Keywords: Privacy · Dimensionality reduction · GAN

1 Introduction

In recent years, the spread of web services and mobile devices has made it possible to collect data on a large scale, and advanced data analysis has become possible using machine learning and other techniques. It is possible to obtain even more value from data by sharing it across institutions and service domains. However, one of the key issues is the risk of private data being exposed. Methods that enable data analysis while protecting the privacy of the data are being developed to reduce the privacy risks associated with data publication and sharing.

Anonymization methods have been proposed to reduce the risk of the re-identification of records through data processing [1,2], and computational methods have been proposed to keep the data encrypted. However, both of these methods are problematic because the dimensions [3] and computational costs involved decrease their utility. Therefore, as a framework for non-model sharing, the method shown in Fig. 1, called data collaboration, has been receiving attention [4,5].

C. Su and K. Sakurai (Eds.): SciSec 2022 Workshops, CCIS 1680, pp. 3–15, 2022.
https://doi.org/10.1007/978-981-19-7769-5_1

Data collaboration enables the utilization of data while protecting privacy by dimensionally reducing it and sharing it as an intermediate representation, removing the effects of dimensionality and the constraints of computational cost. However, the security of intermediate representations is not clear. In this study, we consider the risk that an attacker who does not know the dimensionality reduction algorithm can infer the original data from the intermediate representation. In addition, we suggest measures that data providers can implement to address these risks.

The contributions of this study are as follows.

– We propose a framework for estimating the original data from intermediate representations constructed through data collaboration using a generative adversarial network (GAN). Furthermore, an experimental evaluation using handwritten text data shows that there is a risk of reconstructing the original data from the intermediate representation.
– We propose a method to improve the security of data collaboration by applying privacy measures, namely ϵ-DR privacy [14] to the intermediate representations. We evaluated the effectiveness of this privacy countermeasure in experiments using the proposed attack model.
– We evaluate the relationship between security and data utility for dimensionality reduction algorithms, and show that there is a tradeoff between security and utility.

2   Preliminaries

2.1   Data Collaboration

Data collaboration [4,5] is a method for sharing data collected by multiple institutions. Each institution $i(i = 1, ..., n)$ that collects data X_i compresses its own data X_i with its own dimensionality reduction algorithm f_i. In addition to these data, each organization has common anchor data X^{anc} and shares X_i^{anc} compressed by each institution's dimensionality reduction algorithm f_i. The data analyst generates a projection G_i for n data collection agencies to produce data for analysis based on the anchor data X_i^{anc} compressed by each agency. Using this G_i, the data X_i collected at each institution is projected onto the analysis data, and $\tilde{X}_i$ is obtained for the n data collection institutions. Because $\tilde{X}$ can be handled in the same way as the original data X, $\tilde{X}$ can be used to develop the algorithms. It is also assumed that X will never be reconstructed from $\tilde{X}$ because the algorithm f used for dimensionality reduction is not shared by the institutions.

Data collaboration is a method that can both protect the privacy of the data and make use of it. Because there are no restrictions on the number of computation or algorithms that can be used, it can significantly contribute to the development of data utilization in the future. To investigate the security of data collaboration, we evaluate the possibility of reconstructing the original data from the intermediate representations and propose a method to increase the security.

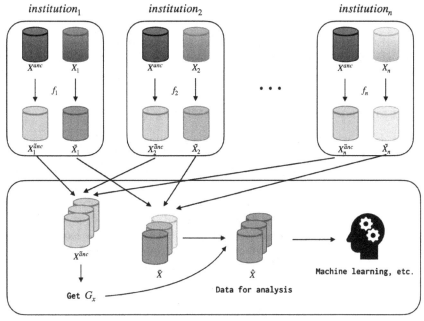

Fig. 1. Diagram of data collaboration.

2.2 Generative Adversarial Network (GAN)

A GAN is a deep learning model for estimating the generative distribution of a given data sample [6]. The advantage of GAN is its ability to accurately estimate the generative distribution of data samples. It can also estimate the generative distribution of complex high-dimensional space images. GAN is an algorithm for learning two models: a generator $\mathcal{G}$ and discriminator $\mathcal{D}$, formulated as a min-max game. The generator generates fake data $\mathcal{G}(z)$ from random noise z. The discriminator $\mathcal{D}$ determines whether the given data are the true data or the fake data produced by the generator. By training both at the same time, the generator $\mathcal{G}$ will eventually produce data that is identical to the true data. Because of their efficacy GANs have been actively studied in recent years. As a result, derived models such as DC-GAN [7] combined with convolutional neural (CNN) networks and cGAN [8] and AnoGAN [9] which can all efficiently learn GAN using class labels have been proposed.

In this study, we reconstruct the original image data used in the data collaboration by employing the features of the GAN to estimate the generation distribution of a given data sample.

3   Related Works

In this section, we introduce a study on reconstructing training data for machine learning models using GAN and a privacy protection method for dimensionality reduction algorithms.

3.1   Reconstruction of Training Data Using GAN

In recent years, with the development of the machine learning, various methods using deep learning have been proposed in the fields of image and natural language processing. In the field of imaging, deep learning has achieved remarkable results for tasks such as image classification, object detection, and face recognition. As a result, models trained with deep learning are sometimes released to the public. For example, a model may be shared in the cloud or a model may be installed and used on a local device. In recent years, there have been concerns about the risk of personal information disclosure from such public models [10,11]. Kusano et al. [12] proposed a classifier-to-generator (C2G) attack model that uses GAN to estimate the image used to train the model from a published image classification model. Because the classification model contained much less information than the data samples used for training, it was difficult to estimate the information in the training data from the classification model. However, they solved this problem by using the GAN of the generative model and data collected from an external source, which was different from the training data.

3.2   DP-PCA

Differential privacy is a privacy mechanism that can protect the original data even if the output or the algorithm itself is made public. Jiang et al. proposed principal component analysis with differential privacy (DP-PCA) [13] as a method for applying apply differential privacy to dimensionality reduction algorithms. PCA satisfies differential privacy by adding noise defined as

$$\hat{A} = A + W(W\ W_d(d+1, C_w)) \tag{1}$$

to the covariance matrix A where W_d is the Wishart distribution, d is the number of dimensions in the data, and C_w is a matrix with d identical eigenvalues $\frac{3}{2n\epsilon}$. The mechanism using the Wishart distribution is less noisy than the mechanism using the Laplace distribution and has higher usefulness. The mechanism based on the Wishart distribution is less noisy than the mechanism based on the Laplace distribution, making it possible to implement a highly useful privacy-preserving dimensionality reduction algorithm.

3.3 ϵ-DR Privacy

Privacy-preserving methods using differential privacy have challenges in terms of data availability and performance degradation relative to the number of queries.

To solve this problem, Nguyen et al. proposed a new privacy protection method called ϵ-DR privacy [14] for dimensionality reduction algorithms. They proposed a method to generate dimensionality reduction data to train machine learning models and to prevent the attacker from estimating the original data. The constraints imposed on the dimensionality reduction algorithm were:

$$E[\|dist(x, R(F(x))\|] > \epsilon \qquad (2)$$

where $F(\cdot)$ is the dimensionality reduction algorithm and $R(\cdot)$ is its inverse map. The ϵ-DR privacy algorithm aims to maximize the distance between the original data and the reconstructed data to protect the privacy of the data owner. They also proposed a framework, called autoencoder generative adversarial nets based dimension reduction privacy (AutoGAN-DRP), to generate data that satisfies ϵ-DR privacy. This method assumes that the attacker will use the auto encoder to reconstruct the original data from the low-dimensional data. Therefore, AutoGAN-DRP generates data that satisfy ϵ-DR privacy by inducing the data reconstructed by the auto encoder to form the desired distribution when the low-dimensional data is generated by the GAN.

4 Proposed Methods

In this section, to evaluate the security of data collaboration, we introduce a framework for reconstructing the original data from intermediate representations using GAN and a method for improving the security of data collaboration.

4.1 Assumptions of Attackers

We assume that the attacker is a person who has access to the intermediate representation of the data collaboration and the anchor data. The attacker does not need to know the dimensionality reduction algorithm used to generate the intermediate representation, nor the original data. The attacker collects external data, which is different from the original data and uses it to estimate the original data.

4.2 Estimating the Original Data Using GAN

We propose an attack model that estimates the original data from an intermediate representation of the data collaboration. An overview of the proposed attack model is shown in Fig. 2. This method is inspired by the Kusano et al. C2G attack model, which was designed to reconstruct training data from machine learning models. The attack model can be split into two phases. In phase 1, the attacker labels the data collected externally. Because the labels of the externally collected data are different from those of the original data, the attacker uses a classification model learned from the original data to label the external data. As the attacker has only intermediate representations of the original data, we mix the intermediate representations of the original data with the intermediate representations of the external data generated by the attacker to perform data collaboration and train the classification model. When labeling the external data, the attacker uses the confidence level of the classification model to select the data to be used as training data for the generative model. In phase 2, the GAN is trained using the data labeled in Phase 1. At this time, the attacker uses the intermediate representation of the original data as the initial value of the generative model. Using the learned generative model, the attacker estimates the original data from the intermediate representation of the data collaboration.

Specifically, this attack model uses the following procedure to estimate the original data from intermediate representations. The attacker uses as input the intermediate representation $\tilde{X}_i = f_i(X_i) \in \mathbf{R}^{n_i \times \tilde{m}_i}$ of each institution i, the intermediate representation $\tilde{X}_i^{anc}$ of the anchor data, the anchor data X^{anc}, and the external data $X_{ex} \in \mathbf{R}^{n_{ex} \times m}$. Here, f_i is the dimensionality reduction algorithm used by each institution i, and the attacker does not need any knowledge of this algorithm.

1. The attacker applies a unique dimensionality reduction algorithm f_{ex} to the external data X_{ex} and anchor data X^{anc} to obtain the intermediate representations $\tilde{X}_{ex}$ and $\tilde{X}_{ex}^{anc}$.
2. The attacker uses a data collaboration algorithm to generate $G_1, ..., G_n, G_{ex}$ from an intermediate representation $\tilde{X}_1^{anc}, ..., \tilde{X}_n^{anc}, \tilde{X}_{ex}^{anc}$ of the anchor data.
3. The attacker uses $G_1, G_2, ...G_1, G_2, ..., G_n$ to generate the analytical data $\hat{X}_i = G_i(\tilde{X}_i)$.
4. The attacker uses $\hat{X}_1^{anc}, \hat{X}_2^{anc}..., \hat{X}_n^{anc}$ to train the classification model C.
5. The attacker uses a classification model C to label the analysis data $\hat{X}_{ex} = G_i(\tilde{X}_{ex})$ generated from external data.
6. The attacker trains a GAN with the labeled external data X_{ex} as the true data and the intermediate representation $\tilde{X}_1^{anc}, \tilde{X}_2^{anc}, ..., \tilde{X}_n^{anc}$ of the original data as the initial value of the generator $\mathcal{G}$.
7. Finally, the attacker obtains an estimate x_{pred} of the original data from the intermediate representation x_i using the generator $\mathcal{G}$ obtained from the learning.

4.3   Improving the Security of Data Collaboration

We propose a method to reduce the risk of sharing intermediate representations produced by data collaboration, assuming the attacker uses the attack model proposed in Sect. 4.2. In the proposed attack model, the only information related to the original data that the attacker has is the auxiliary data and the intermediate representation after the data collaboration was initialized. Because the attacker is expected to infer the original data from the intermediate representation, we apply privacy protection to the shared intermediate representation. Because the GAN generator attempts to estimate the inverse mapping of the dimensionality reduction algorithm that generated the intermediate representation from the

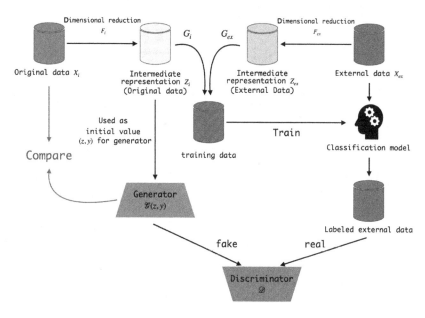

Fig. 2. Overview of the attack model for inferring the original data from intermediate representations of the data collaboration.

original data, the goal is to guarantee that the data far from the original data is recovered even if the inverse mapping is estimated. Therefore, we assume that the attacker has obtained the inverse mapping, and apply a privacy-preserving process. Specifically, we construct the intermediate representation of the data such that the distance between the recovered data and the original data is at least d when the attacker uses the inverse mapping of the dimensionality reduction algorithm. The privacy-preserving process imposed on the dimensionality reduction algorithm is expressed by:

$$min\ dist(x, R(F(x))) = min\frac{\|x - R(F(x))\|_2}{\|x\|_2} \tag{3}$$

where x is one record of the original data, $F(\cdot)$ is the dimensionality reduction algorithm used for the data collaboration, and $R(\cdot)$ is the inverse map of $F(\cdot)$. An illustration of this method is presented in Fig. 3.

5 Experiment and Evaluation

In this section, we present the results of estimating the original data from the intermediate representation of the data collaboration using the following: the proposed method, the effect of ϵ-DR privacy, and the relationship between the privacy guaranteed by ϵ-DR privacy and usefulness. Data collaboration is an algorithm that can maintain the utility of data even if each organization involved

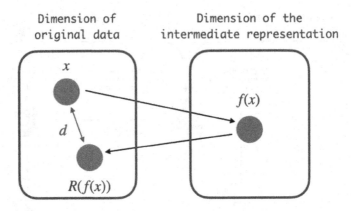

Fig. 3. Diagram of the constraints imposed on the dimensionality reduction algorithm used for the data collaboration.

uses different dimensionality reduction algorithms, which are not disclosed externally as confidential data. However, because attackers can perform brute-force attacks on the dimensionality reduction algorithms, it may be possible to estimate the approximation algorithms. In this experiment, we assumed that the approximation algorithm was estimated, and we conducted the experiment such that the attacker and all the institutions participating in the data collaboration used the same method (PCA) for the dimensionality reduction algorithm.

5.1   Datasets

The datasets used in the experiment are listed in Table 1. The experiment was conducted assuming the data collaboration used "mnist"[1] as the original dataset. The attacker uses one of the following datasets as an external dataset: "digits", "balanced", or "letters" from "emnist"[2]. When using the "digits" dataset as an external dataset, we assume the attacker can easily obtain a dataset similar to the original dataset. With the development of the Internet and the availability of open data, it is a realistic assumption that an attacker can obtain a dataset similar to the original dataset. In the case of using the "letters" dataset as an external dataset, we assume that it is difficult for the attacker to obtain a dataset similar to the original data. Finally, in the case of the "balanced" dataset, we assume a situation in between the two.

5.2   Reconstruction from Intermediate Representations

We conducted an experiment to estimate the original data from the intermediate representation of the data collaboration using the method proposed in Sect. 4. The results of reconstructing the original data from the intermediate

---

[1] http://yann.lecun.com/exdb/mnist/.

[2] https://www.nist.gov/itl/products-and-services/emnist-dataset.

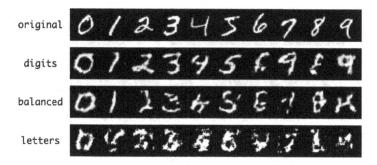

Fig. 4. Results of experiment using the proposed attack model to infer the original data from the intermediate representation of the data collaboration.

Table 1. Datasets used in the experiment.

Dataset	Discription
mnist	Dataset of handwritten numbers
digits	Dataset of handwritten numbers
balanced	Dataset of handwritten numbers and handwritten alphabets
letters	Dataset of handwritten alphabets

representation using the proposed attack model are shown in Fig. 4. It shows that the original data are more likely to be reconstructed in situations in which the attacker is able to obtain a dataset (in this case, "digits") that closely resembles the original data. Even when the attacker cannot obtain images similar to the original data (i.e., the "letters" dataset), we confirmed that the attacker can read certain shapes in the original data. This information may be used by an attacker to determine the domain of the data. The results using the "balanced" dataset as an external dataset are intermediate between the two, and this result most closely resembles a realistic situation.

5.3 Reconstruction from Intermediate Representations with ϵ-DR Privacy

The experimental results in Sect. 5.1 show that an attacker may be able to infer the original data and its domain from the intermediate representation of the data collaboration. Therefore, in this study, we propose a method to secure data collaboration using ϵ-DR privacy. In the experiments described in this section, data collaboration was performed using the constraints on the dimensionality reduction algorithms introduced in Sect. 4.3. We generated multiple datasets by changing the original data and the parameter ϵ. Figure 5 shows the results of the original data estimated by the attack model, and Table 2 shows the results for the evaluation of the RMSE of the estimated and original data. When we checked the estimated image data, we found that there was no significant change

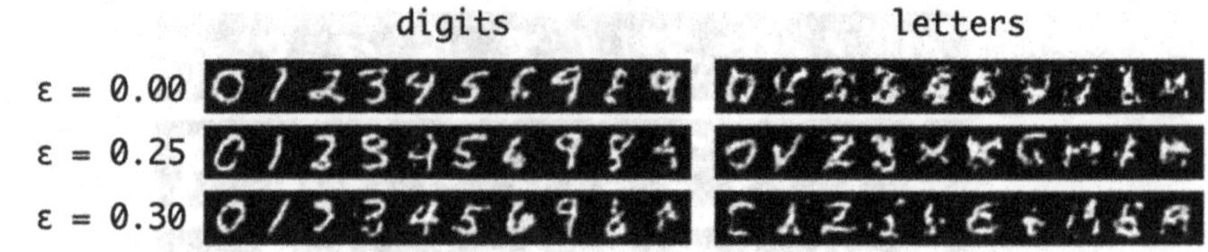

digits   letters

Fig. 5. Results of experiment using an attack model to estimate the original data from the intermediate representation of the data collaboration, applying ϵ-DR privacy.

Table 2. Results of experiment evaluating the RMSE of the original data and the data estimated by the attack model from the intermediate representation of the data collaboration applying ϵ-DR privacy.

ϵ	Dataset	
	Digits	Letters
0.00	139.38	127.25
0.25	136.64	129.60
0.30	137.44	147.92

in the attack results even when we modified the value of ϵ while using the "digits" dataset as the external dataset. There was also no tendency for the value of the RMSE to change. This result confirms that ϵ-DR privacy does not function well. One possible reason for this is that the "digits" dataset is very similar to the "mnist" dataset, which is a situation that favors the attacker. In such a situation, the risk that the attacker may be able to reconstruct the original data must be taken into account. When the "letters" dataset was used as the external dataset, we confirmed that the attack model did not accurately estimate the original data with increasing values of ϵ. The value of the RMSE also increased in proportion to the value of ϵ, confirming that the distance between the original data and the estimated data increases. Therefore, we can confirm that constraining the dimensionality reduction algorithm using ϵ-DR privacy significantly contributes to improving security, assuming that the attacker cannot collect data similar to the original data. Therefore data providers can generate intermediate representations using constraint-imposed dimensionality reduction algorithms, which can hinder the estimation of the original data and domain estimation.

5.4 The Relationship Between Security and Utility in Data Collaboration

We conducted an experiment to test the relationship between ϵ-DR privacy and data utility in data collaboration. In this experiment, the ϵ-DR privacy parameter ϵ was changed, and data collaboration was performed with a dimensional algorithm that imposed constraints on each parameter. We trained a classification model using the analysis data generated from the data collaboration as

Table 3. Relationship between ϵ and the utility of the data in data collaboration.

ϵ	Accuracy
0.0	0.86
0.05	0.86
0.1	0.84
0.2	0.78
0.25	0.62
0.3	0.56
0.4	0.18
Baseline	0.617

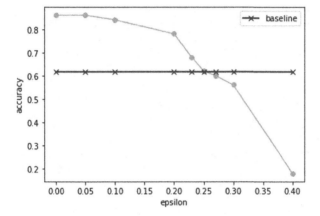

Fig. 6. Relationship between the safety of ϵ-DR privacy and the utility of the data.

training data and evaluated the accuracy of the trained classification model using common validation data. A graph showing the relationship between the ϵ-DR privacy parameter ϵ and the accuracy of the classification model is shown in Fig. 6. A table showing the relationship between the parameter ϵ and the accuracy of the classification model is shown in Table 3. The results of the graphs confirm that as the security of the data increases, the utility of the data decreases, and that there is a trade-off between security and utility. Consequently, the data provider must impose constraints on the dimensionality reduction algorithm and generate intermediate representations while accounting for the utility of the data. The baseline for the results is the accuracy that occurs when the classifier is trained using data owned by only one institution without centralizing the data. The fact that the accuracy of the results is better than that of the baseline results when the data are analyzed indicates the effectiveness of the data collaboration.

6   Conclusion

In this study, we analyzed the security of data collaboration and made suggestions for improving its security. For the security analysis, we proposed an attack model in which an attacker with access to anchor data and an intermediate representation of the original data uses external data to estimate the original data. The results of our experiments confirmed that there is a risk that the domain of the original data will be inferred even if the attacker does not own external data similar to the original data. We also proposed a method that applies ϵ-DR privacy [14] to improve the security of data collaboration. We confirmed that ϵ-DR privacy can reduce the risk of an attacker estimating the original data and that there is a trade-off between security and usefulness.

Acknowledgement. These results were obtained under contract with the New Energy and Industrial Technology Development Organization (NEDO).

References

1. Latanya, S.: k-anonymity: a model for protecting privacy. Int. J. Uncertainty Fuzziness Knowl.-Based Syst. **10**(05), 557–570 (2002)
2. Mimoto, T., Kiyomoto, S., Hidano, S., Basu, A., Miyaji, A.: The possibility of matrix decomposition as anonymization and evaluation for time-sequence data. In:16th Annual Conference on Privacy, Security and Trust (PST) (2018)
3. Aggarwal, C.: On k-anonymity and the curse of dimensionality. In: Proceedings of the 31st International Conference on Very Large Data Bases (2005)
4. Imakura, A., Sakurai, T.: Data collaboration analysis framework using centralization of individual intermediate representations for distributed data sets. ASCE-ASME J. Risk Uncertainty Eng. Syst. Part A: Civil Eng. **6**(2), 04020018 (2020)
5. Ye, X., Li, H., Imakura, A., Sakurai, T.: Distributed collaborative feature selection based on intermediate representation, In: Proceedings of the Twenty-Eighth International Joint Conference on Artificial Intelligence (IJCAI-19) (2019)
6. Goodfellow, I.: Generative adversarial nets. In: Neural Information Processing Systems (NIPS) (2014)
7. Radford, A., Metz, L., Chintala, S.: Unsupervised representation learning with deep convolutional generative adversarial networks. https://arxiv.org/abs/1511.06434 (2015)
8. Mirza, M., Osindero, S.: Conditional generative adversarial nets. https://arxiv.org/abs/1411.1784 (2014)
9. Schlegl, T., Seebock, P., Waldstein, S., Langs, G.: Unsupervised anomaly detection with generative adversarial networks to guide marker discovery. https://arxiv.org/abs/1703.05921 (2017)
10. Shokri, R., Stronati, M., Song, C., Shmatikov, V.: Membership inference attacks against machine learning models. In: IEEE Symposium on Security and Privacy (SP) (2017)
11. Fredrikson, M., Lantz, E., Jha, S., Lin, S., Page, D., Ristenpart, T.: Privacy in pharmacogenetics: an end-to-end case study of personalized warfarin dosing. In: Proceedings of the 23rd USENIX Conference on Security Symposium (2014)

12. Kusano, K., Sakuma, J.: Classifier-to-generator attack: estimation of training data distribution from classifier. https://openreview.net/forum?id=SJOl4DlCZ (2018)
13. Jiang, W., Xie, C., Zhang, Z.: Wishart mechanism for differentially private principal components analysis. In: Thirtieth AAAI Conference on Artificial Intelligence (2016)
14. Nguyen, H., Zhuang, D., Wu, P., Chang, M.: AutoGAN-based dimension reduction for privacy preservation. Neurocomputing **384**, 94–103 (2020)

Encrypted 5G Smallcell Backhaul Traffic Classification Using Deep Learning

Zongning Gao[1,2(✉)] and Shunliang Zhang[1,2]

[1] Institute of Information Engineering, Chinese Academy of Sciences,
Beijing 100093, China
{gaozongning,zhangshunliang}@iie.ac.cn
[2] School of Cyber Security, University of Chinese Academy of Sciences,
Beijing 100049, China

Abstract. 5G small-cell base stations ("Smallcell") have been widely
deployed to enhance network capacity in densely populated city centers.
Generally speaking, IPSec is used to secure the backhaul links between
the Smallcell network and the core network. However, encryption sometimes serves as a tunnel to hide malware. Encrypted traffic classification
of 5G Smallcell backhaul links is rarely discussed in the literature. To
our knowledge, we are the first to classify encrypted 5G Smallcell backhaul links using 1D-CNN. We are able to classify 5G Voice, SMS and
Internet data with 99.99% accuracy rate and above, and the model is
validated using real network data. The work can be used for classifying
real encrypted network traffic in general.

Keywords: 5G smallcell · Deep learning · IPSec · Encrypted traffic
classification

1 Introduction

With the rapid development of mobile communication technology, 5G has
brought great convenience to people's life. Mobile applications affect every aspect
of people's daily life, such as mobile payment, online shopping, take-outs, navi-
gation and the list goes on. However, with convenience come increasing security
risks, such as spam messages, network fraud, mobile phone viruses and tro-
jan implantation. With means for attacking, more and more often disguised as
encrypted data, being able to classify encrypted mobile communication traffic
has become critical, yet challenging.

With continuous acceleration of 5G commercialization, mobile communication traffic will experience explosive growth. 5G mainly uses 3.5G frequency band
and above, therefore the coverage range of 5G macro base station is smaller and
the signal have more difficulty transmitting through buildings. Compared to

---

This work was supported by the National Key R&D Program of China No.
2016QY13Z2306.

Macrocell, 5G Smallcell improves coverage more effectively, increases network capacity and enhances user experience.

5G network has limited network coverage. In contrast, Smallcell complements 5G network in terms of expanding network coverage. Compard to 5G network, Smallcell has following advantages:

– Smaller volume, easier installation, wider signal coverage and lower transmit power.
– Less signal diminution and enhanced signal quality.
– Increased frequency utilization efficiency.

In 5G Smallcell architecture, IPSec tunnel is deployed between Smallcell and security gateway (SeGW), which ensures the privacy and integrity of data communication in 5G access backhaul. IPSec is not used in 2G/3G interface protocols, but is important for 4G/5G network. As shown in Fig. 1.

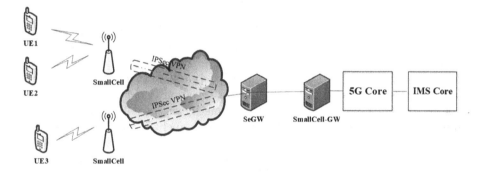

Fig. 1. IPSec tunnel in Smallcell architecture.

We tried different combinations of CNN model type, sampling size and classification methods in order to optimize performance.

The main contributions of our paper can be summarized as follows:

– Firstly, our contribution is to take IP packets as data input and train a 1D-CNN model with 99.99% classification accuracy.
– Secondly, we show that the 1D-CNN model with 500 bytes as sampling length is optimal for Smallcell IPSec encrypted traffic classification, as the classification accuracy is the highest (99.99%).

The remainder of this paper is organized as follows. Section 2 reviews related work. Section 3 presents the models and evaluates model performances. Section 4 concludes the work.

2   Related Work

2.1   SSL Encryption vs. IPSec Encryption

Most research on encrypted traffic classification focus on SSL traffic classification. SSL encrypts traffic above the transport layer, which is convenient for the purpose of classification because researchers can divide packets into session flows based on IP quintuples (source address, source port, destination address, destination port, transport layer protocol). Divided packets are then used to extract model features. Details can be found in [1–3].

Most studies around encrypted traffic analyze SSL encrypted data, while the challenge of applying or generalizing these findings is really data access. SSL encrypted data has to be sourced from the core network, which is difficult or not feasible for most researchers. In contrast, collecting IPSec encrypted traffic data from ratio access network is relatively easy. By taking advantage of this convenience, we are able to build a high-performance traffic classification model. IPSec technology has been widely used in 5G network for network security and therefore it is important to classify IPSec encrypted traffic. However, there is relatively few studies on the identification of IPSec VPN encrypted traffic [4,5].

IPSec encrypts network traffic above the network layer, it is no longer feasible to divide packets into session flows using IP quintuple. IPSec traffic classification relies on different data types as input (packets) and therefore CNN models trained on SSL flows cannot be used for classification in our context(The data type is different because once an IPsec tunnel is successfully established, the addresses and port numbers at both ends of the tunnel between the base station and the gateway are generally fixed during rekey lifetime. The source and destination port numbers are both 4500). Our contribution is to take IP packets as data input and train a 1D-CNN model with 99.99% accuracy.

Based on this, this paper proposes to carry out the research on traffic identification and classification of 5G encrypted communication in Smallcell architecture by taking IP packets as the unit and combining the advantages of CNN classification.

2.2   Network Traffic Classification

Previous traffic classification work for unencrypted networks mainly include classification based on port, packet depth, packet characteristics as well as machine learning models [6].

The diversity of encryption algorithms and methods makes encrypted traffic classification challenging. Past work around encryption traffic classification can be grouped into the following six categories [6]: Effective payload detection based on unencrypted data streams generated during handshake [7]. Payload randomness [8]. Machine learning models based on flow data [9]. Host characteristics [10]. Packet size distribution [11]. Ensemble methods models [1,12].

3   Smallcell Encrypted Traffic Identification Framework

3.1   The Proposed Framework

As shown in Fig. 2, our proposed framework includes two phases.

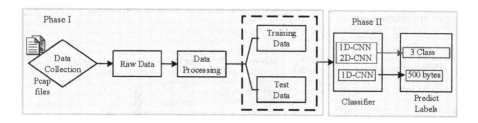

Fig. 2. The framework of proposed model.

Phase I: data collection and data processing
1. We set up a Smallcell network environment to fetch IPSec encrypted traffic data, detailed in Fig. 4. Since the goal is to build a model that enables us to classify traffic into voice traffic, SMS traffic and internet traffic, we fetched the three traffic types separatel, which makes it easy to label the data afterwards.
2. Extract IPSec packets from raw data
3. We then converted IPSec packet data into a format that can be used as model input, by truncating and padding data frames of different lengths into the same length (500, and this is chosen based on model performance). Since we need a unified packet length, the excess part will be trimmed, the part less than 500 bytes will be filled with zeros.

Phase II: model training
We construct a 1D-CNN model shown as Fig. 3 using different data frame lengths (100–600), with interval of 50, and identify the optimal length that balances accuracy and training time is 500.

We splitted the sample into two parts, with 80% used as the training set and 20% as test set.

The 1D-CNN model constructed in this paper includes three 1-D convolution layers and two full connection layers.

- Convolution layer extracts the characteristics of the input byte stream through three layers of convolution operation.
- Full connection layer plays the role of classifier.

We take advantage of the fact that deep learning model can learn high-level features from raw data input. Recent studies [13,14] showed the effectiveness of deep learning models for classifying encrypted traffic. Table 1 shows the 1D-CNN model specification:

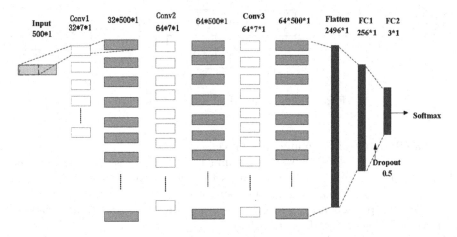

Fig. 3. 1D-CNN model structure.

Table 1. 1D-CNN model parameter list

Layer Num.	Operation	Input Size	Filter Width	Step Size	Padding	Output
1	Conv1	500 * 1	7	2	same	247 * 32
2	Conv2	247 * 32	7	2	same	121 * 64
3	Conv3	121 * 64	7	3	same	39 * 64
4	Full connect	39 * 64	null	null	none	2496
5	Full connect	256	null	null	none	3
6	softmax	3	null	null	none	1

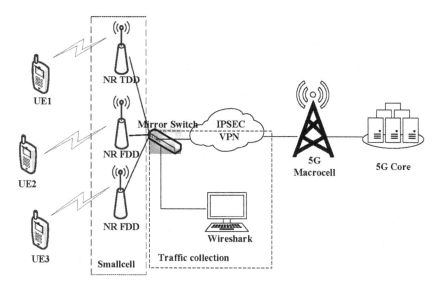

Fig. 4. Smallcell traffic collection diagram.

3.2   Traffic Collection

As shown in Fig. 4, three Smallcell base stations (two NR FDD and one NR TDD) are connected to the mirroring switch, and the data packets of mobile phones are copied to our PC through the mirroring switch. Data packets are saved in pcapng format by wireshark packet capture tool.

3.3   Model Training

We trained the model using the open-source library Pytorch, and the hyperparameters used for training are shown in Table 2:

Table 2. CNN Hyperparameters

Parameter	Value
Dropout	0.5
Loss function	Cross entropy function
Optimization	Adam optimizer
Learning ratet	1e–3
Num. of average train	15

3.4   Performance

Evaluation Metric. The metrics used are pretty standard in the traffic classification literature. We use accuracy, precision, recall and F-measure. They are computed using the confusion matrix shown in Table 3.

Table 3. Confusion matrix

	Predicted: Type I	Predicted: none Type I
Accurate: Type I	TP	FN
Accurate: none Type I	FP	TN

As the follows:

$$Accuracy : A = \frac{TP + TN}{TP + TN + FP + FN} \tag{1}$$

$$Precision : P = \frac{TP}{TP + FP} \tag{2}$$

$$Recall : R = \frac{TP}{TP + FN} \tag{3}$$

$$F1 - Measure : F1 = \frac{2 \times P \times R}{P + R} \tag{4}$$

Accuracy and F1 score reflect the balance between precision and recall.

3.5   2D-CNN Model

We use the same database and parameters to compare the accuracy of 1D-CNN and 2D-CNN in Smallcell IPSec encrypted traffic classification, and found that 2D-CNN is not more efficient in extracting information from the raw data, and therefore is not necessary.

The results for 2D-CNN are as follows:

It can be seen from Fig. 5, 1D-CNN classification accuracy on Smallcell IPSec encrypted traffic(Voice, SMS, Internet) is higher than 2D-CNN model. Therefore, 1D-CNN is more suitable for network traffic data classification. Our guess is that network traffic itself is a 1D data flow, and a 1D model can be used to extract data features well, so as to achieve accurate identification and classification. There is no need to convert 1D data into 2D images first, and then use 2D models for processing.

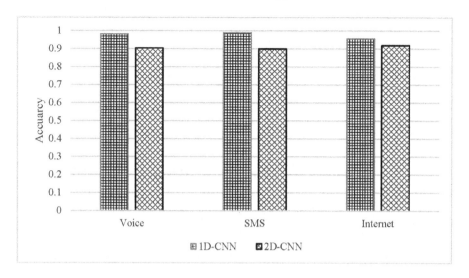

Fig. 5. Traffic classification accuracy of 1D-CNN vs. 2D-CNN.

3.6   Optimizing Sample Size

We trained models on data frame of different lengths, starting from 50 bytes to 600 bytes(step is 50 bytes). We found that for the interval[500,600], a the classification accuracy stabilizes around 99% (Fig. 6 and Fig. 7). Considering that longer data frame lengths leads to longer trainig time, we suggest using 500 as the optimal length.

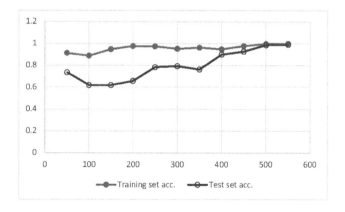

Fig. 6. Traffic classification accuracy between training set and test set.

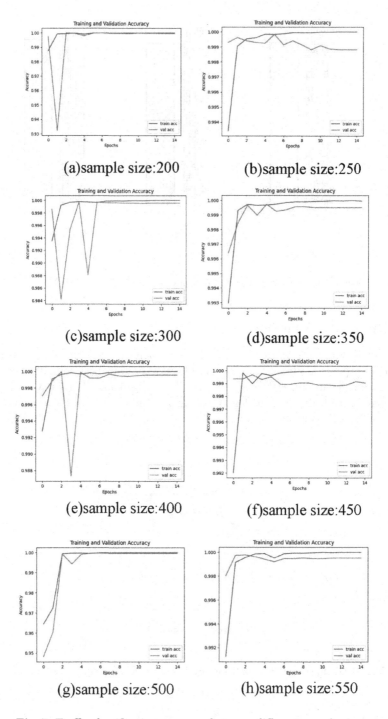

Fig. 7. Traffic classification accuracy between different sample sizes.

3.7 Performance on Traffic Classification of 5G Voice, SMS and Internet Data

(All results listed below correspond to the optimal data frame byte lengths of 500)

Figure 8 shows that 18,642 of the 18,644 packets are correctly classified. Figure 9 and Fig. 10 show that the accuracy and loss curves of the training set and test set becomes stable as the number of training rounds increases.

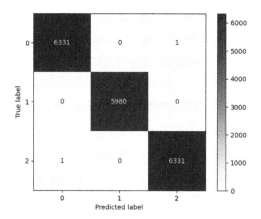

Fig. 8. Confusion matrix.

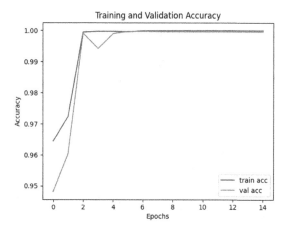

Fig. 9. Accuracy curve.

The results are as follows: Accuracy: 99.99%, Recall: 99.99%, Precision: 99.99%, F1: 99.99%. Experiments show that using the 1D-CNN model, the accuracy, recall rate, precision rate and F1 value can reach 99.99%.

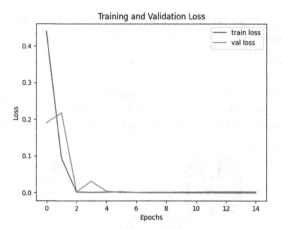

Fig. 10. Loss curve.

4   Conclusion

We demonstrate the feasibility of applying the 1D-CNN model for classifying IPSec encrypted 5G traffic by using deep learning method. Subsequently, the model can be applied to 5G Smallcell architecture to monitor encrypted data traffic in real time. We propose the following areas for future research exploration:

Data set: currently, there is no publicly available IPSec data set for mobile communication networks. Researchers often collect their own data, making it difficult to compare works among different researchers

Model generalizability: the model proposed in this paper is aimed at the classification of 5G IPSec encrypted traffic in Smallcell architecture. However, whether the model can be generalized in classifying encrypted traffic in other mobile network system remains to be explored.

References

1. Lin, W., Huamin, F., Biao, L., et al.: SSL VPN encrypted traffic identification based on hybrid method. Comput. Appl. Softw. **36**(2), 315–322 (2019)
2. Wang, W., Zhu, M.: End-to-end encrypted traffic classification with one-dimensional convolution neural networks. In: 2017 IEEE International Conference on Intelligence and Security Informatics (ISI). IEEE, pp. 43–48 (2017)
3. Guo, S., Su., Y.: Encrypted traffic classification method based on data stream. J. Comput. Appl. **41**(5), 1386–1391 (2021)
4. Yimin, Z., Fangzheng, L., Yong, W.: IPSec VPN encrypted traffic identification based on hybrid method. Comput. Sci. **48**(4), 295–302 (2021)
5. Yildirim, T., Radcliffe, P.J.: VoIP traffic classification in IPSec tunnels. In: 2010 International Conference on Electronics and Information Engineering (ICEIE 2010) (2010)

6. Liangchen, C., Shu, G., Baoxu, L., et al.: Research status and development trends on network encrypted traffic identification. Netinfo Secur. **19**(3), 19–25 (2019)
7. Ruolong, M.A.: Research and Implementation of Unknown and Encrypted Traffic Identification Based on Convolutional Neural Network. Beijing University of Posts and Telecommunications, Beijing (2018)
8. Li, G., Li, W., Li, Q.: Encrypted and compressed traffic classification based on random feature set. J. Jilin Univ. (Eng. Technol. Ed.) (2020)
9. Anderson, B., Mcgrew, D.: Identifying encrypted malware traffic with contextual flow data. In: The ACM Workshop on Artifical Intelligence and Security, 28 Octobor 2016, Vienna, Austria. New York. ACM **2016**, pp. 35–46 (2016)
10. Bermolen, P., Mella, M., Meo, M., et al.: Abacus: accurate behavioral classification of P2P-TV traffic. Comput. Netw. **55**(6), 1394–1411 (2011)
11. Gao Changxi, W., Yabiao, W.C.: Encrypted traffic classification based on packet length distribution of sampling sequence. J. Commun. **36**(9), 65–75 (2015)
12. Sun, Z., Zhai, J., Dai, Y.: An encrypted traffic identification method based on DPI and load randomness. J. Appl. Sci. **9**(05) (2019)
13. D'Angelo, G., Palmieri, F.: Network traffic classification using deep convolutional recurrent autoencoder neural networks for spatial-temporal features extraction. J. Netw. Comput. Appl. **173**, 102890 (2021)
14. Aceto, G., Ciuonzo, D., Montieri, A., et al.: MIMETIC: mobile encrypted traffic classification using multimodal deep learning. Comput. Netw. **165**, 106944.1-106944.12 (2019)

Human Security Behavior Assistance in the Cyber-Physical Space

Ruojin Xiao, Leilei Qu📖, and Wenchang Shi(✉)

Renmin University of China, Beijing, People's Republic of China
{ruojinx,llqu,wenchang}@ruc.edu.cn

Abstract. With the development of human-computer interaction technology, the concept of space is constantly being extended. As technology continues to be embedded in daily life, the boundaries between the physical world and cyberspace are blurring. We consider this composite environment as a cyber-physical space, which is not only closely connected with the external physical world, but also has the characteristics of technology, virtuality and independence. Human security behaviors in cyber-physical space will be affected by more factors in different environments because they occur in parallel in the two spaces. Therefore, in this new socio-technical system, we need to reconsider how to guide and assist human security behavior. In this paper, we focus on the security behavior in cyber-physical space and the research question of how to provide assistance for it. On the one hand, the characteristics of the environment are considered, that is, the cyber-physical space is the product of technological development. On the other hand, human behavior is affected by their own psychological characteristics and bounded rationality, so the characteristics of the behavior subject are also considered. Starting from the tech-psychological and tech-economic perspectives, we propose that by changing motivation, changing ability, providing appropriate triggers, or using people's status-quo bias, regress aversion bias, social influence to assist human security behavior based on the persuasive technology and nudge theory. Finally, we summarize the design ideas of human security behavior assistance in cyber-physical space.

Keywords: Cyber-physical space · Security behavior assistance · Persuasive technology · Nudge

1 Introduction

As Internet usage grows, the technology supporting the structure of the Internet is evolving at an even higher rate. The Web 3.0 era we are entering now brings new opportunities and challenges [28]. The rapid progress of human-computer interaction technology has promoted the integration of virtual cyberspace and reality physical space. The online world that we thought was independent of reality in the past has become a digital living space with a new social system, which we call cyber-physical space. In such a space, human behavior in the

C. Su and K. Sakurai (Eds.): SciSec 2022 Workshops, CCIS 1680, pp. 28–43, 2022.
https://doi.org/10.1007/978-981-19-7769-5_3

physical world will be reflected in cyberspace, while decisions made in the virtual environment will also have an impact on real life. Therefore, the emerging characteristics of the increasingly complex environment make the security issues in this new space also worthy of study.

Cyber-physical space is undoubtedly a socio-technical system, in which security issues are not limited to the attack and defense at the technical level, and the role of human in maintaining the operation of the system should not be underestimated. Since the operation of most security systems are inseparable from the participation of human beings, once there is a problem with the personnel in the system, whether it is an active malicious attack or an unintentional leak of secrets or operational errors, strict protection measures will fail. Humans are considered to be the weakest link in cyberspace security [34]. It is one of the most urgent tasks to strengthen the education and training of relevant personnel and conduct appropriate behavior assistance.

It is gratifying that the current study of human behavior in security systems has attracted the attention of researchers. Since security mechanisms are designed, implemented, applied and breached by people, human factors should be considered in their design [1]. Password security [16,33], phishing [22], privacy protection [35] and other fields have shifted the focus from simply using technical means to strengthen system security protection to how to prevent people from intentional or unintentional insecurity behavior to reduce the overall security of the system. A large number of theories and research methods in psychology, behavioral economics and social science have been applied in the field of security to improve human security awareness or help them make security decisions [2,26,27]. For example, using the nudge theory of behavioral economics, security researchers have designed a dynamic personalized password policy to guide people with different personalities to set passwords that are more difficult to guess [16], which can reduce the risk of information leakage from successful attacks due to a weak password set by a certain account.

However, through the summary and analysis of the existing research on security behavior assistance, we find that although there have been many applications, there is still a lack of systematic summary of the theoretical models behind it. Most of the studies use questionnaires, interviews, user experiments and other methods to propose effective assistance for people's insecurity behavior (eg. using weak password). Although these are certainly valuable results, some of them lack interpretability, which means that the reason why the assistance methods work is still unknown. Therefore, in order to avoid using only experimental data, we prefer methodological guidance. At the same time, as We increasingly live in cyber-physical spaces, spaces that are both physical and digital, and where the two aspects are intertwined. Such spaces are highly dynamic and typically undergo continuous change [31]. Providing assistance for security behavior in this scenario requires us to reconsider how the technical factors that build the entire space interact with the human factors.

We first give an overview of cyber-physical space(see Fig. 1). Cyber-physical space consists of three major parts: cyber space, physical space and human behavior. They are not independent parts, but intermingle and influence each other. Cyber space reflects the state of physical space through information technology, and is also influenced by the state of physical space. A representative manifestation of this phenomenon is online payment. Whether it is the state of cyber space or physical space, it is difficult to represent without the carrier of behavior. At the same time, subtle changes of human behavior can also be fed back into the dynamically changing cyber-physical space. Because of these characteristics of cyber-physical space, in addition to the traditional technical perspective, we propose a comprehensive analysis to research it from a psychological perspective and an economic perspective.

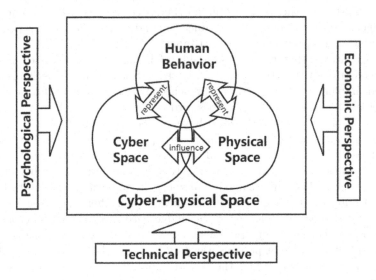

Fig. 1. An overview of human behavior in cyber-physical space

In this paper, we will explore the human security behavior assistance method in cyber-physical space from the perspective of tech-psychological and tech-economic. Focusing on persuasive technology and nudge theory, two theoretical models that have been widely used to guide human security behavior, we hope to analyze the theoretical principles behind them by combing the development history of the models, so as to answer the key research question of how to assist human security behavior. Next, establish the relationship between behavior assistance model and specific security research to provide a set of more scientific and effective design ideas of security behavior assistance from the methodology.

Therefore, the main contributions of the paper are as follows:

a) answer the critical question of how to assist human security behavior in cyber-physical space from a techno-psychological and techno-economic perspective

b) establish the relationship between behavior assistance theoretical model and specific security practices by summarizing existing research, and provide a set of more effective security behavior assistance design ideas from the methodology.

2   A Tech-Psychological Perspective

Human behavior in cyber-physical space is made by people in the physical space, and expressed in the cyber virtual environment through technical means. Therefore, guiding human behavior from a techn-psychological perspective is using information technology methods to influence the psychological factors that determine human behavior, and then provide assistance to human security behavior.

The classic method from this perspective is the persuasive technology proposed by Professor Fogg [10]. It is a user behavior guidance technology that combines the persuasive principles in psychology with computer technology. Its goal is to study, analyze and design intersecting computer products to change people's attitudes and behaviors. The theoretical basis of persuasive technology is Fogg behavior model.

2.1   Fogg Behavior Model

Professor Fogg presented Fogg behavior model [11], which is an effective model to explore the causes of behavior. Its core content can be simply expressed as an equation:

$$Behavior = Motivation + Ability + Trigger(B = MAP) \tag{1}$$

The model states that the occurrence of a behavior must simultaneously satisfy three elements: sufficient motivation, sufficient ability and appropriate trigger. But if you want to prevent a behavior from happening, you can remove any one of the three elements.

As shown in Fig. 2, people's motivation and ability are placed in two directions of the coordinate axis, which increase in turn along the direction of axis. People's motivation and ability in a certain circumstance can be regarded as a point in the coordinate system. The curve identified in the figure means an behavior threshold line, and the part above the curve is "places where the behavior is likely to occur". That is, when people's motivation and ability are sufficiently sufficient to cross the threshold line, supplemented with appropriate triggers, the behavior can occur. However, if either of the two factors, motivation and ability, is insufficient so that the corresponding coordinate point falls below the threshold line, the behavior will not occur even if an appropriate trigger is presented.

These three elements are further explained [11]. Motivation is the source of power for people to behave, which provides a reason for a particular behavior. Fogg behavior model summarizes people's motivation into three types: a) pleasure and pain, that is, people want to experience pleasure or avoid pain; b) hope

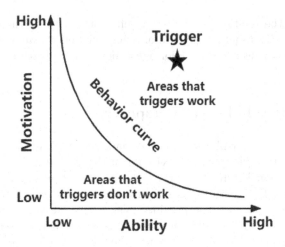

Fig. 2. Fogg behavior model

and fear, that is, people want to increase hope or decrease fear; c) social acceptance and exclusion, that is, people want to receive social acceptance and avoid social exclusion. Ability is the cornerstone of behavior. You must ensure having sufficient ability to complete the behavior once you want to promote it. Ability includes time, money, physical, mental, social acceptance and routine. Finally, trigger is the key to make the behavior happen. Sufficient motivation and ability only increase the possibility of the occurrence of behavior. Whether a behavior finally occurs depends on whether appropriate trigger is provided. Fogg divides triggers into three types: a) sparks, which enhance people's motivation; b) facilitators, which simplify tasks and help people perform behaviors; c) signals, which are some weaker cues serving as reminders.

2.2   Human Behavior Assistance Based on FBM

Fogg behavior model decomposes the necessary conditions for the occurrence of behavior into three factors, which also provides three ideas for human security behavior assistance: a) change motivation, b) change ability and c) provide effective trigger.

Change Motivation. Motivation includes extrinsic motivation and intrinsic motivation. Extrinsic motivation refers to encouragement and rewards from environment and goals. Intrinsic motivation refers to the realization of personal achievement and satisfaction of curiosity. When designing security behavior assistance, if the promotion of both intrinsic motivation and extrinsic motivation can be considered, the behavior assistance scheme may achieve good results. However, because security is often the "second choice" of people, when facing an urgent task, people's motivation to make security decisions tend to be at a lower level and is difficult to improve in a short time. Under the circumstances, it is necessary to rely on the change of extrinsic motivation to improve people's overall behavioral motivation and urge people to make security behaviors.

Alain Forget et al. [12] proposed a persuasive authentication framework, which considers the adaptability of persuasive technology in security. This work summarized the application of persuasive technology in the field of usable security and authentication into five basic principles: simplification, personalisation, monitoring, conditioning and social interaction. The last three principles are motivated by the consideration of changing people's behavioral motivations (whether it is to increase the motivation of performing security behavior or reduce the motivation of performing insecurity behavior). When people know that their passwords are being monitored by security administrators, they may also be motivated to self-monitor and adjust their behavior to make more secure passwords. At the same time, various forms of reinforcement conditioning from the outside can provide people with external motivation to perform security behavior. Attitudes from the external society can also provide additional persuasive effects, such as appreciating and encouraging people's efforts to ensure the security of the organization, or explaining that insecurity behavior will not only harm personal interests but even endanger the whole organization. Thus, people's motivation to take insecurity behavior may be reduced.

The work of Alain Forget et al. [13] developed Persuasive Text Passwords(PTP) by applying the above principles. The security of the password is enhanced by randomly inserting some characters into the password set by the user. Although users can obtain new random character combinations through constantly refreshing, users will feel bored and the motivation to do this will gradually decrease. The PTP system makes insecurity choice, finding a password that is easy to remember but also easy to guess, less attractive to assist users away from insecurity decisions.

George E. Raptis et al. [25] designed GamePass, a graphical password creation mechanism that incorporates gamification. Due to various factors such as task urgency, account value, and people' cognitive and memory capabilities, setting a secure password has often become the secondary goal and most people lack sufficient motivation to set a strong password. GamePass increases people engagement in the password creation process through the process of gamification and turns a secondary goal of creating secure passwords into a primary goal of performing well in the game, which makes a stressful task into a fun activity. This method greatly improves people's behavioral motivation of creating a secure password. It also incorporates scores, ranks and rankings, which are effective incentive strategies to persuade users to actively participate in the game, further providing external motivation of behave securely.

Anirudh Ganesh et al. [14] designed a game to persuade users to improve the security behavior of smartphones for the security and privacy issues of mobile terminals, based on the protection motivation theory. Compared with textual security education materials, gamification makes it easier for users to remember security knowledge. Knowledge of the consequences of security threats also enhances their motivation to behave securely in their lives.

Change Ability. Starting from the Fogg behavior model, we can conclude that there are two ways to enhance the ability: a) educate and train people to help them enrich their knowledge and improve their self-level to achieve the extent that they can complete the target behavior; b) change the difficulty of behavior so that the ability to perform security behaviors is at a level that is easily achievable for people, or makes it more difficult to perform insecurity behaviors that are impossible or very difficult for people to do at their current level of ability.

Among the five persuasive principles under the authentication framework proposed by Alain Forget [12], Simplification is for the purpose of changing the ability of people to perform behaviors. Forget proposed that the security authentication process should be as simple as possible, ensuring that people can complete the entire task in as few steps as possible, thus not burdening the user with additional abilities.

Sonia Chiasson et al. [7,8] improved the difficulty for people to select insecure passwords by providing them with a highlighted window that appears randomly and allowing people to only select points within the window as graph passwords. In other words, it simplifies the process of choosing a secure password without any extra effort. Changes in the ability dimension make it more likely that the desired security behavior will occur.

Article [37] designed a security interactive comic to enhance people's understanding of the concepts of security password guessing attacks, antivirus protection, and mobile online privacy. Article [36] also used infographics and interactive comic to persuade people to update their antivirus software. Since the lack of understanding of security threats and their related impacts is a fundamental reason for preventing security behaviors, effective security education for users can greatly enhance their ability to perform security behaviors when facing security threats from the perspective of the ability dimension in Fogg behavior model.

Provide Effective Trigger. If it is found through the analysis of the situation that the motivation and ability of people to make security behaviors have reached the level of being able to complete, but the security behavior expected by the behavior designer still does not occur. Then it is necessary to consider whether there is a lack of appropriate triggers.

What can trigger people's security behavior? This is a question that behavior designers and researchers must answer. Sauvik Das et al. [9] studied the triggers of people's security and privacy behaviors. It divides the triggers into three types: forced, proactive and social. Force Triggers are external stimuli that force people to make behavior changes beyond their own will. Typically, passwords are required to updated regularly due to organizational mandates. Subject by external conditions, this is the least common type of trigger. Proactive triggers are self-willed or goal-directed behavioral change triggers, such as a routine password update. Social triggers, on the other hand, are the most common triggers found in the study, which refer to direct social interactions that lead to behavioral change when people observe or interact with others, such as receiving advice from friends. Like the classification of triggers in Fogg's model of behavior: sparks, facilitators, and signals, different kinds of triggers play a significant role at different motivation-ability levels. Articial [9] also prove that people of different ages, nationalities and security behavioral intention(SBI) have different triggers when they conduct security privacy behaviors. This provides an idea for us to research the effect of triggers and design what kind of triggers can work on a specific group of people.

Triggers are the easiest to change, but also one of the most overlooked by behavior designers. In the field of security, the researches of triggers that lead people to behave securely will involve nudge theory, which we will discuss next. Nudge theory is often used to design a good trigger. Various successful practices of Fogg behavior model tell us that the appropriate design and utilization of triggers have a good effect on assisting people's behavior. There are many elements that can be used as triggers in cyber-physical space. A pop-up window or even a prompt sound constitutes a trigger for successful behavior. How to use these diverse mediators as effective triggers for security behavior assistance may provide a direction for future research.

3   A Tech-Economic Perspective

Behavioral economics argues that perfectly rational people do not exist. Influenced by various cognitive biases, people develop different cognitive styles and behave differently when making decisions (see Fig. 3 for some examples). Once these cognitive biases are used reasonably, they can guide human behavior to the direction we expect. From the perspective of cyberspace security, it is to assist people make security behavior decisions. The nudge theory in behavioral economics can be a great help for us.

3.1   Nudge Theory

Nudge theory [29, 30] was developed by Thaler and Sunstein. It is also known as libertarian paternalism or soft paternalism, nudge has a paternalistic style in the choice of stimulating behavior, but fundamentally it still allows the subject to have the opportunity to choose freely. It breaks the "rational people" assumption in traditional economics and proposes that people with limited cognition and rationality may not make the most beneficial choices for themselves. Therefore, it is necessary to assist people to make rational decisions on the premise of respecting their free choices.

Using the term NUDGE(S), Thaler [29] breaks down the key principles that influence the choice architecture into six points: a) iNcentives, designers should set different options for different people; b) Understand mapping, which makes the message the designer wants to convey easier to Understand; c) Default,

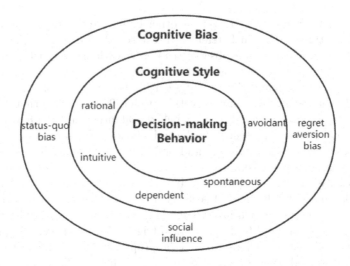

Fig. 3. Cognitive bias and cognitive styles influencing decision-making behavior

people tend to choose the most convenient and effortless default choice in the decision-making process; d) Give feedback, a good choice architecture should provide feedback on the status quo and guidance for follow-up choices to help People improve their behavior; e) Expect error, a good choice architecture should be able to design preventive measures in advance for some foreseeable wrong operations; f) Structure complex choices, structural simplification of complex choices can make choices less difficult.

According to the above principles, behavior assistance designers can change people's behaviors through a proper structure of the selection system, so that it can develop in the direction they want. Nudge is designed based on the consideration of people's behavioral tendency of bounded rationality in a specific choice environment. By changing the environment, that is, making very small changes to the presentation of decision-making options, it is expected to achieve the effect of small cost but large benefit.

3.2   Human Behavior Assistance Based on Nudge Theory

Nudge theory originated from economics. In response to the assumption of rational people in economics, Thaler discussed limited rationality, limited willpower and limited self-interest, and introduced the research of psychology on human into economics and established related theories about behavioral economics. This part of the research was subsequently extended to the field of law and public policy [4]. Because nudges can make designers push people to behave in a favorable direction through the design of the choice system at almost no cost, the nudge theory has attracted widespread attention from governments around the world after it was put forward. For example, changing the organ donation mechanism from "opt-in" to "opt-out", which means setting the choice of organ donation as the default option, would make a large difference in lives saved through transplantation [17]. In this case, although the power of whether or not to donate organs is still in the hands of every citizen, the actual organ donation rate has greatly increased.

As the digital and physical worlds continue to blend, people often face vital choices in the digital environment. In order to assist users in making behavioral decisions, the idea of digital nudge has also been applied in many fields including human-computer interaction [6]. For example, NudgeCred [5] is a browser plug-in that helps users judge the credibility of news on Twitter. It improves users' ability to identify online news by directing users to the authority of information sources and other users' comments on the information. In the field of security, nudge theory has also been further applied. In terms of password authentication, Shipi Kankane et al. [18] found that salience nudge can effectively reduce the user's comfort when using automatic password generation. The study by Leilei Qu et al. [23] found that different nudges have a significant impact on the security decision of whether users turn on 2FA.

Through the analysis of existing nudge studies, we summarize three psychological characteristics that can be used to design nudges: status-quo bias, regret aversion bias and social influence. What follows is a discussion of how these three psychological traits work and how they can be used to design security nudges.

Status-Quo Bias. Status-quo bias is the psychological tendency to maintain the Status quo and resist change. It leads us to follow the path of least resistance, that is, to maintain the choices we have made, rather than to make extra efforts to find uncertain better choices.

Taking advantage of this psychological state, we can design nudges from different perspectives. The core idea is to make the behaviors we expect users to do as the choices of least resistance, exemplified by default options and "opt-out" mechanisms. This design is widely used in cookie consent banners on websites and has been dubbed by researchers as "dark pattern", which means that through web design elements, users make choices that benefit website service providers. Gray C M et al. [15] analyzed the cookie consent banners used by 560 websites from EU member states, and found that during the cookie configuration process, websites often use interface design to affect user's cookie configuration, setting consent to website collection of cookies as the default option, hide the reject button, etc. In article [21], Midas Nouwens et al. found that if the "opt-out" button is removed from the homepage of cookie setting, the probability of user consent can be increased by 22–23%. Although the dark pattern has received various criticisms from users and researchers, its legal and ethical feasibility remains to be further discussed. But we can't deny that this is a typical application of taking advantage of status-quo bias to design nudges and influence people's security behavior.

As a neutral method, the effect of nudges depends entirely on the direction desired by the designer. In most cases, we still hope that nudges can help people make security choices. For example, when visiting dangerous websites, designers of security warnings often hide the insecurity option of "continue to visit", to reduce people's desire to continue to visit. The research of [32] shows that when users need to connect to an unfamiliar Wi-Fi, recommending it combined with the location sequence and color information can effectively assist the user to choose a relatively security Wi-Fi. That is, put the most security option at the top of the list and mark it in green, making it the path of least resistance for the user to make a decision.

Regret Aversion Bias. Regret aversion bias refers to the fact that when faced with the same amount of gain and loss, people tend to perceive the loss as more unbearable for them. Emphasizing the negative utility of losses is 2 to 2.5 times the positive utility of emphasizing gains. Therefore, when people realize that there is a certain level of risk, they may become more prudent to make decisions.

Based on this psychological factor, designers can prompt people to reflect on whether their decisions are correct by prompting the loss consequences of risky behaviors, thereby increasing the possibility of people choosing security behaviors. Saranga Komanduri [19] designed a password meter which can predict in real time the most likely characters that the user will enter next based on the huge database of password text materials and display them When a user is entering a password. This "read your mind" password meter can make users who try to set weak passwords feel like they are easily guessed. Further, if the initiator of the guessing behavior is not the website itself, but an external attacker trying to steal the password, setting a weak password will greatly improve the success rate of guessing. In this case, users are more likely to choose a strong password that is complex and not easy to guess. Also aiming at improving password strength, the research of Leilei Qu et al. [24] proved that, compared with normal security prompts, the preventive nudge prompt combined with the consequences of password theft has a better effect in assisting users to adopt more security passwords.

Hazim Almuhimedi et al. [3] designed an application permission manager for the situation that users are not sensitive to the method, scope and frequency of data acquisition by mobile applications and therefore cannot achieve effective privacy control. Frequencies of sensitive data collection by different applications (e.g. the number of times of accessing location information) are sent to users. When users find that their sensitive data, that is also their virtual property, is frequently accessed by different applications, they are more likely to take some actions out of loss aversion to information leakage. This nudge effectively motivates users to review mobile application permissions. This nudge was demonstrated in a field study where 95% of participants reassessed their permission settings, and 58% took action to further restrict app access.

Social Influence. Social influence refers to people's desire to meet to the expectations that they are expected to do something, that is, people's behavior is influ-

Table 1. Human security behavior assistance approach.

Perspective	Method	Explanation
Tech-Psychological	Change motivation	Increase motivation of security behavior: provide rewards and encouragement from the outside or stimulate the achievement and curiosity. Redeuce motivation of insecurity behavior: provide the consequences of insecurity behavior, especially those related to personal property or groups and organization interests
	Change ability	Improve human ability: educate people to enrich their knowledge and train them to improve their ability. Redeuce ability requirements of the behavior: reduce the difficulty of the behavior so that people can meet the requirements at the current level
	Provide effective triggers	Provide right triggers when people's motivation and ability are sufficient. Displaying triggers should take into account the timing and form of appearance
Tech-Economic	Status-quo bias	The tendency to maintain the status quo and resist change. Taking advantage of this psychological factors, we can offer people an behavior path with least resistance
	Regret aversion bias	When faced with the same amount of gains and losses, people tend to think the losses are harder to bear. Taking advantage of this psychological factors, we can remind them of the serious consequences of insecurity behavior, especially when it comes to actual losses
	Social influence	People want to cater the expectation that they are expected to do something, and their behavior is influenced by people around them. So that we can influence one's decisions and behaviors by taking advantage of the security behaviors of others

enced by the social environment and the perceptions of the people around them. This is similar to the social acceptance and exclusion in the factors that change behavior motivation in Fogg behavior model. People want to be accepted by society and avoid social exclusion, so they are more inclined to behave in accordance with social expectations.

It is difficult for most people living in the society not to develop herd mentality to some extent. Research in psychology and behavioral economics has proven that people tend to follow the behavior of others. When designing nudges based on this factor, we can try to influence the decisions and behaviors of our target person by exploiting the security behaviors of others. Hiroaki Masaki [20] studied the effect of nudges in helping teenagers avoid privacy and security threats on social networks. Nudges to express the opinion of the public are called "social nudges". According to research, this type of nudge is more effective at preventing people from engaging in potentially risky behaviors, such as posting private information on social networks. Based on the idea of social nudge, they designed data-driven nudge - NudgeData and NudgeDummyData, the core of which is to explain to users the choice of others in the same situation through positive

(XX% of users would) or negative (XX% of users would not) description. A user study was then conducted to observe whether it will affect user behavior. Nudge-Data is a social nudge based on real social survey data, and NudgeDummyData introduces virtual data to study the impact of different data on nudge effects. The results demonstrate that the social nudge of negative descriptions can significantly alter adolescent behavior choices in situations with potential privacy and security risks.

Social influence has great potential in nudging human behavior, but it is not omnipotent. Behavioral guiders also need to pay attention to the possible Boomerang effect, which is the behavior result completely opposite to the target expectation, when using it to nudge. This may be due to the incongruity of goals and means, or the adverse effect of emotions caused by inappropriate guidance methods. The research [20] also shows that the social nudge with positive statements can be counterproductive, so it should be avoided as much as possible in practice.

Finally, starting from the two behavioral assistance theories of persuasive technology and nudge theory, we summarize the available ideas of security behavior support from the tech-psychological and the tech-economic perspective, as shown in Table 1. It is expected that this work will provide a more theoretically design approach for security behavior assistance researchers.

4   Conclusion

The integration of physical and cyberspace makes human behavior not limited to a specific space, but parallel in two Spaces at the same time. This paper focuses on security behavior problems in cyber-physical space and analyzes the theoretical models behind the current security behavior assistance researches for the purpose of providing users with auxiliary support for security behavior. Taking persuasive technology and nudge theory as the starting point, we summarize several design ideas that can be used to implement security behavior assistance schemes from the tech-psychological and tech-economic perspectives. Combined with existing researches, the application of these design ideas are explained.

Admittedly, the work of this paper still has some limitations. We only focus on persuasive technology and nudge theory, but there are far more theoretical models for security behavior assistance in practice. However, we hope that this study can help to understand the problem of "how to guide people's security behavior" and provide more systematic design ideas for future research on security behavior assistance.

Acknowledgements. This work was supported by the National Natural Science Foundation of China under Grant No.61472429 and Grant No. 61772538; the National Key R&D Program of China under Grant No. 2017YFB1400702 and Grant No. 2020YFB1005600.

References

1. Adams, A., Sasse, M.A.: Users are not the enemy. Commun. ACM **42**(12), 40–46 (1999)
2. Adjerid, I., Acquisti, A., Brandimarte, L., Loewenstein, G.: Sleights of privacy: framing, disclosures, and the limits of transparency. In: Proceedings of the 9th Symposium on Usable Privacy and Security, pp. 1–11 (2013)
3. Almuhimedi, H.: Your location has been shared 5,398 times! a field study on mobile app privacy nudging. In: Proceedings of the 33rd Annual ACM Conference on Human Factors in Computing Systems, pp. 787–796 (2015)
4. Benartzi, S., et al.: Should governments invest more in nudging? Psychol. Sci. **28**(8), 1041–1055 (2017)
5. Bhuiyan, M.M., Horning, M., Lee, S.W., Mitra, T.: Nudgecred: supporting news credibility assessment on social media through nudges. In: Proceedings of the ACM on Human-Computer Interaction, vol. 5, no. (CSCW2), pp. 1–30 (2021)
6. Caraban, A., Karapanos, E., Gonçalves, D., Campos, P.: 23 ways to nudge: a review of technology-mediated nudging in human-computer interaction. In: Proceedings of the 2019 CHI Conference on Human Factors in Computing Systems, pp. 1–15 (2019)
7. Chiasson, S., Forget, A., Biddle, R., Oorschot, P.V.: Influencing users towards better passwords: persuasive cued click-points. People Comput. XXII Cult. Creativity Interact. **22**, 121–130 (2008)
8. Chiasson, S., Stobert, E., Forget, A., Biddle, R., Van Oorschot, P.C.: Persuasive cued click-points: design, implementation, and evaluation of a knowledge-based authentication mechanism. IEEE Trans. Dependable Secure Comput. **9**(2), 222–235 (2011)
9. Das, S., Dabbish, L.A., Hong, J.I.: A typology of perceived triggers for {End-User} security and privacy behaviors. In: 15th Symposium on Usable Privacy and Security (SOUPS 2019), pp. 97–115 (2019)
10. Fogg, B.J.: Persuasive technology: using computers to change what we think and do. Ubiquity **2002**(December), 2 (2002)
11. Fogg, B.J.: A behavior model for persuasive design. In: Proceedings of the 4th International Conference on Persuasive Technology, pp. 1–7 (2009)
12. Forget, A., Chiasson, S., Biddle, R.: User-centred authentication feature framework. Inf. Comput. Secur. **23**(5), 497–515 (2015)
13. Forget, A., Chiasson, S., Van Oorschot, P.C., Biddle, R.: Improving text passwords through persuasion. In: Proceedings of the 4th Symposium on Usable Privacy and Security, pp. 1–12 (2008)
14. Ganesh, A., Ndulue, C., Orji, R.: Smartphone security and privacy – a gamified persuasive approach with protection motivation theory. In: Baghaei, N., Vassileva, J., Ali, R., Oyibo, K. (eds.) PERSUASIVE 2022. LNCS, vol. 13213, pp. 89–100. Springer, Cham (2022). https://doi.org/10.1007/978-3-030-98438-0_7
15. Gray, C.M., Santos, C., Bielova, N., Toth, M., Clifford, D.: Dark patterns and the legal requirements of consent banners: an interaction criticism perspective. In: Proceedings of the 2021 CHI Conference on Human Factors in Computing Systems, pp. 1–18 (2021)
16. Guo, Y., Zhang, Z., Guo, Y., Guo, X.: Nudging personalized password policies by understanding users' personality. Comput. Security **94**, 101801 (2020)
17. Johnson, E.J., Goldstein, D.: Do defaults save lives? Science **302**(5649), 1338–1339 (2003)

18. Kankane, S., DiRusso, C., Buckley, C.: Can we nudge users toward better password management? an initial study. In: Extended Abstracts of the 2018 CHI Conference on Human Factors in Computing Systems, pp. 1–6 (2018)
19. Komanduri, S., Shay, R., Cranor, L.F., Herley, C., Schechter, S.: Telepathwords: preventing weak passwords by reading users' minds. In: 23rd USENIX Security Symposium (USENIX Security 14), pp. 591–606 (2014)
20. Masaki, H., Shibata, K., Hoshino, S., Ishihama, T., Saito, N., Yatani, K.: Exploring nudge designs to help adolescent SNS users avoid privacy and safety threats. In: Proceedings of the 2020 CHI Conference on Human Factors in Computing Systems, pp. 1–11 (2020)
21. Nouwens, M., Liccardi, I., Veale, M., Karger, D., Kagal, L.: Dark patterns after the gdpr: Scraping consent pop-ups and demonstrating their influence. In: Proceedings of the 2020 CHI Conference on Human Factors in Computing Systems, pp. 1–13 (2020)
22. Petelka, J., Zou, Y., Schaub, F.: Put your warning where your link is: improving and evaluating email phishing warnings. In: Proceedings of the 2019 CHI Conference on Human Factors in Computing Systems, pp. 1–15 (2019)
23. Qu, L., Wang, C., Xiao, R., Hou, J., Shi, W., Liang, B.: Towards better security decisions: applying prospect theory to cybersecurity. In: Extended Abstracts of the 2019 CHI Conference on Human Factors in Computing Systems, pp. 1–6 (2019)
24. Qu, L., Xiao, R., Wang, C., Shi, W.: Design and evaluation of cfc-targeted security nudges. In: Extended Abstracts of the 2021 CHI Conference on Human Factors in Computing Systems, pp. 1–6 (2021)
25. Raptis, G.E., Katsini, C., Cen, A.J.L., Arachchilage, N.A.G., Nacke, L.E.: Better, funner, stronger: a gameful approach to nudge people into making less predictable graphical password choices. In: Proceedings of the 2021 CHI Conference on Human Factors in Computing Systems, pp. 1–17 (2021)
26. Redmiles, E.M., Mazurek, M.L., Dickerson, J.P.: Dancing pigs or externalities? measuring the rationality of security decisions. In: Proceedings of the 2018 ACM Conference on Economics and Computation, pp. 215–232 (2018)
27. Rodríguez-Priego, N., Van Bavel, R., Vila, J., Briggs, P.: Framing effects on online security behavior. Front. Psychol. p. 2833 (2020)
28. Rudman, R., Bruwer, R.: Defining web 3.0: opportunities and challenges. Electron. Libr. (2016)
29. Thaler, R.H., Sunstein, C.R.: Nudge: Improving Decisions About Health, Wealth, and Happiness. Penguin, New York, NY, USA (2009)
30. Thaler, R.H., Sunstein, C.R.: Nudge: The Final Edition. Penguin, New York (2021)
31. Tsigkanos, C., Kehrer, T., Ghezzi, C.: Modeling and verification of evolving cyber-physical spaces. In: Proceedings of the 2017 11th Joint Meeting on Foundations of Software Engineering, pp. 38–48 (2017)
32. Turland, J., Coventry, L., Jeske, D., Briggs, P., van Moorsel, A.: Nudging towards security: developing an application for wireless network selection for android phones. In: Proceedings of the 2015 British HCI Conference, pp. 193–201 (2015)
33. Ur, B., et al.: Design and evaluation of a data-driven password meter. In: Proceedings of the 2017 Chi Conference on Human Factors in Computing Systems, pp. 3775–3786 (2017)
34. Waldrop, M.M.: How to hack the hackers the human side of cybercrime. Nature, 533(7602) (2016)
35. Wang, Y., Gou, L., Xu, A., Zhou, M. X., Yang, H., Badenes, H.: Veilme: an interactive visualization tool for privacy configuration of using personality traits. In:

Proceedings of the 33rd Annual ACM Conference on Human Factors in Computing Systems, pp. 817–826 (2015)

36. Zhang-Kennedy, L., Chiasson, S., Biddle, R.: Stop clicking on "Update Later": persuading users they need up-to-date antivirus protection. In: Spagnolli, A., Chittaro, L., Gamberini, L. (eds.) PERSUASIVE 2014. LNCS, vol. 8462, pp. 302–322. Springer, Cham (2014). https://doi.org/10.1007/978-3-319-07127-5_27

37. Zhang-Kennedy, L., Chiasson, S., Biddle, R.: The role of instructional design in persuasion: a comics approach for improving cybersecurity. Int. J. Human-Comput. Inter. **32**(3), 215–257 (2016)

A Privacy-Preserving Electricity Theft Detection (PETD) Scheme for Smart Grid

Siliang Dong[✉] and Yining Liu[✉]

School of Computer and Information Security, Guilin University of Electronic Technology, Guilin 541004, China
2532202194@qq.com, lyn7311@sina.com

Abstract. There is serious electricity theft in the smart grid, which will cause huge economic losses to the power supplier. Therefore, it is very important to conduct electricity theft detection. Using machine/deep learning-based approaches to conduct electricity theft detection can greatly save the time and cost of manual investigation. Existing machine learning-based electricity theft detection schemes often treat the detector as trusted and directly publish user electricity consumption data to the detector for detection. However, there are generally no trusted detectors in reality, so these electricity theft detection schemes have the problem of leaking user data privacy. In this paper, we propose a privacy-preserving electricity theft detection (PETD) scheme, which adds noise to user electricity consumption data, and then publishes the noise-added electricity consumption data to the untrusted detector for detection, thereby protecting the privacy of user data. Experiments have shown that after adding noise to user data, although the performance of our model has been reduced, it is still within an acceptable range, thus achieving a balance between data privacy and data availability.

Index Terms: Electricity theft detection · Data privacy · Noise · Untrusted detector

1 Introduction

Electricity theft is widespread in smart grids [1, 2], illegal users achieve the purpose of paying less electricity bills by stealing electricity. Electricity theft will destroy the metering and control devices of power supply equipment, causing the power supply equipment to fail to perform correct and effective measurement statistics, leading to the loss of electrical energy, resulting in the loss of power supply enterprises and the country's energy, and disrupting the normal order of electricity use. Moreover, if the thief changes the line, it is easy to cause safety accidents such as electric shock and fire [3, 4]. Therefore, it is necessary to conduct electricity theft detection [5]. With the popularity of smart meters in smart grids [6], users can interact with data centers in real time, and users can upload real-time electricity consumption data to the data centers through smart meters. The data center publishes the data to outsourced detectors for data analysis to identify users who steal electricity.

In recent years, many scholars have done a lot of research on electricity theft detection. The current electricity theft detection schemes are mainly divided into three categories: state estimation [7], game theory [8], and machine/deep learning [9]. Among them, machine/deep learning methods are widely used in electricity theft detection due to their accuracy and efficiency. However, the existing electricity theft detection scheme [10–13] based on machine/deep learning often considers the detector to be trusted. The detector can directly obtain the user's raw electricity consumption data, which may leak the user's data privacy. For example, in [10], the author proposes a support vector machine (SVM) electricity theft detector, which analyzes the user's electricity consumption pattern for a long period, so as to find users who may be stealing electricity. The detector of this scheme can directly obtain the raw electricity consumption data corresponding to the users, so there is a risk of exposing the users' data privacy. In [11], the authors consider both the internal time-series natures and external influence factors of electricity consumption, thereby improving the accuracy of electricity theft detection. However, the detector of this scheme can still directly obtain the user's raw data, so there is also a risk of exposing the user's data privacy [14]. The above schemes all treat the detector as trusted, and the detector can directly obtain the user's raw data, but in reality the detector is often untrusted, so the above schemes have not consider the issue of protecting user data privacy.

In order to protect the privacy of user data, the data should be privately processed first before the user data is published to the detector for detection. The existing data privacy processing technologies mainly include: n-source anonymity [15–17], data aggregation [18, 19] and other methods. Although n-source anonymity can protect user privacy by cutting off the correspondence between users and their data, when the number of users is large, the slot for transmitting data has to be expanded by many times, which causes the problem of excessive storage burden. Therefore, n-source anonymity is not suitable for large-scale users' electricity theft detection. Although data aggregation can protect user data privacy, how to select a reasonable number of aggregated users so that data privacy can be protected and features of electricity theft can be detected is a difficult problem. Therefore, data aggregation is difficult to use in data privacy processing for electricity theft detection. In this paper, we choose reasonable noise to add to the electricity consumption data to achieve a balance between the data privacy and the data availability.

In our PETD scheme, an important attribute of electricity consumption behavior of users is considered: that is periodicity, which means the users usually consume energy cyclically (daily or weekly) [13]; Generally, the users meets the periodicity of electricity consumption. If there are users stealing electricity, it will destroy the periodic electricity consumption feature. We use convolutional neural networks to analyze the overall long-term electricity consumption pattern of the users, identify some users with abnormal electricity consumption feature, thereby identifying users suspected of stealing electricity. Adding noise to the electricity consumption data will cause some interference to the periodicity of user data, thereby affecting the performance of detectors. In our scheme, we choose reasonable noise to protect data privacy, and retain most of the periodicity of user data, so as to protect user data privacy as much as possible under the premise of ensuring the performance of detectors. In this paper, our proposed PETD scheme has the following contribution points.

(1) We propose a electricity theft detection scheme that does not require a trusted detector, making the scheme more applicable since it is difficult to deploy a trusted detector in practical smart grid environments.
(2) Unlike previous works that does not consider data privacy protection, we choose reasonable noise to add to the electricity consumption data and conduct extensive experiments on massive realistic electricity consumption dataset. Experimental results show that we protect user data privacy at the expense of minimal loss of model performance, thus achieving a balance between data privacy and data availability.

The rest of the paper is organized as follows. Preliminaries are introduced in Sect. 2. System model and design goals are discussed in Sect. 3. The proposed PETD scheme is presented in Sect. 4, and its performance evaluated in Sect. 5. Finally, the paper is concluded in Sect. 6.

2 Preliminaries

2.1 Gaussian Noise

Gaussian noise refers to a type of noise whose probability density function obeys a normal distribution [20]. The probability density function of Gaussian noise is as follows:

$$p(x) = \frac{1}{\delta\sqrt{2\pi}} e^{-\frac{(x-\mu)^2}{2\delta^2}}.$$

where x represents the gray value, μ represents the mean of x, and δ^2 represents the variance of x.

2.2 Principal Component Analysis (PCA)

Principal component analysis is often used to reduce the dimensionality of high-dimensional datasets [21], which prevents the model from overfitting and improve the model accuracy. When reducing dimensionality, it retains the features that carry the most information. The information measurement indicator used by PCA is explainable variance. The larger the variance, the more information the feature carries. The feature variance equation is as below:

$$v_{ar} = \frac{1}{n-1} \sum_{i=1}^{n} (x_i - \hat{x})^2.$$

where v_{ar} represents the variance of a feature, n represents the number of samples, x_i represents the value of each sample in a feature, and $\hat{x}$ the mean of this list of samples.

2.3   Convolutional Neural Network (CNN)

Convolutional neural network is a widely used model in the field of deep learning. CNN includes convolutional layers, pooling layers and full connection layers and so on [22]. The common CNN model structure is shown in Fig. 1.

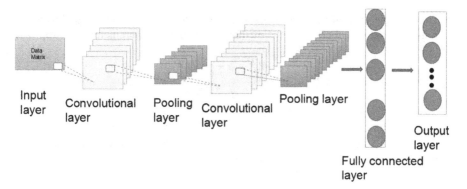

Fig. 1. Classic CNN structure diagram

The convolutional layers include many convolution kernels, which is used to extract the primary features of the data. Then use the Relu activation function to achieve nonlinear classification of data. The equation of Relu performs as follow:

$$f(x) = \begin{cases} 0, \ x < 0; \\ x, \ x \geq 0. \end{cases}$$

The pooling layer is used to reduce the amount of calculation and prevent the model from overfitting. After that, the full connection layer synthesizes the previously extracted features, and outputs the distinguishing features. Then through the softmax function. Assuming that the original output of the neural network is $y_1, y_2,..., y_n$, the output after the softmax function is:

$$y'_i = \frac{e^{y_i}}{\sum_{j=1}^{n} e^{y_i}}.$$

y'_i is the probability output by a single node, and the sum of the output probability of all nodes is 1, that is:

$$\sum_{j=1}^{n} y'_i = 1.$$

the probability of the data belonging to different categories can be output through the softmax function, and the data belongs to the category with the highest probability. The commonly used loss function for neural networks is the cross-entropy loss function. Cross entropy describes the distance between the actual output and the expected output, that is, the smaller the value of the cross entropy, the closer the two probability distributions are. Assuming that the probability distribution p is the expected output, the probability distribution q is the actual output, and $H(p, q)$ is the cross entropy, then:

$$H(p, q) = -\sum_x p(x) \log q(x).$$

The gradient descent method is usually used to update the weight W and bias b of the convolutional neural network, the method of updating the parameters is as follows:

$$\begin{cases} W_{ij}^{(l)} = W_{ij}^{(l)} - \alpha \frac{\partial}{\partial W_{ij}^{(l)}} J(W, b) \\ b_i^{(l)} = b_i^{(l)} - \alpha \frac{\partial}{\partial b_i^{(l)}} J(W, b) \end{cases}.$$

The convolutional neural network randomly initializes the weight parameters W and biases b, and iterates continuously according to this process until the loss function is minimized, where α is the learning rate, which controls the speed of parameter update.

3 System Model and Privacy Threats

3.1 System Model

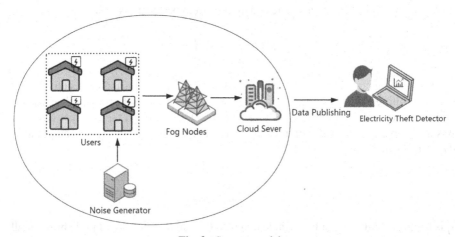

Fig. 2. System model

As shown in Fig. 2, the system model includes users U_i, $i \in ([1, n])$, fog nodes (FN), cloud server (CS), noise generator (NG) and the electricity theft detector.

(1) CS is a server used to store user electricity consumption data, and it outsources user data to the electricity theft detector for electricity theft detection.

(2) The electricity theft detector is an outsourced data analysis organization that receives electricity consumption data published by the CS for electricity theft detection.

(3) FN is an edge computing device that can replace cloud servers for partial computing, and can implement interaction between users and cloud servers according to certain rules [23, 24].

(4) NG is a server used to generate noise and then transmits the noise to the users.

(5) Each user is equipped with a smart meter. The smart meter adds the received noise to the user's real-time electricity consumption data, and then transmits it to the FN.

3.2 Design Goals

There are a series of security problems in the smart grid, such as data injection attack, the denial of service attack, and some other physical threats [25]. In traditional security problems, if the data does not need to be released to the public, but only shared between authorized users, there is no need to consider the problem of privacy protection, only encryption and decryption are required. Authorized users can decrypt the cipher text to get the raw data, while unauthorized users can only get the messy cipher text. However, in a big data environment, the data must be open to the public to be used as much as possible, and the privacy of the data producer must not be leaked. To achieve this, traditional encryption and decryption are not enough. We call this kind of operation privacy processing or privacy computing. We need to remove certain attributes of the data so that it does not reveal user privacy, and at the same time retain some attributes so that it can be used. In our scheme, the detector is untrusted. We cover up the user's raw data by adding noise to the user data, while retaining most of the periodicity feature we need to detect. What we release to the untrusted detector is the noise-added electricity consumption data, thus the detector cannot know the user's raw electricity consumption data. However, the detector can still identify users suspected of stealing electricity by analyzing the periodicity of users' long-term electricity consumption patterns. We assume that there is a secure communication channel between authorized entities, so we only consider privacy problems. In our scheme, privacy threats are as follows.

(1) The electricity theft detector is untrusted, it will sell user data to other organizations for profit.

(2) CS and FN are honest but curious, they will not tamper with user data, but they will attempt to infer valuable information from the data.

(3) Users are also honest but curious. They will execute the protocol honestly, but will try to snoop on other user data.

4   Our Proposed PETD Scheme

This section mainly describes our PETD scheme which includes two parts: electricity privacy preservation part and data detection part. In the electricity privacy preservation part, we add noise to user data to cover up the user's raw electricity consumption data, thereby protecting user data privacy. In the data detection part, we use convolutional neural networks to analyze the periodicity of users' long-term electricity consumption patterns, so as to identify the users suspected of stealing electricity.

Part 1: Electricity Privacy Preservation

(1) The cloud server sends data collection requests to the FN. FN initiates a task request to the users and the NG.
(2) The NG produces noise β_i, $i \in (1, ..., n)$, and sends it to the users U_i, $i \in (1, ..., n)$.
(3) When the users U_i, $i \in (1, ..., n)$ receive the noise β_i, $i \in (1, ..., n)$ from NG, the users adds the noise to their own electricity consumption data, and then send the noise-added electricity consumption data γ_i, $i \in (1, ..., n)$ to the FN.
(4) After FN receives the noise-added electricity consumption data γ_i, $i \in (1, ..., n)$, FN transmits it to the CS in real time, then the CS publishes the noise-added electricity consumption data to the detector for electricity theft detection.

Part 2: Data Detection

4.1 Data Preprocessing

The electricity consumption dataset contains many missing values, which may be caused by the failure of smart meters or the error during the data transmission process. In this paper, we use random forest to fill in the missing values, and the algorithm performs as follows:

(1) Suppose the training set is $D = \{(x_1, y_1), (x_2, y_2), ..., (x_n, y_n)\}$. Take the training set as input, the output $f(x)$ is a continuous variable, and the input is divided into M regions:$R_1, R_2, ..., R_M$ and the output value of each region is:$c_1, c_2, ..., c_m$, then the regression tree model can be expressed as:

$$f(x) = \sum_{i=1}^{M} c_m I(x \in R_m).$$

(2) Use the value s of feature j to divide the input space into two regions, respectively: $R_1(j, s) = \{x | x^{(j)} \leq s\}$ and $R_2(j, s) = \{x | x^{(j)} > s\}$.
(3) In order to make the regression tree optimal, the mean square error (MSE) should be minimized, that is:

$$\min(MSE) = \frac{1}{M} \min_{j,s} [\min_{c_1} \sum_{x_i \in R_1(j,s)} (y_i - c_1)^2 + \min_{c_2} \sum_{x_i \in R_2(j,s)} (y_i - c_2)^2].$$

where c_1, c_2 are the average output values in the region of R_1 and R_2, respectively. In order to minimize the MSE, we need to traverse each value of each feature in turn, calculate the current error of each possible segmentation point, and finally select the point with the smallest segmentation error to divide the input space into two parts, and then recursively the above steps until the end of the segmentation.

After that, we use the Mean Imputation and Zero Imputation methods to fill in the missing values, and calculate their MSE separately, as shown in Fig. 3:

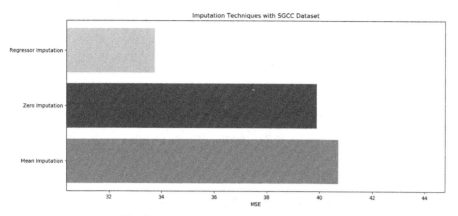

Fig. 3. Mean square error (MSE) comparison

From the Fig. 3, we can see that using random forest to fill in missing values has the smallest MSE, that is, using random forest to fill in missing values has the best effect.

After filling in the missing values, in order to prevent some data from having an excessive influence on the prediction, we use the Z-score standardization method to compress the data to the same scale according to the following equation:

$$x_i = \frac{\overline{x}_i - \hat{x}}{\sigma^2}, \ \forall i.$$

where $\hat{x}$ and σ represent the mean and standard deviation of the training samples. The $\overline{x}_i \in R^n, i = 1, ...N$ represent a training set of points. The $x_i \in R^n, i = 1, ...N$ represent the normalized training samples.

Since the electricity consumption dataset contains the electricity consumption data of users for many days, which will cause a heavy training burden. We use the PCA method to reduce the dimensionality of the dataset, and then convert the data into a matrix of dimensio (p, q, d). p represents the number of rows of the matrix, q represents the number of columns of the matrix, and d represents the number of matrices. The matrix shape of a individual user is $(p, q, 1)$, as shown below:

$$\begin{pmatrix} [C_{1,1}] & \cdots & [C_{1,q}] \\ \vdots & \ddots & \vdots \\ [C_{p,1}] & \cdots & [C_{p,q}] \end{pmatrix}$$

4.2 Our CNN Model

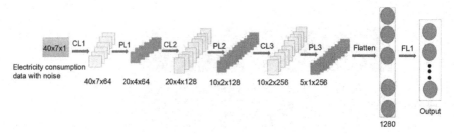

Fig. 4. CNN model framework

As shown in Fig. 4, we use 3 convolutional layers, 3 pooling layers and a full connection layer to build our CNN model. Our model has 3 stages, as described below:

(1) We transform the one-dimensional (1-D) electricity consumption data into a $(f, j, 1)$ matrix to inut the CNN model.
(2) CNN uses the convolution kernel to realize the weight sharing in the feature extraction process to reduce the parameters. The pooling layer reduces the calculation time and prevents the model from overfitting. Assuming that the current matrix shape is (f, j, r), after passing through a convolutional layer containing α convolution kernels, the matrix shape becomes (f, j, α). After the pooling layer, the matrix shape becomes $(f/2, j/2, r)$.
(3) After the pooling layer, we expand the feature into a one-dimensional vector and connect it with a full connection layer of length (λ) to change the matrix shape to (λ). After that, a vector of length (2) is obtained through the softmax function, which is the normal probability and the probability of stealing electricity. If the normal probability is greater than the probability of stealing electricity, it is a normal user, otherwise, it is a user suspected of electricity theft.

5   Privacy Analysis and Performance Evaluation

In this section, we analyze the detection system in two parts. The first part introduces privacy analysis, and the second part introduces performance evaluation.

5.1 Privacy Analysis

In this part, we analyze data privacy in the process of data collection and data publishing. During the data collection process, the noise generator sends the noise to the users. After adding the noise from the noise generator, the user sends the noise-added electricity consumption data to FN, then FN sends the noise-added electricity consumption data to CS. During the data publishing process, the CS publishes the noise-added electricity consumption data to the detector for electricity theft detection.

(1) The NG produces noise $\beta_i, i \in (1, ..., n)$, then sends the noise to the users $U_i, i \in (1, ..., n)$. At this stage, there is no transmission of electricity consumption data, so only the user himself/herself knows his/her real electricity consumption data. Thereby at this stage, user data privacy is guaranteed.

(2) After the users $U_i, i \in (1, ..., n)$ receive the noise $\beta_i, i \in (1, ..., n)$ from the noise generator, they adds the noise to their own electricity consumption data, and then send the noise-added electricity consumption data $\gamma_i, i \in (1, ..., n)$ to FN. At this stage, what FN receives is the noise-added electricity consumption data and cannot obtain the user's raw electricity consumption data, so user data privacy is guaranteed.

(3) FN transmits the noise-added electricity consumption data $\gamma_i, i \in (1, ..., n)$ to the CS in real time. The CS also cannot obtain the user's raw electricity consumption data, so user privacy is guaranteed at this stage.

(4) The CS publishes the noise-added electricity consumption data $\gamma_i, i \in (1, ..., n)$ to the detector for data analysis to identify users suspected of stealing electricity. The detector also cannot obtain the user's raw electricity consumption data, so in the process of data publishing, user data privacy is also protected.

In summary, in the process of data collection and data publishing, except the user himself / herself, no other organization knows the user's real electricity consumption data, so the user's data privacy is protected.

5.2 Performance Evaluation

In this section, we evaluate the proposed PETD scheme by conducting experiments on a 64-bit computer with Intel(R) Core(TM) i5-6500 CPU, 3.2 GHz, 8GB RAM, using Python, Tensorflow and Keras framework. The experiments used the labeled database from State Grid Corporation of China (SGCC) [13], which contains the energy usage data of 42372 customers within 1,035 days. The last column of the dataset is the label corresponding to the user, which is a single binary value (i.e., 0 represents a normal user, and 1 represents a suspected electricity theft user).

We use cross-validation to divide the SGCC dataset into a training set and a test set, and add noise to the 1035-day historical electricity consumption data of users in the test set. Then we use the Z-score standardization method to compress the data to the same scale and use PCA to reduce the dimensionality of the dataset.

As shown in Fig. 5, after we reduce the dimensionality of the 1-D electricity consumption data, when the feature is around 280 dimensions, the cumulative explainable variance ration reaches 99%, which means that 99% of the information of the raw electricity consumption data is retained. In order for the convolutional neural network to more accurately analyze the periodic characteristics of the electricity consumption data, we convert the electricity consumption data into a two-dimensional (2-D) matrix by weekly cycle:

$$\begin{pmatrix} [C_{1,1}] & \cdots & [C_{1,7}] \\ \vdots & \ddots & \vdots \\ [C_{40,1}] & \cdots & [C_{40,7}] \end{pmatrix}$$

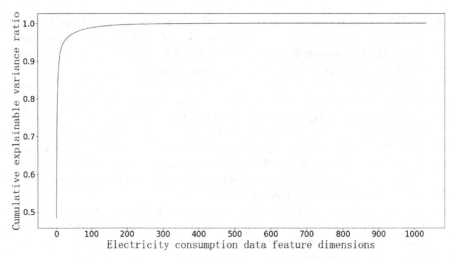

Fig. 5. Cumulative explainable variance ratio

5.2.1 Model training Phase

As shown in Fig. 4, our convolutional neural network model contains 3 convolutional layers, 3 pooling layers, and 1 full connection layer. Our first convolutional layer contains 64 convolution kernels, the size of the convolution kernels is (5, 5). We set the sliding step size to (1, 1) and use the padding method to perform convolution operations. The first convolutional layer outputs a matrix with dimensions (40, 7, 64), and then through the first pooling layer, we set the pooling window size to (2, 2), and the sliding step size to (2, 2).

The first pooling layer outputs a matrix with dimensions (20, 4, 64), then through the second convolutional layer, the second convolutional layer has 128 convolution kernels, the size of the convolution kernels is (5, 5), and the sliding step size is set to (1, 1). The second convolutional layer outputs a matrix with dimensions (20, 4, 128), then through the second pooling layer, we set the pooling window size to (2, 2), and the sliding step size to (2, 2). The second pooling layer outputs a matrix whose shape is (10, 2, 128), then through the third convolutional layer, the third convolutional layer has 256 convolution kernels, the size of the convolution kernels is (5, 5), and the sliding step size is set to (1, 1). The third convolutional layer outputs a matrix with dimensions (10, 2, 256), then through the third pooling layer, we set the pooling window size to (2, 2), and the sliding step size to (2, 2). The third pooling layer outputs a matrix with dimensions (5, 1, 256), after that, we pull the matrix into a vector whose shape is (1280), and connect it to the full connection layer. Then use the softmax function to obtain the data category probability. The model performs gradient descent by comparing the difference between the predicted data label and the real label of the data, and continuously adjusts the model parameters to optimize the model, that is the model training process.

5.2.2 Model Evaluation

The choice of noise is very important, because we identify users who steal electricity by detecting the periodicity of users' long-term electricity consumption behavior pattern. If excessive noise is added, the original periodic characteristics of the data will be disturbed, thereby decreasing the model performance. If the noise is too small, the detector can still infer the user's approximate electricity consumption after receiving the data. Therefore, we must choose a reasonable noise to balance data privacy and model performance. We use cross-validation to test the detection effect of the model on the noise-added test set, as shown in Fig. 6.

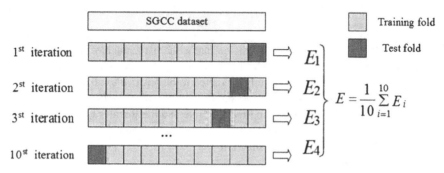

Fig. 6. Cross-validation flowchart

Where E_i, $i = 1, ...10$ represents the accuracy of the i-th iteration, E represents the average accuracy score after 10 iterations. As shown in Table 1, we list the confusion matrix, which is an effective model evaluation tool for supervised learning.

Table 1. Confusion matrix

Predicted value	True value	
	0 (normal user)	1 (offending user)
0 (normal user)	TN (True Negative)	FN (False Negative)
1 (offending user)	FP (False Positive)	TP (True Positive)

TN represents the number of samples whose actual label is 0 and predicted to be 0 by the model, FN represents the number of samples whose actual label is 1 and predicted to be 0 by the model, FP represents the number of samples whose actual label is 0 and predicted to be 1 by the model, TP represents the number of samples whose actual label is 1 and predicted to be 1 by the model. In our CNN-based electricity theft detection scheme, the variance ε of noise has a great influence on the detection results. We use four evaluation metrics to evaluate the electricity theft detection effect of different-variance-noise-added electricity consumption data. The four evaluation metrics are as follows.

$$\text{Accuracy score} = \frac{TP + TN}{TP + TN + FP + FN}$$

$$\text{Precision rate } P = \frac{TP}{TP + FP}$$

$$\text{Recall rate } R = \frac{TP}{TP + FN}$$

$$\text{F1} - \text{score} = \frac{2 \times P \times R}{P + R}$$

The Accuracy score is the percentage of samples that are correctly predicted by the model to the total samples. The Precision rate is the percentage of samples that are actually positive among all the samples predicted to be positive. The Recall rate is the percentage of samples that are correctly predicted to be positive to all samples that are actually positive. The Precision rate and the Recall rate are sometimes contradictory. F1-score is the harmonic mean of the Precision rate and the Recall rate. The larger the value of F1-score, the better the model effect. For different variances ε value, the four model evaluation metrics change as shown in Fig. 7.

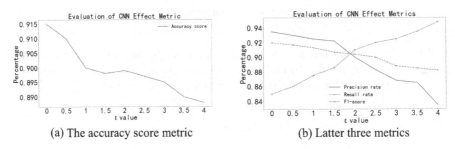

(a) The accuracy score metric   (b) Latter three metrics

Fig. 7. Evaluation metrics of different ε value

From Fig. 7, it can be concluded that as the noise variance ε increases, the detection accuracy generally shows a downward trend. As the noise variance ε increases, the detection effect occasionally increases due to the contingency of the experiment, but overall, the detection rate shows a downward trend. The ideal state of the model is that both the precision rate and the recall rate are high, but the two are contradictory to each other. We use F1-score to balance the precision rate and the recall rate, and F1-score and the accuracy are comprehensive global model evaluation metrics used by us to choose the reasonable ε value. In order to make the user's electricity consumption data more private, the variance of the noise should be as large as possible, but as the variance of the noise becomes larger, the accuracy score and F1-score will become smaller, and the performance of the model will become worse. We must make data privacy and model performance are balanced. When the noise variance ε is 2.5, the accuracy score is around 0.90, and F1-score also maintains a relatively high value, at the same time, the user's raw electricity consumption data can be protected to a certain extent. Therefore, we choose the noise variance $\varepsilon = 2.5$. It is worth noting that the relationship between the variance of the noise and the performance of the model is not completely certain, but will change with the change of the dataset. For example, in other datasets, the detection effect may still be very good when the noise with a larger variance (such as 4, 5, 6) is added. In this paper, our main idea is to reflect the idea of adding noise to achieve a balance between data availability and privacy.

5.2.3 Performance Comparison

In this section, we compare our scheme with the performance of existing mainstream schemes on the given dataset, the schemes we choose to compare are as follows:

(1) Support Vector Machine (SVM): Support vector machines classify data by constructing a spatial classification hyperplane. There have been many previous studies [26–28] using support vector machines to identify users who steal electricity.
(2) Random Forest (RF): Random Forest [29] is an ensemble learning model, which integrates many decision trees, and its performance is often better than a single decision tree.
(3) Extreme Gradient Boosting (XGBoost): XGBoost is one of the boosting algorithms. The idea of Boosting algorithm is to integrate many weak classifiers to form a strong classifier. Because XGBoost is a boosted tree model, it integrates many tree models to form a strong classifier. The tree model used is the classification and regression trees (CART) model.
(4) Convolutional Neural Networks (CNN): This scheme can be regarded as a variant of our PETD scheme. Note that the training data and the test data for CNN is the raw electricity consumption data, while the training data for our PETD scheme is the raw electricity consumption data and the test data is the noise-added electricity consumption data.
(5) Wide & Deep CNN: The Wide & Deep CNN [13] uses a wide component to learn the features of the one-dimensional (1-D) data, and use a deep component to learn the periodic features of the two-dimensional (2-D) data, then use the features learned from the 1-D data and the 2-D data as the basis for identifying the thieves.

We use the Mean Average Precision (MAP) and the Area Under Curve (AUC) as model performance comparison metrics. AUC is a commonly used model evaluation metric, the equation is as follows:

$$AUC = \frac{\sum_{i \in positiveClass} Rank_i - \frac{M(1+M)}{2}}{M \times N}$$

where M, N represent the number of positive samples and negative samples, respectively, $Rank_i$ represents the rank value of sample i.

Table 2. Performance comparison with other existing schemes

Methods	Training ratio = 50%			Training ratio = 70%			Training ratio = 80%		
	AUC	MAP@100	MAP@200	AUC	MAP@100	MAP@200	AUC	MAP@100	MAP@200
SVM	0.718	0.675	0.601	0.727	0.728	0.591	0.730	0.735	0.623
RF	0.720	0.908	0.867	0.737	0.926	0.853	0.739	0.895	0.854
XGBoost	0.732	0.910	0.876	0.757	0.938	0.889	0.767	0.916	0.873
CNN (raw data)	0.775	0.905	0.883	0.788	0.958	0.920	0.782	0.925	0.875
Wide&Deep CNN	0.785	0.936	0.895	0.796	0.968	0.932	0.785	0.950	0.909
Our PETD scheme	0.725	0.900	0.870	0.750	0.913	0.910	0.770	0.915	0.860

We show the performance comparison between our scheme and other schemes in Table 2. We conducted three groups of experiments, the training ratio of each experiment is 50%, 70%, and 80% respectively. In our scheme, we need to add noise to the test set. In each group of experiment, we compare the evaluation metrics (AUC and MAP) with the other five schemes. In the MAP evaluation, the number of test samples we choose is 100 and 200, respectively. It can be concluded from Table 2 that after adding noise, the performance of our scheme is slightly worse than that of deep learning methods, but it is better than some ordinary machine learning methods that detect raw data such as (SVM and RF). We selected reasonable noise for users in the test set to protect user data privacy and control the loss of performance effects within an acceptable range, thus achieving a balance between the data availability and data privacy.

5.2.4 Comparison with Existing Schemes

This section describes the comparison between our scheme and the electricity theft detection schemes of Yao et al. [30], Zheng et al. [13], Punmiya et al. [12], and Zhang et al. [31]. Yao et al.'s scheme proposes that the electricity consumption of neighboring users is similar to that of neighboring users, that is, the electricity consumption behavior of a single user should be similar to that of neighboring users. If a user deviates from the similarity of group electricity consumption for a long time, it is suspected of stealing electricity. The scheme improves the accuracy of electricity theft detection by detecting group similarity. In Zheng et al.'s [13] scheme, they converts one-dimensional (1-D) electricity consumption data into two-dimensional (2-D) data, so as to better discover the periodic characteristics of electricity consumption. The features learned from the 1-D data and the features learned from the 2-D data are combined with the Wide & Deep Convolutional Neural Network as the basis for identifying users who steal electricity. Punmiya et al.'s [12] scheme does feature engineering on electricity consumption data, creating features that make it easier to detect electricity theft for the model. However, the ensemble learning model used in the scheme can only process data of a general scale, and is not suitable for massive data processing. In Zhang et al.'s scheme, the authors decomposes the electricity sequences into trend, seasonal and residual views, and uses a recurrent neural network to fully analyze the time characteristics of the electricity consumption data. However, the above schemes are all from the perspective of how to make it easier for the model to learn electricity consumption features, and the detectors can directly obtain the user's raw electricity consumption data. Different from the above schemes, our PETD scheme starts from the perspective of protecting user privacy. In our scheme, before publishing the data to the detector, the data is added with reasonable noise, so that user privacy is protected, at the same time, the detector can also ensure an acceptable electricity theft detection performance. We have realized that not only the privacy of data is protected, but also the data can be used for normal analysis. In addition, our PETD scheme is scalable, as shown in Table 3.

Table 3. Characteristics comparison

	Proposed scheme	Yao et al. [30]	Zheng et al. [13]	Punmiya et al. [12]	Zhang et al. [31]
Relying on trusted detectors	No	Yes	Yes	Yes	Yes
User privacy	Yes	No	No	No	No
Massive data processing	Yes	Yes	Yes	No	Yes

6 Conclusion

In this paper, we proposed a privacy-preserving electricity theft detection (PETD) scheme for smart grid. In our scheme, we add reasonable noise to the users' electricity consumption data to conceal the users' real electricity consumption data, thereby realizing electricity theft detection without relying on a trusted organization. Experiments have proved that after adding noise, although the performance of our model has been reduced, it is still within an acceptable range, thus achieving a balance between data privacy and data availability. However, the computational burden in the process of adding noise to the data is a bit heavy. In future work, we will further optimize the process of adding noise to reduce the computational burden.

Acknowledgment. This work was supported by Natural Science Foundation of China under grant No. 62072133, Key projects of Guangxi Natural Science Foundation under grant No. 2018GXNSFDA281040.

References

1. Shokoya, N.O., Raji, A.K.: Electricity theft: a reason to deploy smart grid in South Africa. In: 2019 International Conference on the Domestic Use of Energy (DUE), Wellington, South Africa, pp. 96–101 (2019)

2. Ayub, N., Aurangzeb, K., Awais, M., Ali, U.: Electricity theft detection using cnn-gru and manta ray foraging optimization algorithm. In: 2020 IEEE 23rd International Multitopic Conference (INMIC), Bahawalpur, Pakistan, pp. 1–6 (2020)
3. Presnal, J., Houston, H., Maberry, G.: The electrical safety program and the value in parterning with health & safety professionals. In: 2020 IEEE IAS Electrical Safety Workshop (ESW), Reno, NV, USA, pp. 1–7 (2020)
4. Brenner, B., Majano, D.: Expanding workplace electrical safety to non-electrical occupations. In: 2020 IEEE IAS Electrical Safety Workshop (ESW), Reno, NV, USA, pp. 1–5 (2020)
5. Boucetta, C., Flauzac, O., Haggar, B.S., Nassour, A.N.M., Nolot, F.: Smart grid networks enabled electricity-theft detection and fault tolerance. In: 2020 8th International Conference on Wireless Networks and Mobile Communications (WINCOM), Reims, France, pp. 1–6 (2020)
6. Sirojan, T., Lu, S., Phung, B.T., Ambikairajah, E.: Embedded edge computing for real-time smart meter data analytics. In: 2019 International Conference on Smart Energy Systems and Technologies (SEST), Porto, Portugal, pp. 1–5 (2019)
7. Wen, M., Yao, D., Li, B., Lu, R.: State estimation based energy theft detection scheme with privacy preservation in smart grid. In: 2018 IEEE International Conference on Communications (ICC), Kansas City, MO, USA, pp. 1–6 (2018)
8. Cárdenas, A.A., Amin, S., Schwartz, G., Dong, R., Sastry, S.: A game theory model for electricity theft detection and privacy-aware control in AMI systems. In: 2012 50th Annual Allerton Conference on Communication, Control, and Computing (Allerton), Monticello, IL, pp. 1830–1837 (2012)
9. Pereira, J., Saraiva, F.: A comparative analysis of unbalanced data handling techniques for machine learning algorithms to electricity theft detection. In: 2020 IEEE Congress on Evolutionary Computation (CEC), Glasgow, United Kingdom, p. 18 (2020)
10. Jokar, P., Arianpoo, N., Leung, V.C.M.: Electricity theft detection in AMI using customers' consumption patterns. IEEE Trans. Smart Grid $7(1)$, 216–226 (2016)
11. Chen, Z., Meng, D., Zhang, Y., Xin, T., Xiao, D.: Electricity theft detection using deep bidirectional recurrent neural network. In: 2020 22nd International Conference on Advanced Communication Technology (ICACT), Phoenix Park, Korea (South), pp. 401–406 (2020)
12. Punmiya, R., Choe, S.: Energy theft detection using gradient boosting theft detector with feature engineering-based preprocessing. IEEE Trans. Smart Grid $10(2)$, 2326–2329 (2019)
13. Zheng, Z., Yang, Y., Niu, X., Dai, H., Zhou, Y.: Wide and deep convolutional neural networks for electricity-theft detection to secure smart grids. IEEE Trans. Industr. Inf. $14(4)$, 1606–1615 (2018)
14. Esquivel-Quiros, L.G., Barrantes, E.G., Darlington, F.E.: Measuring data privacy preserving and machine learning. In: 2018 7th International Conference on Software Process Improvement (CIMPS), Guadalajara, Mexico, p. 85–94 (2018)
15. Zhang, Y., Chen, Q., Zhong, S.: Privacy-preserving data aggregation in mobile phone sensing. IEEE Trans. Inf. Forensics Secur. $11(5)$, 980–992 (2016)
16. Liu, Y., Wang, Y., Wang, X., Xia, Z., Xu, J.: Privacy-preserving raw data collection without a trusted authority for IoT. Comput. Netw. 148, 340–348 (2019)
17. Chen, J., Liu, G., Liu, Y.: Lightweight privacy-preserving raw data publishing scheme. IEEE Trans. Emerg. Top. Comput. $9(4)$, 2170–2174 (2020)
18. Liu, Y., Guo, W., Fan, C., Chang, L., Cheng, C.: A practical privacy-preserving data aggregation (3pda) scheme for smart grid. IEEE Trans. Industr. Inf. $15(3)$, 1767–1774 (2019)
19. Song, J., Liu, Y., Shao, J., Tang, C.: A dynamic membership data aggregation (dmda) protocol for smart grid. IEEE Syst. J. $14(1)$, 900–908 (2020)
20. Ma, X., Song, B., Lin, F.:Passivity analysis for neural networks perturbed by poisson noise and gaussian noise. In: 2019 Chinese Control Conference (CCC), Guangzhou, China, pp. 8778–8782 (2019)

21. Wu, C., Huang, L., Wang, W.: De-noising method of joint empirical mode decomposition and principal component analysis. In: 2020 IEEE International Conference on Power, Intelligent Computing and Systems (ICPICS), Shenyang, China, pp. 193–195 (2020)
22. Xin, R., Zhang, J., Shao, Y.: Complex network classification with convolutional neural network. In: Tsinghua Science and Technology, vol. 25, no. 4, pp. 447–457 (2020)
23. Lin, Y., Shen, H.: Cloud fog: towards high quality of experience in cloud gaming. In: 2015 44th International Conference on Parallel Processing, Beijing, pp. 500–509 (2015)
24. Lyu, L., Nandakumar, K., Rubinstein, B., Jin, J., Bedo, J., Palaniswami, M.: PPFA: privacy preserving fog-enabled aggregation in smart grid. IEEE Trans. Industr. Inf. **14**(8), 3733–3744 (2018)
25. Sanjab, A., Saad, W., Guvenc, I., Sarwat, A., Biswas, S.: Smart grid security: threats, challenges, and solutions.arXiv:1606.06992 (2016)
26. Nagi, J., Yap, K.S., Tiong, S.K., Ahmed, S.K., Mohammad, A. M.: Detection of abnormalities and electricity theft using genetic support vector machines. In: TENCON 2008 - 2008 IEEE Region 10 Conference, pp. 1–6 (2008)
27. Depuru, S.S.S.R., Wang, L., Devabhaktuni, V.: Support vector machine based data classification for detection of electricity theft. IEEE/PES Power Syst. Conf. Exposition **2011**, 1–8 (2011)
28. Nagi, J., Yap, K.S., Tiong, S.K., Ahmed, S.K., Nagi, F.: Improving SVM-based nontechnical loss detection in power utility using the fuzzy inference system. IEEE Trans. Power Deliv. **26**(2), 1284–1285 (2011)
29. Svetnik, V., Liaw, A., Tong, C., Culberson, J.C., Sheridan, R.P., Feuston, B.P.: Random forest: a classifification and regression tool for compound classifification and qsar modeling. J. Chem. Inf. Comput. Sci. **43**(6), 1947 (2003)
30. Yao, D., Wen, M., Liang, X., Fu, Z., Zhang, K., Yang, B.: Energy theft detection with energy privacy preservation in the smart grid. IEEE Internet Things J. **6**(5), 7659–7669 (2019)
31. Zhang, Y., Ji, Y., Xiao, D.: Deep attention-based neural network for electricity theft detection. In: 2020 IEEE 11th International Conference on Software Engineering and Service Science (ICSESS), Beijing, China, pp. 154–157 (2020)

Design and Implementation of VCP Network for Open Flow

Jie Ke, Changhong Zhu, and Yisen Lin[✉]

School of Computer Science and Engineering, Guilin University of Aerospace Technology,
Guilin 541004, Guangxi, China
linyisen0409@163.com

Abstract. The traditional TCP congestion control mechanism is implicit feedback. In the high-speed network environment, it is easy to have problems such as unclear congestion indication and low efficiency, resulting in low link utilization. To solve this problem, this paper designs and implements a feedback Variable-structure congestion Control Protocol (VCP) network based on Open Flow to improve the link utilization in the high-speed network environment. Firstly, based on the POX controller, a new OpenFlow switch and controller is designed to replace the router to realize the network intermediate node function of the VCP protocol. Secondly, the TCP/IP protocol stack of Linux is studied, and the end system function of the VCP congestion control mechanism is realized by using the modular architecture of the Linux kernel function, so as to realize the VCP network terminal. Finally, the VCP is deployed on the mininet platform for the operation and test verification, and the network is built on the mininet platform to test the efficiency and fairness of the VCP. The experimental results show that the VCP protocol can achieve higher link utilization and ideal fairness in Gbit/s network.

Keywords: Congestion control mechanism · Open Flow · VCP · Linux

1 Introduction

The TCP protocol adopts the conservative congestion window growth method AIMD [1, 2] (Additive Increase Mutilplicative Decrease), which cannot effectively utilize the network bandwidth, and with the increase of high-latency data streams, the unfairness of TCP is increasingly prominent. The focus of congestion control mechanisms can be divided into two categories: based on end systems and based on intermediate nodes (based on implicit feedback [3, 4] and based on explicit feedback [5]). Implicit feedback mechanisms rely solely on end nodes to gather information (usually packet loss and delay increases) to guess the state of network congestion. The research of congestion control protocol based on explicit feedback mechanism has become an important research trend for network congestion problems.

　　In IP network, there are mainly two types of explicit feedback mechanisms: one is based on congestion notification feedback, such as ECN [6–8], Anti-ECN [9], Multilevel

© The Author(s), under exclusive license to Springer Nature Singapore Pte Ltd. 2022
C. Su and K. Sakurai (Eds.): SciSec 2022 Workshops, CCIS 1680, pp. 62–79, 2022.
https://doi.org/10.1007/978-981-19-7769-5_5

ECN [10], MaxNet [11, 12], the routing node marks a few bits in the data packet header according to the network load information, the marking information is fed back by the data receiving end to the data sending terminal, and the sending terminal adjusts the sending rate according to the marking information. The second is based on explicit rate feedback, such as Quick Start [13, 14], XCP [15, 16], VCP [17, 18], RCP [19], CADPC [20], ACP [21], JexMax [22]. These algorithms transmit data flow state information and network state information between end systems and intermediate routing nodes by introducing congestion headers, achieving high network utilization and better fairness. Whether it is an implicit congestion control mechanism or an explicit congestion control mechanism, the focus is on the traditional network architecture. In recent years, a new network architecture, namely SDN [23] (Software Defined Network), has been proposed, which abstracts all network devices in the network as a whole and abstracts them into a network operating system, separates the control layer and the forwarding layer, and provides a global Regulates network traffic and efficiently utilizes network bandwidth, which alleviates network congestion to a certain extent.

Among the many protocols of SDN, OpenFlow is only one of the most respected and widely recognized protocols, but it is not the only way for SDN. At this stage, SDN is difficult to promote, and the implicit congestion control mechanism has shown many deficiencies. Therefore, the research on explicit congestion control protocols is still an important trend to solve congestion control. Among many explicit congestion control protocols, it is possible to The Variable-structure Congestion Control Protocol (VCP) can maintain high efficiency, fairness, and stability in both traditional and high-speed networks, and its network load feedback requires only two ECN bits. Mark. This paper studies the VCP protocol uses the OpenFlow technology to realize the VCP network intermediate node, uses the Linux TCP/IP protocol stack to realize the VCP terminal node, forms the VCP network, and verifies the performance of the VCP protocol in the high-speed network environment.

2 Related Works

2.1 VCP Protocol

Typical representatives of explicit rate-based feedback methods include VCP and XCP. This kind of algorithm transmits information such as network state information and data flow state by introducing congestion headers between network terminal systems and network intermediate nodes. However, XCP has many problems, such as increasing the load of the network, not using a promotion, increasing the burden of routers, and relatively complex network promotion projects.

(1) Load factor VCP divides the degree of network congestion into three levels: Low Load, High Load, and Overload. The Load Factor is used to reflect the degree of congestion in the network. VCP uses different combinations of the two bits of ECN in the data packet header to indicate the three levels of network congestion respectively: $(00)_2$ indicates that the sending terminal does not support the VCP protocol; $(01)_2$ indicates that the network congestion level is low load; $(10)_2$

indicates that the network congestion level is high load; (11) 2 network congestion level is overload. The formula for calculating the VCP load factor is:

$$\rho_l = \frac{\lambda_l + \kappa_q \cdot \tilde{q}_l}{\gamma_l + C_l \cdot t_p}$$

Among them, research shows that the RTT value of 75%–90% of the data flow on the Internet is less than 200 ms, so take 200 ms; t_p is the incoming traffic (in bytes) within the time; λ_l is the steady-state queue length during this time; κ_q take 0.5; γ_l is the expected utilization rate of the link, take 0.98; C_l is the link bandwidth. The ECN bits are encoded according to ρ_l: when $0 \le \rho_l < 80\%$, mark (01) 2; when $80\% \le \rho_l < 100\%$, mark (10) 2; when $\rho_l \ge 100\%$, mark (10) 2.

(2) Adjustment of congestion window

The sending terminal dynamically adjusts the congestion window cwnd according to the encoding of the ECN bits in the returned ACK, and the adjustment algorithm of the congestion window is as follows: ① The ECN code is (01)2, indicating that the current network load index belongs to the low load range, and the MI algorithm is used. The expression of the congestion window cwnd is: $cwnd(t + rtt) = cwnd(t) \times (1 - \xi)$. Among them, $\xi = 0.0625$. Since each data stream has a different RTT, adjust the parameter ξ to $\xi \leftarrow (1 + \xi)^{\frac{rtt}{t_p}} - 1$. ② The ECN code is (10)2, indicating that the current network load index belongs to the high load range, and the AI algorithm is used. The expression of the congestion window cwnd is: $cwnd(t + rtt) = cwnd(t) + \alpha$. ③ The ECN code is (11)2, indicating that the current network load index belongs to the overload range, and the MD algorithm is used. The original calculation expression of the congestion window cwnd is: $cwnd(t + \delta_t) = cwnd(t) \times \beta$. Among them, $\beta = 0.875$, $\delta_t \to 0_+$. Since MD is to recover the network from congestion and must be performed quickly, similar to an impulse behavior, the parameter β is independent of RTT, so it is not necessary to adjust according to the different RTT of each data stream.

2.2 OpenFlow Technology

The OpenFlow technology was first proposed in the literature [24]. This technology enables the network to have programmability. Nick Mckeown and his team further proposed the concept of SDN (Software Defined Network, Software Defined Network), which aims to enable users to develop applications through software, only focusing on the upper management interface without considering the underlying complex network topology. With the in-depth study of SDN, control platforms such as NOX, POX, Onix [25], Floodlight, Beacon, and Maestro have emerged. These current mainstream controllers are encapsulating the OpenFlow protocol that communicates with switches. In this paper, the network intermediate routing node is the OpenFlow switch and controller based on the OpenFlow protocol. The switch and the controller communicate through the OpenFlow secure channel. The controller configures and manages the switch functionally. The datagram is sent to the controller for processing.

2.3   OpenFlow Technology

Mininet [26] is a lightweight software-defined network and test platform, which uses lightweight virtualization technology to make a single system look like a complete network running the corresponding kernel system and user code, or simple It is understood as a process-based virtualization platform in the SDN network system, which supports various protocols such as OpenFlow and OpenvSwitch.

In summary, OpenFlow switches and controllers can be designed using OpenFlow technology to replace routers to implement intermediate nodes in VCP networks.

3   Design and Implementation of OpenFlow-Oriented VCP Network

This paper designs and implements the VCP network terminal system based on the Linux protocol stack, and designs and implements the VCP network intermediate nodes based on the Mininet platform for OpenFlow, namely the OpenFlow switch and the OpenFlow controller.

3.1   Design and Implementation of Intermediate Nodes in the VCP Network

The middle node design of the VCP network adopts the third-party controller POX, and based on the POX controller, new OpenFlow switches and controllers are designed. The new OpenFlow switch required in this paper can be designed using the POX controller. In addition, the POX controller supports compiling new controllers. Therefore, this paper uses the POX controller to design a new OpenFlow switch and controller to replace the router to realize the intermediate node of the VCP network. In this paper, the intermediate routing node is divided into a control management part and a data processing part. Among them, the control management part is responsible for the new OpenFlow controller designed according to the POX controller, responsible for the calculation of the VCP load factor, monitoring the real-time information of the switch and the modification of the flow table information; and the data processing part is responsible for the data channel function. From Fig. 1, it can be seen that the OpenFlow switch needs to realize the identification, ECN marks and forwards data packets to the corresponding ports.

This paper uses the controller POX to design a new OpenFlow switch. In order to meet the required functions, refer to the switch under the /pox/forwarding file to design a new OpenFlow switch, and its source code is also placed in the corresponding In the /pox/forwarding file, namely vcp_of_switch.py, in addition to the normal switch function, the functions that need to be implemented are as follows:

① Check whether the incoming data packet is a VCP data packet, that is, check whether the protocol number field of the IP header of the data packet is marked as the VCP protocol.

② Data collection, that is, record the length of each output queue and the data flow of each port.

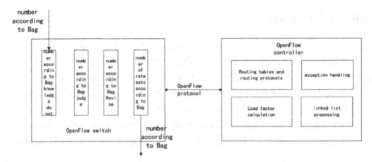

Fig. 1. The overall design structure of the intermediate routing node of VCP based on OpenFlow

③ Update the ECN mark of the packet header. When a packet passes through the OpenFlow switch, it must be matched by the flow table before it can be forwarded. The design of the flow table matching rule is shown in Fig. 2:

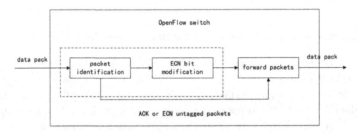

Fig. 2. OpenFlow switch packet matching rules

In order to implement the OpenFlow switch, this paper defines three classes in vcp_of_switch.py, namely VCP_Of_Switch (object), OF_Connection (object) and Switch_Features (object).

A. Class OF_Connection (object)

When the entire network starts up, the OpenFlow switch needs to establish a connection with the controller through a secure channel and maintain communication. And OF_Connection (object) is responsible for encoding and decoding the information between the switch and the controller. The main functions are shown in Table 1.

Table 1. Main functions in OF_Connections (object)

Function	Features
__init__ (self, io_worker)	Initialize the module
set_message_handler (self, handler)	set message processor
send_message (self, data)	Send information to the switch
read_message (self, io_worker)	Decode the information sent by the switch
_error_handler (self, reason, info)	Handling error messages
_extract_message_xid (self, message)	Extract the information sent by the switch
close (self)	Turn off the information processor
get_controller_id (self):	Get switch ID

B. VCP_Of_Switch (object)

VCP_Of_Switch (object) is the core part of the whole module and the main class of the OpenFlow switch function implementation. Its functions can be divided into three parts: one is the setting of the basic parameters of the switch, such as port, buffer size and flow table, etc.; The operation of the flow table entry; the third is the interaction between the switch and the controller. The implementation of these three parts is described below.

① Setting of the basic parameters of the switch The OpenFlow switch is different from the traditional switch. In addition to the basic functions of the traditional switch, it also includes the function of the flow table and the function of communicating with the controller. It is not only necessary to define the information of each port and cache of the switch in the VCP_Of_Switch (object), but also need to define the flow table in the OpenFlow protocol. The definition of each parameter of the switch and the definition of the parameters of the information that the switch interacts with the controller, in VCP_O_Switch (object), the core function that implements the above functions is __init__ (self, dpid, name, ports, miss_send_len, max_buffers, max_entries, features), in the header of the class, that is, the parameters that the initialization switch must have.

② Flow entry In order to further improve the definition and operation of the flow table, the control POX compiled the library file flow_table.py, which defines the basic composition of the flow table entry in detail, such as the definition of matching settings, instruction sets, and counters, and also defines the convection table. The operation includes adding, modifying, and deleting the flow table. The controller calls this library file, sends information to the switch, and sets the flow table, and the switch reconfigures the flow according to the information sent by the controller according to this library file. Surface. Therefore, in VCP_Of_Switch (object), the functions and functions of the controller to the flow table direction management are shown in Table 2.

Table 2. Flow table operation functions

Function	Features
_handle_FlowTableModification (self, event)	Process flow table
_flow_mod_modify (self, flow_mod, connection, table, strict=False) _flow_mod_modify_strict (self, flow_mod, connection, table)	Modify the flow table modification of the switch
_flow_mod_delete (self, flow_mod, connection, table, strict) flow_mod_delete_strict (self, flow_mod, connection, table)	Delete the flow table of the switch
_flow_mod_add (self, flow_mod, connection, table)	Add new flow table

③ Interaction between switch and controller After the switches and controllers in the network are turned on, they need to interact to establish connections. First, the switch and the controller are connected through a secure channel, and the switch will default the secure channel as a local connection. Once the secure channel is established, both the switch and the controller will send a "hello" message to each other. At the same time, the switch and the controller can send each other a message. The "echo" message measures the delay, whether the connection is maintained, etc. These two kinds of messages belong to the symmetric message, and some functions that implement the definition of the symmetric message are shown in Table 3.

Table 3. Switch and controller message part functions and functions

Function	Features
rx_message (self, connection, msg)	Process the message sent by the controller
set_connection (self, connection)	Secure Channel Connection Settings
send (self, message, connection=None)	Send a message to the controller
_rx_hello (self, ofp, connection):	process hello message
_rx_echo_request (self, ofp, connection)	Handling echo requests
_rx_echo_reply (self, ofp, connection)	Reply to the echo message sent by the controller
send_hello (self, force=False)	Send a hello message to the controller
rx_packet (self, packet, in_port, packet_data)	Handling secure channel information

In this paper, the controller not only needs to manage the flow table regularly, but also needs to obtain the port information regularly, that is, the controller calculates the average queue length every 200 ms. The calculation formula is: Among them, the weight; represents the current read average queue length; represents the weighted average queue length. Therefore, the switch must count the buffer queue length of each output queue. The controller needs to obtain the statistical information of each output port, and the controller obtains the statistical information by sending a read-state message to the switch.

2) OpenFlow controller design and implementation

The OpenFlow controller designed and implemented in this paper mainly realizes three functions: the first is the interaction between the controller and the switch; the second is the flow table management of the switch; the third is the calculation of the VCP load factor. The controller POX defines a large number of library files to support its own implementation. This paper uses it to compile a new OpenFlow controller. The implementation of the controller function is in the compiled VCP_Of_Controller.py module, which defines three classes to implement the controller. The functions are Of_Connection (object), VCP_Of_Controller (event) and Load_Factor_Computing (event). The three classes are described below. ① Of_Conection (object) The controller's class Of_Connection (object) is used to encode and decode the information that the controller communicates with the switch. Its design and implementation are the same as the function of the class Of_Connection (object) in the switch. It realizes the "hello" message when the controller communicates with the switch. At the same time as the encoding and decoding of the "echo" message, this class also needs to encode and decode the controller-to-switch message, and the sub-messages "Features", "Configuration", "Read-State", "Modify-State" under the message" and "Send-Packet" play an important role in the controller controlling the switch. ② VCP_Of_Controller (event) VCP_Of_Controller (event) is one of the core functions of the controller. It realizes the operation of the controller on the switch flow table, including the deletion, addition, and modification of the switch flow table entry, the matching rules in the flow table entry, and the action command of the instruction set. Its basic parameter settings are set according to the library file of the controller POX. In the design of this paper, the switch is connected to three hosts, so the data packet goes through the flow table matching process in Table 4.

The controller needs to delete the flow table rules of the switch and define the function _handle_table (event) to delete the flow table rules of the switch and add flow table entries. The parameters of msg, which represents a message, that is, a carrier that carries information in the communication between the controller and the switch. ③ Load_Factor_Computing(event) The main functions implemented by the defined class Load_Factor_Computing (event) are: first, the counter should keep synchronized with the switch, regularly obtain the output port queue information of the switch, and calculate the load factor; the second is to calculate the load factor, and realize the function of the calculation of its load factor in Table 5.

Table 4. Flow table matching process

Flow table ID	Flow table matching description
0	If the ECN bit of the header of the matching data packet is 00, the data packet does not support the ECN protocol and enters the flow directly; if it is not 00, it enters the next flow table 8
1	Whether the matching data packet is a returned ACK or a sent data packet, if the ACK enters the flow table 5 and matches, otherwise, it enters the next flow table;
2–3	Match the source address of the data packet, if the match is successful, enter flow table 6, otherwise enter the next flow table
4	Match the source address of the data packet, if the match is successful, enter the flow table 7, otherwise send the data packet to the controller
5–7	The ECN tag of the matching data packet matches. If the value of the data packet is less than the ECN value of the switch, the ECN of the data packet is updated to the ECN value of the switch, and then it enters the flow table 8
8	Match the source address of the packet, send the packet to the output queue of the corresponding port and wait

Table 5. Functions for calculating load factor calculations

Function	Function description
_timer_func ()	timer, synchronized with the switch
_handle_flow_stats_received (event)	Get information about each flow of the switch
_handle_ports_tats_received (event)	Obtain the traffic information of each port of the switch
_load_factor_computing (event)	Calculate persistent output queues and load factors

After the load factor is calculated, the calculated load factor should be sent to the switch, that is, the controller sends the switch flow table entry modification command, that is, to modify the switch flow Table 2, 3, 4 and 5, and define the function _flow_modify(event) to implement.

3.2 Design and Implementation of OpenFlow Monitoring Module

After completing the design and implementation of the intermediate nodes and terminals of the VCP network, the VCP network is built on the Mininet platform to verify the efficiency, fairness, and stability of the VCP protocol. This article uses the Netfilter-iptables mechanism of the Linux kernel. When the host of the Linux kernel receives and sends data packets, the data packets must be processed by Netfilter. As shown in Fig. 3, Netfilter provides four mechanisms, namely Filter, NAT, Mangle, and Raw. When the data packets pass through the linked list under each mechanism, Netfilter operates on the data packets according to the rules of the linked list. Among them, Filter is the core mechanism of Netfilter, which performs the filtering operation on the data packets. Filtering, for example, all data packets that can be specified to the TCP Port 80 of the machine are discarded. Since this article does not need to compile Netfilter, it just uses the configuration tool iptables for Netfilter, adds rules through the command line, counts the packets sent by each sender, and calculates the rate of the packets sent by each sender at the receiver.

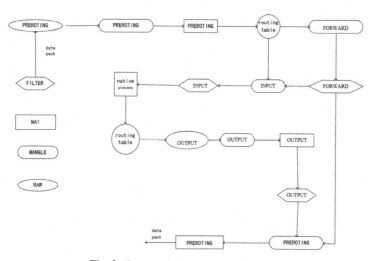

Fig. 3. Data packets go through Netfilter

In addition to realizing the above functions, the monitoring module also needs to monitor the output queue information of each output terminal. In this paper, a python program is used to write a monitoring module to monitor the bandwidth rate of the link and the output queue of each port. Its important function definitions are shown in Table 6.

3.3 Design and Implementation of VCP Terminal System

In this paper, VCP is regarded as a congestion control protocol belonging to TCP, and when the datagram is processed in the VCP part and sent to TCP, the datagram will be treated as a normal TCP datagram. When sending a data packet, TCP calls the vcp_queque_xmit() function instead of the ip_queque_xmit() function, and passes it to the VCP, which processes the data packet and forwards it to the IP. In this process, the VCP is responsible for adding the data header added at the IP layer and marking the protocol code bit used to mark the upper-layer protocol number in the header as 200 and marking the ECN mark. When implementing the VCP congestion control module, call the int inet_add_protocol (struct net_protocol *prot, unsigned char protocol) function to establish a connection with the IP. In this way, in the congestion control part of the TCP protocol, a new congestion control algorithm is defined: tcp_vcp. The function of this algorithm is to calculate and adjust the cwnd of TCP through AI, MI, and MD algorithms according to the load factor marked in the ACK header.

Table 6. Monitoring module functions

function	parameter	Function description
monitor_qlen()	iface, interval_sec, fname,	Use TC to monitor the output queue size of each port of the switch and write it into the qlen.txt of the current file
monitor_count()	ipt_args, interval_sec, fname,	Use iptables to monitor the rate at which the receiver receives the data sent by each sender, and write it into the txt file of the current file
monitor_devs()	dev_pattern, interval_sec, fname	Use /proc/net/dev to monitor the speed of sending and receiving packets on each port, and write it into the current file txt file
monitor_dev_ng	interval_sec, fname	Command line call bwm-ng network tool to monitor bandwidth and bandwidth speed

1) Send terminal For a datagram to be sent: after the user data of the application layer is added with the application header and the TCP header and encapsulated into a TCP datagram, the datagram is transmitted to the VCP by calling the vcp_queue_xmitt() function, where the member variable sk_protocol in the vcp_queue_xmitt() function = 200 (VCP protocol number), the IP header (IP_VCP) of the VCP protocol registration datagram. The VCP marks "01" in the ECN bit of the IP_VCP header, and marks the transport layer protocol number as 200, indicating that the datagram supports the VCP protocol. Calling the function ip_queue_xmit(), the VCP transmits the datagram to the IP layer. Figure 4 shows the encapsulation process of a datagram to be sent.

2) Receiving terminal For a datagram to be received: If the transport layer protocol number is marked as VCP, the IP datagram enters the VCP processing part through the IP layer. After reading the congestion level information marked by the ECN in the datagram header, the VCP forwards the processed datagram to TCP. If the transport layer protocol is marked as TCP, the datagram is passed directly to the TCP layer. The TCP protocol stack processes standard TCP datagrams. Figure 5 shows the processing of a datagram to be received. In the standard data packet receiving process, if it is confirmed that the data packet is a TCP data packet, TCP will call the tcp_v4_rcv function to receive the data packet. From the Linux kernel version 2.6.9, the data structure of the TCP protocol is no longer modularized. If it needs to be modified The data structure of TCP can only recompile the source code of the kernel. Therefore, in order to reduce the workload, a modular congestion control algorithm is used. Therefore, in the receiving process of VCP data packets, VCP is sent from IP to VCP for the first time. The VCP reads and saves the ECN mark of the data packet, the data packet is returned to the Backlog again, and the data packet

is processed again according to the standard receiving process of the data packet. As shown in Fig. 5.

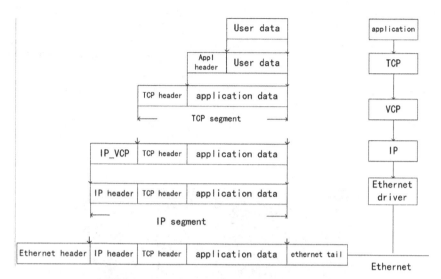

Fig. 4. Sending datagram encapsulation process

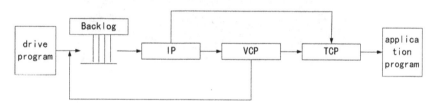

Fig. 5. Received datagram processing process

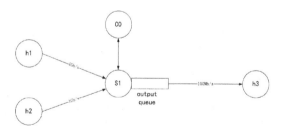

Fig. 6. Experimental topology

4   Validation Experiments

4.1   Construction of the Experimental Network

A PC with a CPU frequency of 3.2 GHz is used as the platform, and VirtualBox is installed to build a Mininet platform to simulate a small VCP single-bottleneck local area network to verify the efficiency and fairness of the VCP congestion control protocol. As shown in Fig. 6, a typical VCP network topology is constructed for verification, in which h1, h2, and h3 respectively represent three end systems, namely hosts; s1 represents an OpenFlow switch; c0 represents a controller. Among them, the link bandwidth between h1 and h2 and the switch is 1 Gbps, and the link bandwidth between h3 and the switch is 100 Mbps, that is, the bottleneck bandwidth. The Mininet platform runs on Ubuntu 13.04 that supports the VCP protocol, and its simulation network is built as shown in Fig. 7.

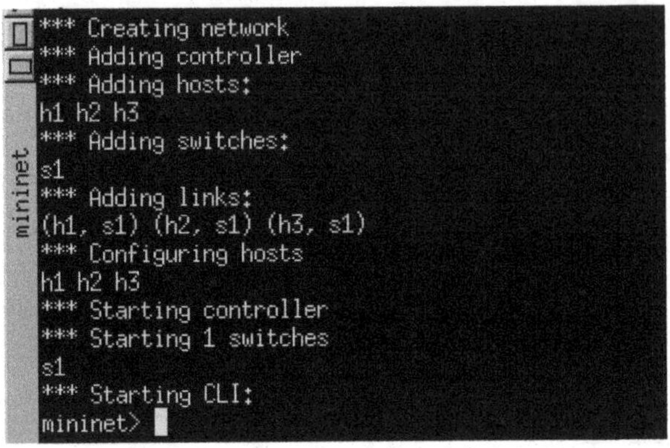

Fig. 7. Network topology simulated by Mininet

4.2   VCP Efficiency Test

1) Link utilization test In the VCP network, the network bottleneck is set on the s1-h3 link, and the bandwidth utilization of the VCP protocol on the s1-h3 link is tested. The bandwidth is set to 100 Mbps, and the bandwidth of the s1-h1 and s1-h2 links is is 1Gbps. Use the command line commands of the xterm interface of the host h1 and the host h2 to continuously send data to the host h3 to test the link bandwidth utilization of the switches s1-h3. In the Mininet platform, the Drop Tail mechanism, namely TCP/DT, is implemented. When output queues are full, all subsequent datagrams are discarded. In the experiment, the utilization ratio of VCP network and ordinary TCP (TCP/DT) network in the bottleneck section is compared. The experimental results are shown in Fig. 8, and the horizontal axis represents time.

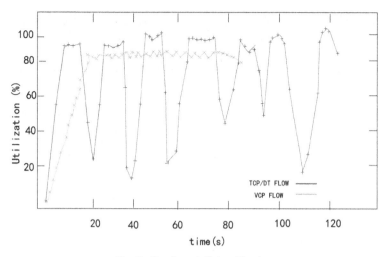

Fig. 8. Bottleneck link utilization

2) Transmission delay test In order to test the link transmission delay of the VCP protocol as the throughput changes, in the experiment, the host h1 sends the data packet to the host h3, and the bandwidth of the link s1-h1 and s1-h3 segments is set to the default value of 1Gbps. Mininet simulates the network that supports the VCP mechanism and the traditional TCP (TCP/DT) network, respectively, and calculates the change of the packet transmission delay with the throughput, as shown in Fig. 9: the horizontal axis represents the throughput (%), and the vertical axis represents the link transmission Delay (ms). It can be seen from Fig. 9 that when the throughput is low (below 60%), both the VCP and TCP/DT mechanisms can maintain a low transmission delay. However, as the throughput increases, the transmission delay of the TCP/DT congestion control mechanism increases significantly, almost showing an exponential growth trend. When the throughput is high, it even reaches 13ms; relatively speaking, the transmission delay of the VCP protocol increases with the change in throughput does not fluctuate significantly, and it can basically be kept below 3ms. The experimental results show that the VCP protocol can maintain a relatively ideal transmission delay.

4.3 VCP Fairness Test

In order to test the fairness of the VCP protocol, that is, to measure whether each user or each link in the network bottleneck link segment can share network resources fairly, the test still adopts the configuration in Sect. 3.1: the experimental bottleneck is the s1-h3 segment. The link bandwidth of the bottleneck segment is set to 100 Mbps, and the link bandwidth of the s1-h1 segment and the s1-h2 segment is 1Gbps. After the experiment starts, the host h1 and the host h2 send data packets to the host h3 at the same time. By testing the bandwidth utilization of the intermediate network segment between the switch s1 and the host h3, it is checked whether the flow1 sent by the sending host h1 and the flow2 sent by the sending host h2 are fair. Share the bandwidth of the bottleneck link s1-h3 segment. Figure 9 shows the change of the bottleneck link utilization rate of flow1 and flow2 with time, the horizontal axis represents time, and the vertical axis is the bandwidth utilization rate of each sending host on the link bottleneck s1-h3 segment link.

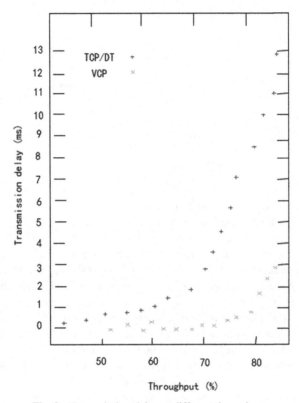

Fig. 9. Transmission delay at different throughputs

Figure 10 VCP fairness test As can be seen from Fig. 10, the total utilization of VCP flow 1 and VCP flow 2 to the bottleneck link s1-h3 is still relatively ideal. Although it fluctuates slightly after stabilization, it can generally be maintained between 35% and 45%. Although there is a slight inequity in the allocation of network resources, on the whole, the two links can better share the bandwidth of the bottleneck link. 5 Conclusion This paper designs and simulates a realistic VCP network verification platform. First, the Linux network protocol stack is used to implement the VCP network end system; secondly, the VCP network intermediate routing node composed of OpenFlow switches and controllers is implemented using POX; Mininet platform builds a typical VCP experimental verification network. Among them, the host in the network runs the VCP network end system, the OpenFlow switch and the controller realize the intermediate routing node of the VCP network, and an experiment is designed to verify the efficiency and fairness

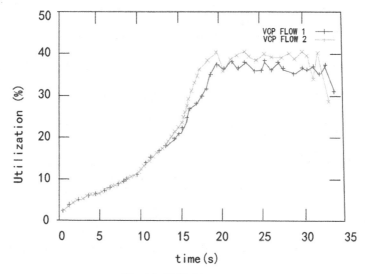

Fig. 10. VCP fairness test

of the VCP protocol in the real network environment. The experimental results show that, compared with the traditional TCP/DT mechanism, the VCP protocol can make better use of the resources provided by the link, the efficiency of the protocol is still higher; and the VCP protocol can better realize the network resources without the link. The distribution among the roads has better fairness. The VCP protocol only uses two binary bits of the ECN to encode the congestion level information, which can achieve relatively good performance in a real network environment.

Acknowledgments. This work is supported in part by Guangxi Young and Middle-aged Research Capacity Enhancement Project "Research and Application on The Key Technology of Intelligent Experiment Management Platform (Grant No. 2020ky21026) and the 2020 school-level Scientific Research Project in Guilin University of Aerospace Technology (Grant No. XJ20KT18: Research on Technology of Error-tolerance Recognition of Channel Coding parameters in non-cooperative communication).

References

1. Dah-Ming, C., Raj, J.: Analysis of the increase and decrease algorithms for congestion avoidance in computer networks. Comput. Netw. ISDN Syst. **17**(1), 114 (1989)
2. Yang, Y.R., Lam, S.S.: General AIMD congestion control. In: Proceedings of IEEE ICNP, pp. 187–198 (2000)
3. Lefelhocz, C., Lyles, B., Shenker, S., Zhang, L.: Congestion control for best-eort service: why we need a new paradigm. IEEE Netw. **10**(1), 10–19 (1996)
4. Gevros, P., Crowcroft, J., Kirstein, P., Bhatti, S.: Congestion control mechanisms and the best effort service model. IEEE Netw. **15**(3), 16–26 (2001)

5. Bakshi, B.S., Kirshna, P., Vaidya, N.H., Pradhan, D.K.: Improving performance of TCP over wireless networks. In: Proceeding of the 1st Annual International Conference on Mobile Computing and Networking, pp. 2–11. ACM, New York (1995)

6. Ramakrishnan, K., Floyd, S., Black, D.: The addition of explicit congestion notification (ECN) to IP (2001)

7. Oljira, D.B., Grinnemo, K.J., Brunström, A., et al.: MDTCP: practical latency-aware multipath congestion control for datacenter networks (2020)

8. Chen, C., Fang, H.C., Iqbal, M.S.: QoSTCP: provide consistent rate guarantees to TCP flows in software defined networks. In: ICC 2020-2020 IEEE International Conference on Communications (ICC), pp. 1–6. IEEE (2020)

9. Hu, J., Huang, J., Li, Z., et al.: AMRT: anti-ECN marking to improve utilization of receiver-driven transmission in data center. In: 49th International Conference on Parallel Processing-ICPP, pp. 1–10 (2020)

10. Durresi, A., Sridharan, M., Liu, C., Goyal, M., Jain, R.: Traffic management using multilevel explicit congestion notification. In: Proceedings of SCI (2001)

11. Gronát, P., Aldana-Iuit, J.A., Bálek, M.: MaxNet: neural network architecture for continuous detection of malicious activity. In: 2019 IEEE Security and Privacy Workshops (SPW), pp. 28–35. IEEE (2019)

12. Wydrowski, B., Andrew, L., Mareels, I.: MaxNet: Faster Flow Control Convergence. In: Mitrou, N., Kontovasilis, K., Rouskas, G.N., Iliadis, I., Merakos, L. (eds.) NETWORKING 2004. LNCS, vol. 3042, pp. 588–599. Springer, Heidelberg (2004). https://doi.org/10.1007/978-3-540-24693-0_49

13. Floyd, S., Allman, A., Jain, M., Sarolahti, P.: Quick-Start for TCP and IP. Draft-ietf-tsvwg-quickstart-07 txt (2006)

14. Zhang, D., Zheng, K., Zhao, D., et al.: Novel quick start (QS) method for optimization of TCP. Wirel. Netw. **22**(1), 211–222 (2016)

15. Katabi, D., Handley, M., Rohrs, C.: Congestion control for high bandwidth-delay product networks. In: Proceedings of the 2002 SIGCOMM Conference, vol. 32, pp. 89–102. ACM, New York (2002)

16. Jiang, N., Huang, J., Liu, S., et al.: Achieving fast convergence and high efficiency using differential explicit feedback in data center. In: ICC 2020–2020 IEEE International Conference on Communications (ICC), pp. 1–6. IEEE (2020)

17. Xing, S., Yin, B., Yao, J., et al.: A VCP-based congestion control algorithm in named data networking. In: 2018 IEEE 3rd Advanced Information Technology, Electronic and Automation Control Conference (IAEAC), pp. 463–468. IEEE (2018)

18. Zhang, H., Zhou, H., Chen, C., et al.: Fast fairness convergence through fair rate estimation in Variable-structure congestion control protocol. Comput. Commun. **70**, 54–67 (2015)

19. Barreto, L.: XCP-Winf and RCP-Winf: improving explicit wireless congestion control. J. Comput. Netw. Commun. (2015)

20. Teymoori, P., Welzl, M., Gjessing, S., et al.: Congestion control in the recursive internetworking architecture (RINA). In: 2016 IEEE International Conference on Communications (ICC), pp. 1–7. IEEE (2016)

21. Shreedhar, T., Kaul, S.K., Yates, R.D.: ACP: age control protocol for minimizing age of information over the internet. In: Proceedings of the 24th Annual International Conference on Mobile Computing and Networking, pp. 699–701 (2018)

22. Zhang, Y., Leonard, D., Loguinov, D.: Jetmax: scalable max-min congestion control for high-speed heterogeneous networks. Comput. Netw. **52**, 1193–1219 (2008)

23. Jasim, M.N.: A proposed adaptive least load ratio algorithm to improve resources management in software defined network OpenFlow environment. Karbala Int. J. Mod. Sci. **7**(1), 6 (2021)

24. McKeown, N., et al.: OpenFlow: enabling innovation in campus networks. ACM SIGCOMM Comput. Commun. Rev. **38**(2), 69–74 (2008)

25. Lanversin, J.T., Kütt, M., Glaser, A.: ONIX: an open-source depletion code. Ann. Nucl. Energy **151**, 107903 (2021)
26. Chaudhary, R.: Software-defined networking based control flow optimization for multi-cloud environment (2021)

Theory and Application of Blockchain and NFT Workshop (TA-BC-NFT)

Medical Waste Treatment Process Based on Blockchain Technology - A Case Study of Covid-19 Waste Handling in Vietnam

Nguyen Huyen Tran[✉], Khoi Le Quoc, Hong Khanh Vo,
Luong Hoang Huong, The Anh Nguyen, Khoa Tran Dang, Khiem Huynh Gia,
Loc Van Cao Phu, Duy Nguyen Truong Quoc, Hieu Le Van,
Huynh Trong Nghia, Bang Le Khanh, and Kiet Le Tuan

FPT University, Can Tho, Vietnam
trannhce161052@fpt.edu.vn

Abstract. Medical waste management is a challenging problem that not only directly affects the environment but also people's health. This urgent issue is getting more and more attention in the context of the Covid-19 pandemic. New infections are increasing exponentially in all countries globally, especially developing countries with large populations (e.g., India, Brazil, Bangladesh). Studies on the spread of the disease have listed one of the causes of this crisis as the Covid-19 waste treatment process not being followed correctly and the difficulty of data retrieval. Vietnam was also severely damaged by the Covid-19 epidemic, although the government initially controlled the disease very well. The Covid-19 waste treatment process in Vietnam is still being processed manually and with a combination of many departments. Data sharing and tracking are also tricky because they are centrally stored in different facilities/departments. In addition, there is a lack of synchronization and transparency of shared data. This paper is one of the first attempts to fill that gaps by applying Blockchain technology and decentralized storage. Relevant parties will retrieve all data, and the source of waste can be easily traced. We also implemented a proof-of-concept based on the Hyperledger Fabric platform to demonstrate the idea's feasibility. In the evaluation, we observe the process of initializing and querying data. These initial efforts will lay the groundwork for more in-depth studies to create an initiative for Vietnam's medical waste treatment process when faced with a new wave of infections or another epidemic.

Keywords: Covid-19 waste · Medical waste treatment · Blockchain · Hyperledger fabric · Covid-19 in Vietnam

1 Introduction

Inefficient medical waste management can lead to negative impacts on the environment and public health [1,2]. This pressure adds to the challenge for developing countries with large populations, where medical waste management processes are still manual and lack cooperation from stakeholders [3]. A few notable

C. Su and K. Sakurai (Eds.): SciSec 2022 Workshops, CCIS 1680, pp. 83–96, 2022.
https://doi.org/10.1007/978-981-19-7769-5_6

examples have been studied on the effects of medical waste management practiced in India [4] and Bangladesh [5]. Vietnam is also on the list of developing countries with a high population rate. Several studies on the management and harms related to medical waste have been carried out in Vietnam [6–8]. The medical waste treatment process has received more attention than ever since the outbreak of the "Coronavirus disease 2019" (a.k.a Covid-19) pandemic from the end of 2019 until now, not only in developing countries like Vietnam but the whole world. Specifically, Covid-19 by coronavirus-2 causes new severe acute respiratory syndrome (SARS-CoV-2), which is a burden on the medical waste treatment process in particular and the health system in general [9,10]. Indeed, the management of medical waste that is not paid enough attention to and resolved will spread the disease to the community and directly affect people's health [11]; thereby continue to put pressure on the health system of a country and make the disease outbreak stronger [12]. This cycle will continue until the complete collapse of a country's health system. To prevent the above risk, we can think of upgrading the existing medical infrastructure or completely solving the problem of medical waste treatment. The second solution is said to save money and time for developing countries, including Vietnam [13].

The medical waste treatment process is managed by two ministries, the Ministry of Health and the Ministry of Natural Resources and Environment, according to Joint Circular 58/2015/TTLT-BYT-BTNMT[1] (Medical waste management regulation), approved in 2015. Meanwhile, updated minutes for the medical waste treatment process related to the Covid-19 pandemic (i.e., waste from treatment facilities, isolation, etc.) were issued by the National Steering Committee (NSC) on August 5, 2020, based on Circular 36/2015/TT-BTNMT (Regulation of hazardous waste collection and treatment) and Decision 3455 /QD-BCDQG (Guidance on waste management and sterilization for COVID-19 prevention and control). In the above documents, it is stipulated that all waste related to the treatment of Covid-19 patients is called "potentially SARS-CoV-2 contaminated waste" (called Covid-19 waste). In addition to waste with a high risk of infection, Decision 3455 also separates domestic waste into concentrated isolation areas or households with sick people.

The manual waste treatment process without transparency in management can cause significant risks and disease outbreaks, as pointed out in the study by Das et al. [14]. One of the two best examples of how waste management can contain disease outbreaks in Brazil [15] and Taiwan [16] has also demonstrated the same. Therefore, the control of the waste treatment process needs transparency and easy verification of data and origin throughout the process. To be able to meet these requirements, this paper proposes a Covid-19 waste treatment process based on Hyperledger Fabric platform[2].

One of the highlights that makes Blockchain technology widely deployed not only in the medical environment such as healthcare at medical facilities [17,18] or in emergencies [19,20], blood donate [21,22] but also in other supply

---

[1] The documents used in this section do not propose the English version.

[2] https://www.hyperledger.org/use/fabric.

chain management areas, for example cash-on-delivery [23, 24], logistic [25, 26] is the transparency and ease of confirmation of any information stored on the distributed ledger. Data is also stored decentralized, minimizing data loss and speeding up data access for the entire system [27]. Contribution of this paper consists of three-factor i) analyzing the current Covid-19 waste treatment process according to Decision 3455; ii) providing a Covid-19 waste treatment model for Vietnam based on Blockchain technology to increase transparency and security for data stored in a decentralized manner; iii) proposing proof-of-concept to demonstrate the feasibility of the idea.

Following this introduction, the next section describes the background of blockchain and its related techniques. The state-of-the-art is presented in Sect. 3 to summarize blockchain-based medical waste treatment system approaches as well as that system for Covid-19 waste in Vietnam. Then, we analyze the current Covid-19 waste treatment process and our architecture before presenting the execution algorithm in Sect. 4. Section 5 focuses on the analysis and evaluation. Finally, suggestions for future research and conclusion are made in the last section.

2   Background

2.1   Blockchain Technology

Blockchain was well-known for the success of Bitcoin [28] and is commonly characterized as a transparent, reliable, and decentralized ledger on a peer-to-peer network that manages transaction data on several computers at the same time. As a result, blockchain is seen as a trust circle that allows parties to be autonomous without relying on a single third-party confirmation [29]. We receive several benefit when design the system based on blockchain as below.

- **Security:** Blockchain is a highly secure system due to its digital signature and encryption. The system has been specially designed to ensure safety, convenience, and tamper-proof.
- **Fraud control:** A system based on data stored in multiple locations is invulnerable to hackers. In this case, all records may efficaciously recover.
- **Transparency:** Both the provider and the customer will be informed of the completion of the transaction immediately, which is convenient and reliable.
- **No hidden fees:** Because the system is decentralized and does not need to pay intermediary fees, there is no need to worry about costs and commissions.
- **Access levels:** The user must choose between a public blockchain network that anyone can access and a network with the necessary permissions, first authorizing the user to log in to each node.
- **Speed:** Transactions are processed much faster than usual as there is no need to integrate payment systems, reducing costs and increasing processing speed.
- **Account reconciliation:** The participants' validity is checked and confirmed by the participants, whereby they also verify their authenticity.

2.2   Smart Contract

A smart contract (a.k.a chaincode) is a term that describes a particular set of protocols capable of automatically executing the terms and agreements between the parties in a contract with the help of Blockchain technology. The whole process of a Smart Contract is done automatically without external intervention. Smart Contract term is equivalent to a legal contract and is recorded in a computer's language. The Smart Contract routine has the following characteristics.

- **Distributed:** Replicated and distributed in all nodes of the Ethereum network. This is one difference from other solutions based on centralized servers.
- **Deterministic:** Only take actions that they are designed to perform if the conditions are satisfied. Besides, the results of Smart Contracts remain the same no matter who the executor is.
- **Automate:** Able to automate all kinds of tasks, and it works like a self-executing program. However, in most cases, if the Smart Contract is not activated, it will remain "inactive" and will not perform any action.
- **Non-modifiable:** Smart Contract cannot be modified after deployment. They can only be "deleted" if this function has been added before. Therefore, it can be said that Smart Contract is like an anti-forgery code.
- **Customizable:** Before deployment, Smart Contracts can be encoded in different ways. So, they can be used to create many types of decentralized applications (Dapps). Ethereum is a blockchain that can be used to solve any computational problem (Turing complete).
- **No need to rely on trust:** Two or more parties in a contract can interact through a Smart Contract without knowing or trusting each other. In addition, blockchain technology ensures the accuracy of data.
- **Transparency:** Since Smart Contracts are based on a public blockchain, no one can change their source code, although anyone can view it.

3   Related Work

3.1   Blockchain-Based Medical Waste Treatment System

The removal or segregation of wastes, especially medical waste, continues to contaminate our ecosystem [30]. As an obvious example, 99% of items (including medical equipment and supplies) become trash after use within the first six months of first use [31]. This problem can be viewed as a catastrophic failure in material recovery. In particular, the circular economy (CE) introduces the elimination of waste and misuse of resources. This system focuses on reusing, repairing, and recycling in a secure method. Thereby, we can ultimately reduce input materials and prolong the time of usage (instead of only six months on average) of equipment and supplies, minimizing pollution and other wastes into the environment. Morseletto et al. [32] have defined a circular economy as "an economic model directed at the efficient use of resources through waste minimization, long-term value retention, and resource minimization primary and closed-loop of products, product parts, and materials within the boundaries of environmental protection and socio-economic benefits." According to the above definition, a CE-based production and consumption system focuses on maintaining the utility, the value of products, and materials.

To this end, the Ellen MacArthur Foundation [**ECdetail**] has introduced a series of principles (e.g., reuse, repair, refurbish, remanufacture, recover, recycle, recover, and regenerate from waste streams). The primary purpose of the CE system is toward a World without waste. Besides, CE is considered a model of the future where toward a green economy. For example, to reduce waste and increase recycling, Amazon[3] has created CE loops based on partnerships and offers options for customers to reuse, repair, and recycle their products [33].

The management and classification system of medical equipment and supplies acts as a decentralized trading environment in the current context. The system consists of participants who share data and authenticate and are solely responsible for the shared data. That data can be inventory data, digital assets, types of equipment, supplies, or any other kind of information [34] used in a healthcare environment. Understanding the demand for medical equipment and supplies is extremely important; it contributes to reducing the spread of Covid-19 disease in the community [35]. Blockchain-based management systems were introduced to address this problem. The next part focuses on exploiting waste management systems and medical supplies developed based on Blockchain technology.

Gupta et al. [36] proposed an Ethereum-based system called Electronic Waste Management (EWM). Based on the constraints defined in the smart contract, EWM has ensured compliance with waste disposal guidelines for electrical and electronic equipment (EEE). In EWM, the author proposed three main stakeholders offered by the system: manufacturers, consumers, and retailers of electronic components. Smart Contracts calculate, record, report, and provide incentives for consumers to send back EEE waste to retailers to address the post-use waste problem. Besides, in the aspect of retailers, smart contracts focus on verifying that waste is received for all sold EEEs. Specifically, the retailer ships the EEE waste to the producer and pays a portion of the original cost of the EEE to the consumer. Smart Contracts have also imposed penalties on EEE manufacturers if waste is not collected from retailers within a predetermined period.

3.2 Covid-19 Waste Treatment

There are some studies to assess the level of Covid-19 waste in Vietnam [7] and developing countries [37] as well as offer solutions in the pre-treatment process and after the pandemic with these dangerous wastes [38,39]. Besides, the method of applying Blockchain is very widely used. Specifically, studies have applied Blockchain's transparency to store detailed information during the treatment of Covid-19 disease, such as providing food supply chains to avoid disruptions

---

[3] www.amazon.com.

during the pandemic. [40], applying circular economy model [34], providing vaccine [41]. In addition, the Covid-19 waste treatment processes are also applied Blockchain, which can be found in the [42] which stores waste information from medical equipment during testing and vaccination; medical waste monitoring model [43].

4   Approach

4.1   Covid-19 Waste Treatment Process in Vietnam

Figure 1 details the treatment process and responsible place for Covid-19 waste in Vietnam. In general, there are five sources of Covid-19 waste generation, including isolated treatment places (e.g., hospitals), isolated places (e.g., military barracks or the public facilities are requisitioned for quarantine purpose), testing places, vaccination places, and personal places under quarantine (e.g., household). The Covid-19 waste treatment process includes five steps, from identification to incineration of hazardous waste. Besides, the waste originating from the personal place under quarantine is not recognized as COVID-19 waste (e.g., masks, tissues, and cloths removed by quarantined individuals). These types of waste are required to be temporarily stored indoors and then treated with municipal solid waste after seven days of quarantine. If a member is confirmed to be infected, this waste is treated as COVID-19 waste. According to Decision 3455, all Covid-19 waste belonging to medical facilities must be managed in these medical facilities' existing waste treatment system. Waste in the remaining area must be managed by the People's Committee of the province or city. This process requires both the waste transportation to the designated treatment facilities and the entities responsible for the respective waste disposal. Finally, companies and waste treatment plants must process (e.g., incineration) hazardous wastes from two sources (i.e., municipality, medical facility).

The disadvantage of the above model can come from the connection between the parties involved in the process of transportation to waste treatment, for example, from collection to transportation and from transportation to treatment. This transfer may encounter some mistakes in the transportation or waste treatment stage if the information transferred between the parties concerned is not strictly checked and monitored. All activities are carried out manually, and there is a lack of transparency in determining the origin and processing time of various types of waste.

Furthermore, the treatment process must also strictly adhere to time requirements (e.g. 7-day quarantine for personal place under quarantine) and treatment level (e.g., destruction or recycling). The connection between stages can increase the risk of disease outbreaks on a large scale. Checking and identifying information is also extremely difficult because everything is processed manually, and the information is difficult to verify the authenticity. Moreover, it is challenging to check the waste treatment process (e.g., steps taken in the required time) of the Ministry of Health and the People's Committee of the province or the city level

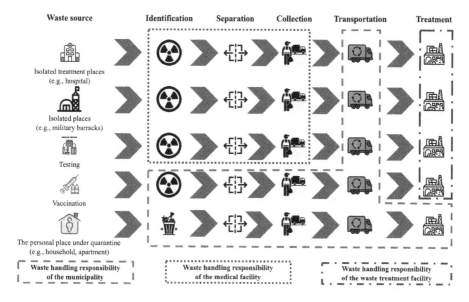

Fig. 1. The current Covid-19 waste treatment process in Vietnam [7]

must be handled manually, and no system can support the verification process. Besides, the centralized data storage can easily be attacked by malicious users or lose data when a problem occurs. Due to the above drawbacks, this paper propose a Covid-19 waste management model based on Blockchain technology.

4.2 Covid-19 Waste Treatment Process Based on Blockchain Technology

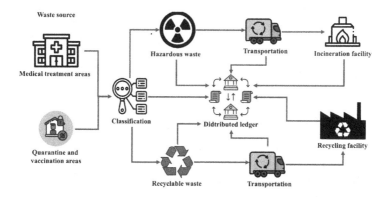

Fig. 2. The Covid-19 waste treatment process based on Blockchain technology

Figure 2 depicts the Covid-19 waste treatment process based on Blockchain technology. The method includes six main steps, from classification to medical waste treatment. Depending on how dangerous the waste is, we incinerate or recycle it. Besides, all steps in the treatment process are updated in the distributed ledger so that stakeholders can verify and check the progress of waste treatment. Specifically, step 1 presents the process of classifying medical waste as either Covid-19 waste or regular waste. Step 2 labels hazardous for Covid-19 waste (2a) and recyclable waste for the rest (2b). All information about time, place, volume, etc., is stored in a distributed ledger (2c). Step 3 transports hazardous waste (3a) and stores their information and the corresponding type of transport (3b). The same goes for the recycling type in steps 4a and 4b. Step 5 focuses on tracking the state of the transportation. The parties involved can track the location and distance travelled by the vehicle. Step 6 presents the waste treatment process, including incinerating (6a) or recycling (6b). All information is recorded and updated in the distributed ledger.

4.3   Algorithm

4.3.1   Data Creation

The data initialization step is described in Algorithm 1. Each kind of waste was generated and declared in the management system of the medical facility. They classify and label based on their hazard level[4]. Then the information corresponding to the waste was stored in the distributed ledger through the smart contract of the APIs in the Blockchain system.

The data includes the overview information of the waste and the status - state. With a value of **0**, the waste is described as being stored at the medical center. When value equals **1** indicating that the waste has been identified and separated, and **2** means the waste has been collected. Besides, we consider the time and date for each step of the waste treatment process. In addition, the "transport" field change from **0** to **1** if the status of waste is transportation; the data field indicates the waste is moved to the waste incineration/recycling facilities.

The data structure of waste stored includes information about the medical facility, quantity, day, time, state and transport status of the transportation which specifically described as follows:

```
wasteDataObject = {
"wasteID": waste001,
"name": waste_name001,
"quantity": waste_quantity001,
"medicalFacility": facility001,
"packageID": waste_packageID001,
```

---

[4] For example, Covid-19 waste is represented by the hazardous waste code "13-01-01". COVID-19 waste types are eligible for acceptance at industrial hazardous waste incinerators without any legal restrictions under Circular 36.

Algorithm 1: Create data

1: Input: wasteID, name, quantity, medicalFacility, packageID, time, date, state, transport
2: Output: response success/failed
3: **for** Each package which contain medical waste **do**
4:     create data of package
5:     create new data corresponding waste
6:     store data of package and waste to ledger
7: **end for**

```
"time": 10:00:00 AM,
"date": 01/01/2022,
"state": 0,
"transport": 0
};
```

4.3.2   Query Data

To query data from the distributed ledger, we propose the query function of the system described in Algorithm 2. For each waste stored at the medical center, the system checks the waste status. If the waste can be identified or separated, the "state" was updated to **1**. If the waste is transported to the waste facilities, the "state" was updated to **2**.

Algorithm 2: Query data

1: Input: wasteID
2: Output: JSON object corresponding to wasteID
3: **for** each waste store in medical facility **do**
4:     storing ID of waste unit with correspondence ID of delivery unit
5:     **if** identified or separated **then**
6:         query data of waste corresponding id
7:         update "state" = 1 transported
8:         update state transportation id
9:         update "state" = 2
10:    **end if**
11: **end for**

---

5   Evaluation

5.1   Environment Setting

Our paradigm is deployed on the Hyperledger Fabric network maintained inside docker containers. In this section, we measure the performance of the chaincode of the two scenarios in the algorithms (i.e., 4.3), namely initializing and querying data. The experiments are deployed on Ubuntu 20.01 configuration, core i5 2.7 Ghz, and 8 GB RAM.

To prove the effectiveness of our model, we also define several experiments by exploiting the Hyperledger Caliper[5] that is used to design the test scenarios and collect all the information regarding the performance.

5.2 Experimental

5.2.1 Initializing Data

In this scenario, the study measures the performance of the data initialization function performed through chaincode, the number of requests sent simultaneously from three users[6].

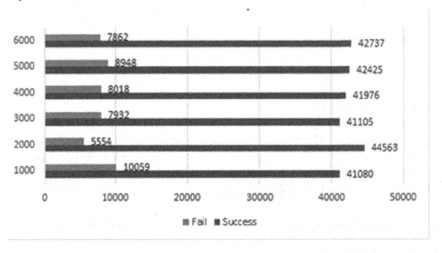

Fig. 3. The execution result of processing request creation

Figure 3 shows the execution result of the waste information initialization function. The data initialization script is conducted with three users simultaneously making 1000–6000 requests to the system. Based on the execution results in the image above, one can see that the number of successful and failed requests is kept at a stable level. In the create package function, the number of failed requests ranges from 5554–10059, while the number of request success is maintained at a much higher rate, from 41080–44563 requests.

5.2.2 Querying Data

In this scenario, we measure the querying function of stored waste data after initializing process.

---

[5] https://www.hyperledger.org/use/caliper.

[6] This paper assumes the three users from the three different process, i.e., waste source (e.g., medical facility officer), transportation (e.g., truck driver), and waste incineration/recycle facility (i.e., factory officer).

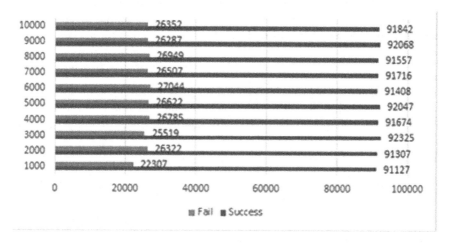

Fig. 4. The result of query waste data

Figure 4 shows the execution results of query data of waste requests made by ten users, with the number of requests increasing from 1000 to 10000. The number of failed requests ranges from 22307 – to 27044. It can be seen that the percentage of failed requests accounts for very little compared to successful requests that fluctuate at over 90000 requests.

6 Conclusion

This paper proposed an initial attempt to build a Covid-19 waste treatment process based on Blockchain technology (i.e., Hyperledger Fabric). All information related to the waste treatment process (e.g., time, institution, status, transportation) is recorded and updated in the distributed ledger. Thereby, the data stored from the classification stage to the waste treatment stage are strictly checked by the relevant parties. Information of related parties is stored transparently with other parties in the same transaction. This protocol makes it easy for participants to track the relevant information of the source through the corresponding metadata, queried from the ledger. Besides, our solution can prevent information tampering and make Covid-19 waste management more transparent by solving problems in traditional medical facilities, such as centralized data storage, which makes it difficult to trace the origin. Furthermore, the solution supports waste transactions between medical centers and waste centers, and recycling plants and sorting plants can easily manage and query related data. The evaluation of the ability to generate and retrieve data proved the effectiveness of the proposed plan.

In the upcoming work, we plan to implement Smart Contract constraints, i.e., any violations would be sanctioned without a trusted arbitrator/third party supports. Besides, there are many issues that can be further studied with this topic; for instance, deploying tests in a real-world environment or analyzing scenarios can increase system-wide latency.

References

1. Romero, I., Carnero, M.C.: Environmental assessment in health care organizations. Environ. Sci. Pollut. Res. **26**(4), 3196–3207 (2019)
2. Mardani, A., et al.: Application of decision making and fuzzy sets theory to evaluate the healthcare and medical problems: a review of three decades of research with recent developments. Expert Syst. Appl. **137**, 202–231 (2019)
3. Zurbrügg, C., Caniato, M., Vaccari, M.: How assessment methods can support solid waste management in developing countries-a critical review. Sustainability **6**(2), 545–570 (2014)
4. Sharma, S.K., Gupta, S.: Healthcare waste management scenario: a case of Himachal Pradesh (India). Clin. Epidemiol. Glob. Health **5**(4), 169–172 (2017)
5. Alam, O., Qiao, X.: An in-depth review on municipal solid waste management, treatment and disposal in Bangladesh. Sustain. Urban Areas **52**, 101775 (2020)
6. Dang, H.T.T., Dang, H.V., Tran, T.Q.: Insights of healthcare waste management practices in Vietnam. Environ. Sci. Pollut. Res. **28**(10), 12131–12143 (2021)
7. Nguyen, T.D.T., Kawai, K., Nakakubo, T.: Estimation of COVID-19 waste generation and composition in Vietnam for pandemic management. Waste Manag. Res. **39**(11), 1356–1364 (2021)
8. Salhofer, S., et al.: Plastic recycling practices in Vietnam and related hazards for health and the environment. Int. J. Environ. Res. Public Health **18**(8), 4203 (2021)
9. World Health Organization et al.: Water, sanitation, hygiene, and waste management for the COVID-19 virus: interim guidance, 23 April 2020. Technical report, World Health Organization (2020)
10. Zhu, Z., et al.: Waste management during the COVID-19 pandemic: from response to recovery (2020)
11. Mol, M.P.G., Caldas, S.: Can the human coronavirus epidemic also spread through solid waste? Waste Manag. Res. **38**(5), 485–486 (2020)
12. Nzediegwu, C., Chang, S.X.: Improper solid waste management increases potential for COVID-19 spread in developing countries. Resour. Conserv. Recycl. **161**, 104947 (2020)
13. Praveena, S.M., Aris, A.Z.: The impacts of COVID-19 on the environmental sustainability: a perspective from the southeast Asian region. Environ. Sci. Pollut. Res. **28**(45), 63829–63836 (2021)
14. Das, A.K., et al.: COVID-19 pandemic and healthcare solid waste management strategy-a mini-review. Sci. Total Environ. **778**, 146220 (2021)
15. Penteado, C.S.G., de Castro, M.A.S.: COVID-19 effects on municipal solid waste management: what can effectively be done in the Brazilian scenario? Resour. Conserv. Recycl. **164**, 105152 (2021)
16. Tsai, W.-T.: Analysis of medical waste management and impact analysis of COVID-19 on its generation in Taiwan. Waste Manag. Rese. **39**(1_suppl), 27–33 (2021)
17. Duong-Trung, N., et al.: On components of a patient-centered healthcare system using smart contract. In: Proceedings of the 2020 4th International Conference on Cryptography, Security and Privacy, pp. 31–35 (2020)

18. Duong-Trung, N., et al.: Smart care: integrating blockchain technology into the design of patient-centered healthcare systems. In: Proceedings of the 2020 4th International Conference on Cryptography, Security and Privacy, pp. 105–109 (2020)

19. Son, H.X., Le, T.H., Quynh, N.T.T., Huy, H.N.D., Duong-Trung, N., Luong, H.H.: Toward a Blockchain-Based Technology in Dealing with Emergencies in Patient-Centered Healthcare Systems. In: Bouzefrane, S., Laurent, M., Boumerdassi, S., Renault, E. (eds.) MSPN 2020. LNCS, vol. 12605, pp. 44–56. Springer, Cham (2021). https://doi.org/10.1007/978-3-030-67550-9_4

20. Le, H.T., et al.: Patient-chain: patient-centered healthcare system a blockchain-based technology in dealing with emergencies. In: Shen, H., et al. (eds.) PDCAT 2021. LNCS, vol. 13148, pp. 576–583. Springer, Cham (2022). https://doi.org/10.1007/978-3-030-96772-7_54

21. Quynh, N.T.T., et al.: Toward a design of blood donation management by blockchain technologies. In: Gervasi, O., et al. (eds.) ICCSA 2021. LNCS, vol. 12956, pp. 78–90. Springer, Cham (2021). https://doi.org/10.1007/978-3-030-87010-2_6

22. Le, H.T., et al.: Bloodchain: a blood donation network managed by blockchain technologies. Network 2(1), 21–35 (2022)

23. Le, N.T.T., et al.: Assuring non-fraudulent transactions in cash on delivery by introducing double smart contracts. Int. J. Adv. Comput. Sci. Appl. 10(5), 677–684 (2019)

24. Le, H.T., et al.: Introducing multi shippers mechanism for decentralized cash on delivery system. Int. J. Adv. Comput. Sci. Appl. 10(6) (2019)

25. Ha, X.S., et al.: DeM-CoD: novel access-control-based cash on delivery mechanism for decentralized marketplace. In: 2020 IEEE 19th International Conference on Trust, Security and Privacy in Computing and Communications (TrustCom), pp. 71–78. IEEE (2020)

26. Son, H.X., et al.: Towards a mechanism for protecting seller's interest of cash on delivery by using smart contract in hyperledger. Int. J. Adv. Comput. Sci. Appl. 10(4), 45–50 (2019)

27. Sunny, J., Undralla, N., Pillai, V.M.: Supply chain transparency through blockchain-based traceability: an overview with demonstration. Comput. Ind. Eng. 150, 106895 (2020)

28. Nakamoto, S.: Bitcoin: a peer-to-peer electronic cash system. Decentralized Bus. Rev. 21260 (2008)

29. Ha, X.S., Le, T.H., Phan, T.T., Nguyen, H.H.D., Vo, H.K., Duong-Trung, N.: Scrutinizing trust and transparency in cash on delivery systems. In: Wang, G., Chen, B., Li, W., Di Pietro, R., Yan, X., Han, H. (eds.) SpaCCS 2020. LNCS, vol. 12382, pp. 214–227. Springer, Cham (2021). https://doi.org/10.1007/978-3-030-68851-6_15

30. Jiang, P., et al.: Spatial-temporal potential exposure risk analytics and urban sustainability impacts related to COVID-19 mitigation: a perspective from car mobility behaviour. J. Clean. Prod. 279, 123673 (2021)

31. Leonard, A.: The Story of Stuff: How Our Obsession with Stuff is Trashing the Planet, Our Communities, and Our Health-and a Vision for Change. Simon and Schuster (2010)

32. Morseletto, P.: Targets for a circular economy. Resour. Conserv. Recycl. 153, 104553 (2020)

33. How amazon is investing in a circular economy. https://www.aboutamazon.com/news/sustainability/how-amazon-is-investing-in-a-circular-economy. Accessed 30 Mar 2022

34. Nandi, S., Sarkis, J., Hervani, A.A., Helms, M.M.: Redesigning supply chains using blockchain-enabled circular economy and COVID-19 experiences. Sustain. Prod. Consum. **27**, 10–22 (2021)
35. Govindan, K., Mina, H., Alavi, B.: A decision support system for demand management in healthcare supply chains considering the epidemic outbreaks: a case study of coronavirus disease 2019 (COVID-19). Transp. Res. Part E: Logist. Transp. Rev. **138**, 101967 (2020)
36. Gupta, N., Bedi, P.: E-waste management using blockchain based smart contracts. In: 2018 International Conference on Advances in Computing, Communications and Informatics (ICACCI), pp. 915–921. IEEE (2018)
37. Oyedotun, T.D.T., et al.: Municipal waste management in the era of COVID-19: perceptions, practices, and potentials for research in developing countries. Res. Global. **2**, 100033 (2020)
38. Sharma, H.B., et al.: Challenges, opportunities, and innovations for effective solid waste management during and post COVID-19 pandemic. Resour. Conserv. Recycl. **162**, 105052 (2020)
39. Singh, E., et al.: Solid waste management during COVID-19 pandemic: Recovery techniques and responses. Chemosphere **288**, 132451 (2022)
40. Khan, H.H., et al.: Blockchain technology for agricultural supply chains during the COVID-19 pandemic: benefits and cleaner solutions. J. Clean. Prod. **347**, 131268 (2022)
41. Antal, C., et al.: Blockchain platform for COVID-19 vaccine supply management. IEEE Open J. Comput. Soc. **2**, 164–178 (2021)
42. Ahmad, R.W., et al.: Blockchain-based forward supply chain and waste management for COVID-19 medical equipment and supplies. IEEE Access **9**, 44905–44927 (2021)
43. Wang, H., et al.: Research on medical waste supervision model and implementation method based on blockchain. Secur. Commun. Netw. **2022** (2022)

Blockchain Technology-Based Management of Blood and Its Products - A Case Study in Vietnam

Hieu Le Van[(✉)], Khoi Le Quoc, Hong Khanh Vo, Luong Hoang Huong,
The Anh Nguyen, Khoa Tran Dang, Khiem Huynh Gia, Loc Van Cao Phu,
Duy Nguyen Truong Quoc, Nguyen Huyen Tran, Huynh Trong Nghia,
Bang Le Khanh, and Kiet Le Tuan

FPT University, Can Tho, Vietnam
lehieu99666@gmail.com

Abstract. Blood and its products are one of the products that have not found an alternative and play a huge role in the treatment of diseases today. The current supply is obtained from the volunteers' blood (called donors). However, this supply is also very limited and must go through a rigorous inspection process before reaching the recipient. Depending on the type of product extracted from the blood (e.g., red blood cells, white blood cells, platelets, plasma), we have different preservation procedures and requirements (e.g., duration, temperature, humidity). Therefore, it is extremely necessary to build blood and its products management system. The process is now done manually, where all data entry is done by medical staff without the technique supported. Furthermore, data relating to donors and the centrally stored blood donation process are difficult to assess reliably. In addition to the above difficulties, developing countries (including Vietnam) face infrastructural barriers in managing the supply chain w.r.t blood and its products. In this paper, we introduce a blockchain technology-based blood and its products management model applied to provinces/cities in Vietnam. Specifically, the paper introduces the limitation of the current blood collection and blood-based treatment process, thereby proposing a new approach based on blockchain technology. We also implemented our proofs-of-concept on the Hyperledger Fabric platform. This paper is considered the first attempt to introduce blockchain-based blood and blood product management processes to developing countries (i.e., Vietnam).

Keywords: Blood donation in Vietnam · Blockchain · Hyperledger fabric · Blood products supply chain

1 Introduction

Today, the demand for care and treatment is constantly increasing. It contributes to a drastic change in treatment methods from traditional to modern. The recov-

C. Su and K. Sakurai (Eds.): SciSec 2022 Workshops, CCIS 1680, pp. 97–111, 2022.
https://doi.org/10.1007/978-981-19-7769-5_7

ery process is also shortened thanks to the development of science and technology applied in the medical environment. However, there are products that cannot be replaced during that treatment. One of the prime examples of this type of product is blood. Indeed, blood and its products are an important medical resource in long-term treatment as well as in emergencies [1], for example blood is often required for trauma victims, surgeries, organ transplants, childbirth and for patients being treated for cancer, leukemia and anemia. Each unit of blood is very precious and gives a lot of hope to the patients for example a liter of blood can sustain the life of a premature baby for two weeks; 40 or more units of blood may be required for the survival of an accidental blood loss trauma victim; or 8 platelets per day is the minimum for the treatment regimen of blood cancer patients.

However, the only way to replenish blood for health care purposes is to obtain it from donors because there is currently no product that can replace blood and its products. In addition, more and more advanced treatments are being developed, but most of them require blood and blood products instead of alternative products. Besides, the time requirements for use are also very strict to ensure the safety of the recipient. Specifically, blood and its products cannot be stored for long periods of time (e.g., red blood cells must be used up to 42 days after collection; whereas, platelets have a shelf-life within five days of collection). All three of the above reasons are the main reasons for the scarcity of supply according to Chapman et al. [2]. The above article also shows that the best way to optimize the use of blood and blood products is to save the amount of blood available to be received from the donors.

Nevertheless, all blood collected must be rigorously tested to reduce the risk of transmission of infection by blood transfusion (e.g., hepatitis B and C (HBV - HCV) or human immunodeficiency virus (HCV) (HIV)) before transmission to the recipient [3]. In addition to the above obstacles affecting the blood supply chain management process, time requirements are also extremely important. Specifically, no one expects blood, but if it's not available when it's needed, the consequences can be deadly. While donors may tell you there's no better feeling than saving a life, only about 5% of eligible donors actually donate [4]. Therefore, it is imperative to maximize the amount of blood stored in the warehouse.

In addition to the above obstacles, one of the main obstacles in blood collection and storage for developing countries is supply (i.e., volunteers still do not have a positive attitude towards blood donation) [5] and infrastructure for blood and its products' storage [6]. Vietnam is also on the list of developing countries and suffers from a shortage of supply. As far as we know, there is only one hematology hospital that supplies blood to the whole Mekong Delta.

To solve the first problem, it is necessary to raise the awareness of a majority of people about blood donation. To this end, within the framework of this paper, we only focus on technological solutions. In particular, we aim to share donor data in a controlled manner; for example, reduce the medical declaration time from the second blood donation onwards. Indeed, each user can only donate blood at least 28 days after their previous blood donation (i.e., about a month) [7]. Therefore, previously stored information must be stored decentralized and volunteers can donate blood at a different location without providing the previous information. Besides, data sharing between hospitals and blood donation sites makes donor management easier. Health workers have more choices in contacting volunteers for the next blood donation, thereby contributing to promoting the blood donation movement in the community. To solve the second problem, we aim to verify the transparency of blood and its products data. Since storage conditions (e.g., temperature, humidity) and storage times vary depending on the blood product collected (e.g., red blood cells must be used up to 42 days after collection); whereas, platelets have a shelf life of within five days of collection). The storage and transportation of blood and its products from storage to hospitals (or vice versa) will be difficult to determine the relevant information including time, location, health notes donor's and so on.

To solve the above issues, many methods have proposed blockchain technology to increase transparency and traceability of information about blood and blood products. The benefit of the blockchain approach is proved in several system (e.g., CoD [8–13]; Healthcare [14–17]) Besides, data is stored decentralized is also a plus point compared to the current traditional storage model. Where all data is shared and easily traceable to identify the source of blood and blood products. However, current models cannot fully address the requirements for storing different information about blood and its products [18, 19] for proper storage (i.e., shelf-life of usage, temperature, humidity). Furthermore, there has not been an in-depth study to assess the appropriateness of the application of advanced technologies in supply chain management w.r.t blood and its products in Vietnam. To address these problems, this paper proposes a blood and its product management process applying blockchain technology and decentralized storage for medical facilities in Vietnam. In particular, the main contribution of the paper consists of three parts: i) analyzing the current management mechanism of blood and its products in the provinces and cities in the Mekong Delta (southern Vietnam); ii) propose a solution to manage the supply chain of blood and blood products based on blockchain technology; iii) implement the proposed model based on Hyperledger Fabric platform and evaluate their feasibility.

Following this introduction, the next section describes the background of blockchain and two current common platforms (i.e., Hyperledger Fabric and Ethereum) as well as our selection for the proof-of-concepts. The state-of-the-art is presented in Sect. 3 to summarize blockchain-based blood supply chain system approaches as well as that system for blood and its products management in Vietnam. Then, we analyze the current blood and its products supply chain system and our architecture before presenting the execution algorithm in Sect. 4. Section 5 focuses on the analysis and evaluation. Finally, suggestions for future research and conclusion are made in the last section.

2   Background

2.1   Blockchain Technology

Blockchain was well-known for the success of Bitcoin [20] and is commonly characterized as a transparent, reliable, and decentralized ledger on a peer-to-peer network that manages transaction data on several computers at the same time. As a result, blockchain is seen as a trust circle that allows parties to be autonomous without relying on a single third-party confirmation [21].

The Public, Private, and Consortium blockchains are three universally acknowledged forms. Bitcoin and Ethereum are examples of public blockchains. Any anonymous users may join the network, view the blockchain's content, execute a new transaction, or check the integrity of the blocks. Meanwhile, GemOS, Multi-Chain, and Eris are typical examples of a private blockchain in which only permitted users can join the network and write or send transactions to the blockchain [22]. A consortium blockchain is semiprivate on the border between public and private blockchains. It is typically connected with the use of enterprise to better business. Hyperledger fabric [23] is a business consortium blockchain framework. Ethereum [24] also allows for the creation of consortium blockchains (Golang).

Numerous terms and components make blockchain technology functional and advantageous to the participated stakeholders. The smallest data unit on the blockchain that includes records, contracts, and information is called a transaction [25]. Any entity connecting to the blockchain is referred to as a node [25], and transactions are confirmed by particular nodes (known as miners) by examining the sender as well as the transaction's content. The nodes combine the complete transactions into blocks [25, 26] and are in charge of determining if the transactions are valid and should be stored on the blockchain.

2.2   Blockchain Platform

2.2.1   Ethereum Ethereum [27] is a decentralized platform to run smart contracts with the support of Turing-complete programming languages. Ethereum is executed by the Ethereum Virtual Machine (EVM) and written in high-end programming languages such as Solidity, Serpent, Low-level Lisp-like Language (LLL), and Mutan. Withdrawal limitations, loops, financial contracts, and gambling markets are possible on the Ethereum platform. Ethereum is now the most popular platform for smart contract development.

2.2.2   Hyperledger Fabric Hyperledger Fabric [23] is an open-source enterprise-grade permission distributed ledger technology (DLT) platform designed for large-scale commercial use. It has a few essential features that set it apart from other DLT or blockchain systems. Similar to Ethereum, Hyperledger Fabric is also Turing complete. However, unlike Ethereum, which executes smart contracts on virtual machines, Hyperledger code is executed in Docker containers, allowing smart contract applications to run with minimal overhead while sacrificing isolation (i.e., applications in one container are running on top of one operating system). Fabric succeeds in supporting traditional high-end programming languages such as Java and Go (aka Golang) rather than building Ethereum's smart contract languages.

The support of multiple programming languages facilitates the development and maintaining the Fabric platform. Additionally, Fabric assists in mitigating operating costs, including storing and querying information inside the blockchain and quickly setting requirements for security features and user authorization.

This paper apply Hyperledger Fabric to implement our proof-of-concept since three main reason.

- The Hyperledger Fabric architecture based on a modular architecture separates the transaction processing into three phases: distributed logic processing and agreement called chaincode (i.e., smart contract), transaction ordering, validation, and commit transaction. This separation offers several advantages, such as less trust and verification levels required across node types, and optimized performance and network scalability.
- The data structure requires on a need-to-know basis. In particular, personal data security which considers the necessity of certain data elements' privacy, can be achieved through data partitioning on the blockchain. Channels, supported in Hyperledger Fabric, allow data to reach only those parties that need to know.
- Hyperledger Fabric supports a massive of queries based on an immutable distributed ledger where the ledger is a sequenced record of state transitions for a blockchain application. Each transaction results in a set of asset key-value pairs that are committed to the ledger upon creation, update, or deletion.

3 Related Work

3.1 Blood Supply Chain Management Systems Not Applying the Blockchain Technology

Supply chain management integrates core business processes and information. These processes use a central server to handle visibility and traceability issues. The system combines a very complex process that requires synchronization of different operations, leading to randomness and supply chain risk [28,29]. For example, Nagurney et al. [30] proposed a model to minimize costs and risks by expressing the breakdown properties of blood as supply coefficients. Armaghan and Pazani [31] proposed a blood supply chain to handle urgent requests from blood units during the Iran earthquake. The authors build a multi-level, multi-objective model to find an optimal route based on the selected routes to transport blood. The main contribution of [31] is to reduce the cost of the blood supply chain network and maximize reliability. In addition, Eskandari-Khanghahi et al. [32] has developed a model that provides a combination of integer mixed linear programming while considering location, allocation, inventory, and distribution. On the other hand, Delen et al. [33] has integrated GIS (geographic information systems) and data mining techniques to build blood supply chain processes. The main purpose of [33] work is to build an optimal blood transport model to be applied in the military environment.

One disadvantage of centralized storage in the above approaches is transparency [34]. To address this issue, Lam et al. [35,36] demonstrated the implementation of a microservices-oriented software architecture for middleware that collects, stores, and traces data in a centralized manner in order to provide data analyst. To apply these advantages, a centralized blood donation management solution has been proposed in [37]. This approach not only reduces the amount of information collected from blood donors, but also improves the efficiency of blood donation management.

3.2 Blood Supply Chain Management Systems Based on Blockchain Technology

Trieu [18] and Nga [19] propose a cold-blooded supply chain system based on Hyperledger Fabric called BloodChain. The proposed system supports verification of blood related transactions from donors to recipients. Moreover, Blood-Chain allows to display the necessary information during the blood donation process. Specifically, the actors in the system only receive enough information to verify information about donors as well as recipients. Similarly, Lakshminarayanan et al. [38] proposes a blood supply chain management system based on Hyperledger Fabric. Similar to BloodChain, it also ensures transparency of donated blood by tracking blood units between donors and recipients. Moreover, Toyoda et al. [39] has integrated the RFIDs into the blood bags using the EPC stored in the tag. This integration helps to ensure reliability and avoid tampering by tracking products and checking their tags.

However, there are some limitations to the aforementioned solutions. For example, the verification of the system proposed in [18,19] is incomplete due to the lack of evaluation analysis. Furthermore, the monitoring solution proposed in [39] is limited to monitoring blood bags only, and it does not guarantee traceability of blood components (i.e., red blood cells, platelets, white blood cells, platelets and plasma). Since different blood components have different shelf lives and storage temperatures, the order of use preference should also be considered.

4   Approach

4.1   The Current Blood Donate Process in Vietnam

To get the most unbiased view of the traditional blood donation and blood handling process, we collected information about the process in hospitals and healthcare facilities in the Mekong Delta, Vietnam. We conducted a short interview of the medical officers working at the hematology hospital in Can Tho, which supplies blood and blood products to hospitals and healthcare facilities not only in Can Tho city but also neighbouring provinces (e.g., Vinh Long, Ben Tre, Hau Giang).

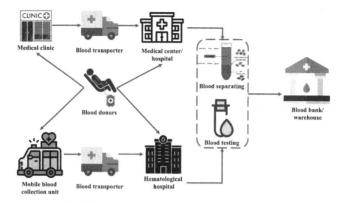

Fig. 1. The current blood donation process

Figure 1 presents the current blood donation process. In particular, the donors are able to donate blood through four ways, including medical clinic, mobile blood collection unit, medical facility (e.g., hospital), and hematology hospital. Except for the second blood donation method (i.e., mobile blood collection unit) which is held in public places for a short time (usually 1 day), donors can donate blood at any time at the three remaining medical facilities. For blood donation at the medical clinic and mobile blood collection unit, the collected products are transferred to the storage facility at the hematology hospital. Here, blood is separated into several components including plasma, red blood cells, white blood cells, and platelets, and then stored according to the specific conditions of the blood product (e.g., temperature, humidity, duration). For the two remaining ways of donating blood, the collected blood does not need to go through a transportation step because these medical facilities have the facilities/equipment to conduct separation and storage. Finally the blood and its products are delivered to the hospital for recipients. All these steps are performed manually and stored locally at each location (e.g., hematology hospital, medical clinic, hospital).

Although the traditional approach is simple and easy to apply to all medical facilities because it does not require high support technology as well as easy to deploy in a practical environment. However, the above approaches face many inherent risks for systems based on centralized management. Verifying the reliability of the data is admissible to this approach. In particular, any data displayed is only taken from the data available in the database which is provided by the central server. Moreover, the important information that affects the treatment process can be lost if the central server is hacked. This is an extremely dangerous thing for medical/healthcare organizations. Due to these dangerous risks, it is urgent to find a decentralized storage solution as well as increase the authenticity of data. Blockchain technology can fulfill both of these issues. The next sections will detail the blockchain-based management models to address the current blood management model.

4.2   Blood Donation Process Based on Blockchain Technology

The biggest difference between the proposed model based on blockchain technology and the traditional model is that all data and retrieval requests are stored in a distributed ledger. Specifically, Fig. 2 shows the storage process of the stakeholder who have a role in the system, i.e., medical facilities (e.g., hospital, medical clinic or hematology hospital); donors; blood products (e.g., red blood cells, white blood cells, platelets); transportation; and blood bank. All data related to blood/blood products are stored, but also all requests for data retrieval from relevant parties (e.g., healthcare workers, carriers) are stored in a log book. dispersion one. This increases transparency for the whole system. Data owners easily know which users can access their data. As for blood records, all information about donors is stored in a distributed ledger. Information about blood type, time, date, and other preservation information are all stored and processed in a decentralized form. Thereby, medical facilities can retrieve and confirm data related to the treatment process. Besides, the data of medical centers/hospitals is also very important. Instead of local storage, our proposed model is towards a decentralized model, where data can be shared for healthcare purposes. Specifically, medical centers/hospitals can exchange information on blood volume and blood products that can be shared in an emergency, reducing requirements for hematology hospitals. On the other hand, information about donors donated at one medical facility in the past can be easily retrieved by another facility, thereby increasing the quality of treatment for patients.

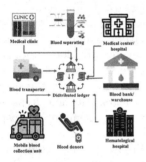

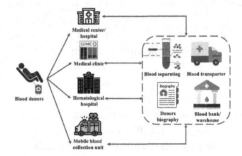

Fig. 2. The distributed storage of blood donation process

Fig. 3. The blood donation process based on Blockchain technology

Figure 3 details the process of sharing donor data between different health facilities. Specifically, basic information (i.e., biography) about addresses and phone numbers is shared for health care purposes. In addition, information about the amount of blood in stock is shared with other medical facilities. In addition, the conversion process is always up to date if there are any shipping requirements for healthcare purposes. However, the results of donor blood tests are not shared in the current model to limit privacy violations. The information shared by donors is only related to health care needs. In unsatisfactory blood test results, the donor's personal data will be deleted from the distributed ledger. We do not support off-chain executions (i.e., out-of-scope) in the current approach, so data sharers (i.e., medical officers) must secure on-chain data uploads.

4.3 Algorithms

In the proposed blockchain-based system, we have two main algorithms to control the process. As explained in Sect 2.2, our methods apply the Hyperledger Fabric platform to conduct the transactions. Moreover, due to these approaches are suitable for a hybrid business environment [13], we exploit JavaScript structure for the data structure and the blockchain network for the process structure below:

```
bloodRecords = {
"donorID": donor ID,
"bloodID": blood and its production ID,
"bloodGroup": blood group,
"bloodProduction": blood production,
"temp": temperature,
"humidity": humidity,
"time": time,
"date": date,
"duration": duration,
"state": 0,
"medicalFacility": locate of medical facility,
"amount of blood unit": 350
};
```

This section targets two main algorithms, including Algorithm 1 describing the data creation to store the blood and its products; whereas Algorithm 2 presents the delivering blood samples from the donation place to the hematological hospital/medical facility).

Algorithm 1 consists of five main steps. It describes the mechanism to gather the blood and its products collected from the donors. Blood and its products, once collected, are identified by the donorID of the respective donor. Each blood and its product has a separate bloodID to avoid duplicating data inside the ledger; the blood is then stored at the medical facility after being donated. Finally, The blood and its products have updated the status in the ledger.

Algorithm 2 summarizes delivering blood samples from the donation place to the medical center, i.e., this process can be repeated based on the context. After storage, the blood samples will be transported to different medical facilities in the donation place. To this end, the shipper information will be stored in the ledger to determine which company transports the blood and how many units of blood have been transported, i.e., updates the metadata. The process's input is the data of the delivery unit, and the output of the algorithm is the data of delivery and the new medical center, which receives the blood from Volunteer. Its corresponding ID_Center further identifies each step.

Algorithm 1: The blood and its products data creation

1: Input: Donor ID, blood group, blood production, blood donation metadata (i.e., time, date), storage requirements (i.e., temperature, humidity, duration), and amount of blood unit
2: Output: data of donor and their blood is stored into ledger
3: **for** unit of blood **do**
4:    storing data of donor, blood and its products to ledger;
5: **end for**

Algorithm 2: Transportation of blood samples from donation places to medical center

---

1: Input: data of delivery unit
2: Output: data of delivery is stored to ledger, new medical center also updated
3: **for** delivery unit **do**
4:    **for** blood samples **do**
5:       storing ID of blood unit with correspondence ID of delivery unit
6:    **end for**
7:    **for** blood samples **do**
8:       update location of new medical center of blood samples
9:    **end for**
10: **end for**
11: **return** Encrypted hash

---

5   Evaluation

5.1   Environment Setting

Our paradigm is deployed on the Hyperledger Fabric network maintained inside docker containers. In this section, we measures the performance of chaincode of the two scenarios in the algorithms (Sect. 4.3), namely initializing and querying data. The experiments are deployed on Ubuntu 20.01 configuration, core i5 2.7 Ghz, 8 GB RAM.

To prove the effectiveness of our model, we also define several experiments by exploiting the Hyperledger Caliper[1] that is used to design the test scenarios and collect all the information regarding the performance.

5.2   Experimental

In the data creation scenario, we measure the response time (i.e., second) of the requests sent to the create data function; with one worker being initialized in the system, the initial number of requests is 1000/s. The number of requests is continuously sent to the system within 2 min and gradually increases to 10,000 requests/s. The measurement results are shown in Fig. 4. We observe that the number of successfully executed requests is relatively high; whereas the failed

---

[1] https://www.hyperledger.org/use/caliper.

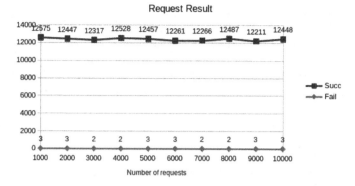

Fig. 4. The results of the create data functions

requests are negligible. In particular, the successful requests are above 12,000 request/s while the number of failed requests only ranges from 2–3 requests.

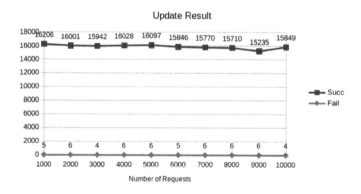

Fig. 5. The results of the update data functions

Figure 5 shows the measurement results of requests that perform the data update function for blood and it products. In this feature, the number of workers increased by 2 workers compared to the initial data creation requests; the number of requests is also increased from 1000 requests to 10,000 requests for worker/second. The number of successful requests increased slightly between 15,235 and 16,206 requests per second. However, the number of failed requests is higher than that in scenario number one because the number of workers has increased. It means that the system takes longer when the number of users increases. It takes more time to process the received requests, and when the number of failed requests increases.

For the data query, Fig. 6 describes the results and number of requests to query the blood and its products recorded in the database. In the second scenario, the numbers of workers increase to 10 workers[2]. For each worker, in turn, sends from 1000 requests to 10,000 requests/second to the system. The system's data query results are still stable, in which the number of successful requests ranges from the lowest level of 37,204 to the highest 42,169 requests, while the number of failed data query requests is at most 1 request (negligible). This further proves the outstanding advantages of the distributed system compared to the traditional centralized ones.

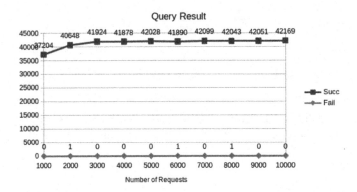

Fig. 6. The results of the request data functions

6   Conclusion

The article applies the benefits of Blockchain technology (i.e., transparency, decentralized storage) to propose a blood and blood product processing process based on the limitations of the current traditional process in Vietnam. Vietnam. The paper provides a proof-of-concepts based on the Hyperledger Fabric platform, which stores information about blood and its products during the storage and transport processes. The information is stored transparently for easy verification in transit and storage. This is an initial effort in applying the benefits of blockchain technology in designing and managing the supply chain of blood and its products for Vietnam in particular and developing countries in general.

In future work, we aim to manage stakeholders based on constraints defined in the form of Smart Contracts. Moreover, this research result is only the first step to build a system based on blockchain technology in a real environment. Therefore, we aim to deploy the proposed model for exporting in more complex scenarios where there are multiple-role of users and off-chain executions (i.e., out of scope for current version) processes of the medical facilities.

---

[2] We assume that the workers are the doctor/nurse/officer in the medical facilities.

References

1. Colvin, B.T., et al.: European principles of haemophilia care. Haemophilia **14**(2), 361–374 (2008)
2. Chapman, J.: Unlocking the essentials of effective blood inventory management. Transfusion **47**, 190S-196S (2007)
3. Sullivan, P.: Developing an administrative plan for transfusion medicine—a global perspective. Transfusion **45**, 224S-240S (2005)
4. Importance of the blood supply. https://www.redcrossblood.org/donate-blood/how-to-donate/how-blood-donations-help/blood-needs-blood-supply.html. Accessed 30-Apr-2022
5. Lownik, E., et al.: Knowledge, attitudes and practices surveys of blood donation in developing countries. Vox sang. **103**(1), 64–74 (2012)
6. Mammen, J.J., et al.: The clinical demand and supply of blood in India: a national level estimation study. Plos One **17**(4), e0265951 (2022)
7. Blood donation frequently asked questions. https://www.mayoclinic.org/blood-donor-program/faq. Accessed 30-Apr-2022
8. Son, H.X., et al.: Towards a mechanism for protecting seller's interest of cash on delivery by using smart contract in hyperledger. Int. J. Adv. Comput. Sci. Appl. **10**(4), 45–50 (2019)
9. Duong-Trung, N., et al.: Multi-sessions mechanism for decentralized cash on delivery system. Int. J. Adv. Comput. Sci. Appl **10**(9), 563–617 (2019)
10. Le, H.T., et al.: Introducing multi shippers mechanism for decentralized cash on delivery system. Int. J. Adv. Comput. Sci. Appl. **10**(6), 1–8 (2019)
11. Le, N.T.T., et al.: Assuring non-fraudulent transactions in cash on delivery by introducing double smart contracts. Int. J. Adv. Comput. Sci. Appl. **10**(5), 677–684 (2019)
12. Ha, X.S., Le, T.H., Phan, T.T., Nguyen, H.H.D., Vo, H.K., Duong-Trung, N.: Scrutinizing trust and transparency in cash on delivery systems. In: Wang, G., Chen, B., Li, W., Di Pietro, R., Yan, X., Han, H. (eds.) SpaCCS 2020. LNCS, vol. 12382, pp. 214–227. Springer, Cham (2021). https://doi.org/10.1007/978-3-030-68851-6_15
13. Ha, X.S., et al.: DeM-CoD: novel access-control-based cash on delivery mechanism for decentralized marketplace. In: 2020 IEEE 19th International Conference on Trust, Security and Privacy in Computing and Communications (TrustCom), pp. 71–78. IEEE (2020)
14. Le, H.T., et al.: Patient-chain: patient-centered healthcare system a blockchain-based technology in dealing with emergencies. In: Malek, Manu (ed.) PDCAT 2021. LNCS, vol. 13148, pp. 576–583. Springer, Cham (2022). https://doi.org/10.1007/978-3-030-96772-7_54
15. Son, H.X., Le, T.H., Quynh, N.T.T., Huy, H.N.D., Duong-Trung, N., Luong, H.H.: Toward a blockchain-based technology in dealing with emergencies in patient-centered healthcare systems. In: Bouzefrane, S., Laurent, M., Boumerdassi, S., Renault, E. (eds.) MSPN 2020. LNCS, vol. 12605, pp. 44–56. Springer, Cham (2021). https://doi.org/10.1007/978-3-030-67550-9_4
16. Duong-Trung, N., et al.: Smart care: integrating blockchain technology into the design of patient-centered healthcare systems. In: Proceedings of the 2020 4th International Conference on Cryptography, Security and Privacy, pp. 105–109 (2020)
17. Duong-Trung, N., et al.: On components of a patient-centered healthcare system using smart contract. In: Proceedings of the 2020 4th International Conference on Cryptography, Security and Privacy, pp. 31–35 (2020)

18. Le, H.T., et al.: BloodChain: a blood donation network managed by blockchain technologies. Network **2**(1), 21–35 (2022)
19. Quynh, N.T.T., et al.: Toward a design of blood donation management by blockchain technologies. In: Gervasi, O., et al. (eds.) ICCSA 2021. LNCS, vol. 12956, pp. 78–90. Springer, Cham (2021). https://doi.org/10.1007/978-3-030-87010-2_6
20. Nakamoto, S.: Bitcoin: a peer-to-peer electronic cash system. Decentralized Bus. Rev. 21260 (2008)
21. Uddin, M.A., et al.: A survey on the adoption of blockchain in IoT: challenges and solutions. Blockchain Res. Appl. **2**(2), 100006 (2021)
22. Alharby, M., Van Moorsel, A.: Blockchain-based smart contracts: a systematic mapping study. arXiv preprint arXiv:1710.06372 (2017)
23. Elli Androulaki, et al.: Hyperledger fabric: a distributed operating system for permissioned blockchains. In: Proceedings of the Thirteenth EuroSys Conference, p. 1–15 (2018)
24. Shi, S., et al.: Applications of blockchain in ensuring the security and privacy of electronic health record systems: a survey. Comput. Secur. **97**, 101966 (2020)
25. Casino, F., Dasaklis, T.K., Patsakis, C.: A systematic literature review of blockchain-based applications: current status, classification and open issues. Telematics Inform. **36**, 55–81 (2019)
26. Monrat, A.A., Schelén, O., Andersson, K.: A survey of blockchain from the perspectives of applications, challenges, and opportunities. IEEE Access **7**, 117134–117151 (2019)
27. Zheng, Z., et al.: An overview on smart contracts: challenges, advances and platforms. Futur. Gener. Comput. Syst. **105**, 475–491 (2020)
28. Shahbaz, M.S., et al.: What is supply chain risk management? A review. Adv. Sci. Lett. **23**(9), 9233–9238 (2017)
29. Lavastre, O., Gunasekaran, A., Spalanzani, A.: Effect of firm characteristics, supplier relationships and techniques used on supply chain risk management (SCRM): an empirical investigation on French industrial firms. Int. J. Prod. Res. **52**(11), 3381–3403 (2014)
30. Nagurney, A., Masoumi, A.H., Yu, M.: Supply chain network operations management of a blood banking system with cost and risk minimization. Comput. Manage. Sci. **9**(2), 205–231 (2012)
31. Armaghan, N., Pazani, N.Y.: A model for designing a blood supply chain network to earthquake disasters (case study: Tehran city). Int. J. Qual. Res. **13**(3), 605–624 (2019)
32. Eskandari-Khanghahi, M., et al.: Designing and optimizing a sustainable supply chain network for a blood platelet bank under uncertainty. Eng. Appl. Artif. Intel. **71**, 236–250 (2018)
33. Delen, D., et al.: Better management of blood supply-chain with GIS-based analytics. Ann. Oper. Res. **185**(1), 181–193 (2011). https://doi.org/10.1007/s10479-009-0616-2
34. Luong, H.H., et al.: IoHT-MBA: an internet of healthcare things (IoHT) platform based on microservice and brokerless architecture (2021)
35. Thanh, L.N.T., et al.: SIP-MBA: a secure IoT platform with brokerless and microservice architecture (2021)
36. Nguyen, L.T.T., et al.: BMDD: a novel approach for IoT platform (broker-less and microservice architecture, decentralized identity, and dynamic transmission messages). PeerJ Comput. Sci. **8**, e950 (2022)

37. Alharbi, F.: Progression towards an e-management centralized blood donation system in Saudi Arabia. In: 2019 International Conference on Advances in the Emerging Computing Technologies (AECT), pp. 1–5. IEEE (2020)
38. Lakshminarayanan, S., Kumar, P.N., Dhanya, N.M.: Implementation of blockchain-based blood donation framework. In: Chandrabose, A., Furbach, U., Ghosh, A., Kumar M., A. (eds.) ICCIDS 2020. IAICT, vol. 578, pp. 276–290. Springer, Cham (2020). https://doi.org/10.1007/978-3-030-63467-4_22
39. Toyoda, K., et al.: A novel blockchain-based product ownership management system (POMS) for anti-counterfeits in the post supply chain. IEEE Access 5, 17465–17477 (2017)

Application of the Elimination Competition Mechanism Based on Blockchain Multi-supervision in Vehicle Data Sharing

Ke Chen[1], Entao Luo[2(✉)], Yong Liu[2], Shuqi Shangguan[2], Ming Wu[3], Tao Peng[4], and Wushour Silamu[1(✉)]

[1] College of Information Science and Engineering, Xinjiang University, Urumqi 830046, China
wushour@xju.edu.cn

[2] College of Information Engineering, Hunan University of Science and Engineering, Yongzhou 425199, China
luoentaohuse@163.com

[3] Intel (China) Co., Ltd., Shanghai 200241, China

[4] School of Computer Science and Network Engineering, Guangzhou University, Guangzhou 510006, China

Abstract. With the rapid development of the Internet of Vehicles and the advent of the 5G era, it is essential to share traffic information among vehicles quickly, securely, and efficiently. Data sharing among vehicles can not only improve driving safety but also alleviate traffic congestion and enhance traffic efficiency. Although existing hybrid blockchain-based vehicle information sharing schemes have improved the transmission speed of vehicle information sharing from various perspectives, there are still challenges in the security of data transmission and transaction settlement rate. In this paper, we propose a vehicle data sharing model based on blockchain multi-supervision, in which the vehicle data and transaction records will be packaged and uploaded by the Road Side Unit (RSU) to the blockchain supervisory committee for review, thus improving the security of the scheme. The experimental results show that this scheme can achieve fast updates and secure storage of vehicle data. At the same time, the built hierarchical strategy can effectively reduce the load and system overhead of the blockchain, thus meeting the security and performance requirements of the current Internet of Vehicles application scenario.

Keywords: Blockchain supervisory committee · Byzantine data security sharing · Data security preserving · Competitive elimination mechanism

1 Introduction

In the Internet of Vehicles, the shared data generally includes important road information such as road facility information, vehicle condition information, and traffic accident information. Intelligent vehicles can analyze this shared data to help vehicle owners understand the surrounding driving environment and achieve safe driving to reduce traffic accidents. However, today's Internet of Vehicles faces two key challenges [1, 2]. Firstly, data between vehicles are vulnerable to attack and theft by unscrupulous elements. Secondly, vehicle network communication is intermittent and lacks high-speed sharing channels, and data sharing efficiency and quality need further improvement [3]. Therefore, achieving secure and efficient data sharing in vehicular networks is a critical problem that needs to be solved now and in the future [4].

Recently, blockchain technology has gained traction in the Internet of Things, artificial intelligence, Internet of Vehicles, and healthcare with its excellent features such as anonymity, traceability, and security [5–8]. Several researchers have used blockchain technology to share data on the Internet of Vehicles. For example, Jia et al. used federated blockchain and innovative contract technologies to achieve secure data storage and sharing in vehicle edge networks, facilitating the convergence of edge computing and vehicle networks and providing powerful computing and storage capabilities for vehicles [9]. Cui et al. proposed a federated block-based V2V data sharing scheme to achieve efficient data sharing for V2V in vehicular networks by combining federated chain with 5G technology and predetermining multiple nodes to establish a distributed shared database [10]. Yang et al. designed a blockchain-based fair non-repudiation service provisioning scheme that enables secure data transactions without authority by implementing a dispute resolution mechanism based on blockchain smart contract technology [11]. Yun et al. proposed a novel blockchain-enabled collaboration framework that reduces data leakage risk by sharing data among multiple distributed parties [12]. While the above schemes can use blockchain technology to enhance the security of existing data, the additional computation and communication overhead may impact the system's overall efficiency. In addition, a common feature of the above schemes is that they do not include data correctness in the evaluation, which means that the data present in the server may have been tampered with or be false data. Such malicious information can seriously damage the relevant interests of information users.

Based on this, this paper proposes a blockchain multi-supervisory-based vehicle sharing mechanism to solve the problems existing in traditional vehicular networks by integrating blockchain and RSU sites into vehicular networks. The contributions of this paper can be summarized as follows:

1) The innovative introduction of the concept of the multi-supervisory committee, based on the research of the multi-supervisory Byzantine data security sharing mechanism, achieves the purpose of secure sharing of data and further accelerates the processing efficiency of block data requests.
2) Based on the comprehensive credit evaluation mechanism, the node dynamic selection and elimination scheme is innovatively proposed to discard low credit inferior nodes and introduce high credit excellent nodes, effectively improving the stability of blockchain operation.
3) By using the improved Byzantine algorithm, and all nodes of the supervisory committee cannot exchange any data during the voting period, this scheme not only ensures fairness in the results but also avoids the emergence of "Inner Ghost" nodes in the supervisory committee.

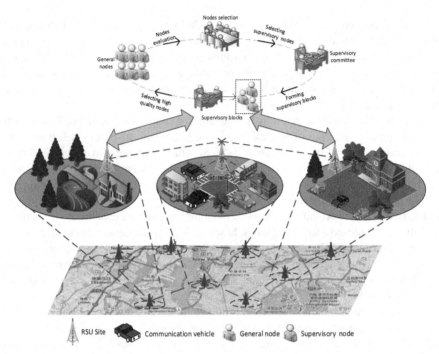

Fig. 1. In-vehicle network interaction model based on improved Byzantine multi-supervisory mechanism

2   Blockchain-Based Multi-regulatory Committee Solution

This paper proposes an on-board network interaction model based on an improved Byzantine multi-supervisory mechanism. The system model is shown in Fig. 1, and the supervisory committee operation process is shown in Fig. 2. This design introduces the concept of the multi-supervisory committee, based on the research of the multi-supervisory Byzantine data security sharing mechanism, to achieve the purpose of secure data sharing and further accelerate the processing efficiency of block data requests. The committee nodes are selected based on that block node's comprehensive workload and equity income rate. This selection method can significantly improve the rate of the regulatory committee in processing RSU requests, promoting the blockchain efficient, stable, and reliable operation.

1) In order to ensure the fairness of the voting results and prevent the appearance of "Inner Ghost" nodes in the regulatory committee, this scheme uses the improved Byzantine algorithm. It adopts the committee voting mechanism when the block receives a request from RSU.

2) The sharing behavior and transaction records between data will be stored on particular servers. The servers involved in this design are divided into the upload server, transaction server, and backup server. The upload server is used to accept data uploaded by users, and the transaction server is used to record each transaction's

information. The backup server is for data backup and data verification. When the regulatory committee detects the occurrence of illegal acts, it can trace the transaction data on the transaction server and hold the relevant participants accountable according to the characteristics of blockchain, such as non-tamperability.

3) Nodes can dynamically enter or exit. The trustworthiness of nodes is evaluated before consensus using the trustworthiness timely evaluation model. After each round of consensus, new nodes are dynamically recruited to join the block based on specific criteria, and nodes with low credit value are abandoned, thus achieving the purpose of the survival of the fittest.

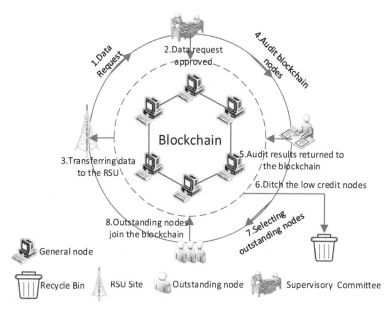

Fig. 2. Supervisory committee operation process

3   Design of a Shared Multi-regulatory Board Program

Based on Blockchain multi-supervisory committee scheme mechanism, an in-vehicle network interaction scheme based on an improved Byzantine multi-supervisory mechanism is designed for the complex data sharing needs of the Internet of Vehicles. Firstly, the blockchain elects nodes, and the election criteria integrate the workload of nodes in the block (POW) and the equity income rate of nodes in the block (POS) for merit selection and will select the outstanding nodes to become supervisory members and form the supervisory committee.

1) Node workload POW the algorithm adopted for this design is:

$$POW = \sum_{i=0}^{n} WT_i * CO_i * \frac{CS_i}{TT}$$

Where WT_i (Work Time) is the work time of the node in round i, CO_i (Current Number of Operations) is the number of operations performed by the node during round i, CS_i (Total Number of Current Node Successes) is the total number of node successes by round i, TT (Total Number of Times) the total number of times the current node has run.

2) Nodal Equity Income Rate the algorithm used in this design is:

$$POS = GB * \frac{TA}{TK}$$

where GB (Get Benefit) is the equity acquired by the node, TA (Total Time For Equity Acquisition) is the total time of equity acquisition by the node, and TK (Total Working Time) is the total working time of the node.

4 Evaluation

This section evaluates the operating performance of the blockchain multi-supervision-based scheme. The operating performance of the initial blockchain nodes is tested first, and then the operating performance of the multi-supervisory Committee-based nodes is tested. This experiment does not consider factors such as block creation time and node communication latency, and 100 times consensus was performed based on the processing efficiency before and after node selection, respectively. The comparison of the changes in the transaction efficiency of the tested nodes before and after the improvement is shown in Fig. 3. The horizontal coordinates indicate the number of the tested nodes, and the vertical coordinates indicate the time spent by the nodes on transactions. Through the comparison graph, we can see that the transaction processing efficiency of the nodes is generally low and inefficient before the nodes participate in the election. In contrast, after the nodes undergo the election of the regulatory committee, the efficiency of the nodes in processing transaction requests is significantly improved, and the processing time is significantly reduced. This experiment can initially prove that the solution proposed in this paper can effectively improve the processing efficiency of node data requests and reduce the data communication overhead.

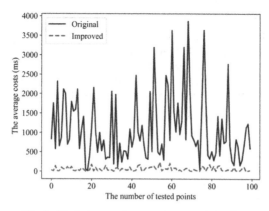

Fig. 3. Node transaction speed comparison chart

5 Conclusion

In this paper, we proposed a blockchain multi-supervision-based vehicle sharing model, which achieves secure sharing of data while accelerating vehicle data interaction by packaging and uploading vehicle data and transaction records from roadside units to the blockchain supervisory committee for review. Experimental results show that the scheme can effectively improve data transaction efficiency and reduce data communication overhead while guaranteeing block creation and data transaction security under the same data request.

References

1. Mollah, M.B., Zhao, J., Niyato, D., et al.: Blockchain for the internet of vehicles towards intelligent transportation systems. IEEE Internet Things J. **8**(6), 4157–4185 (2020)
2. Hussain, R., Zeadally, S.: Autonomous cars: research results, issues, and future challenges. IEEE Commun. Surv. Tutor. **21**(2), 1275–1313 (2019)
3. Grover, H., Alladi, T., Chamola, V., et al.: Edge computing and deep learning enabled secure multitier network for internet of vehicles. IEEE Internet Things J. **8**(19), 14787–14796 (2021)
4. Ghane, S., Jolfaei, A., Kulik, L., et al.: Preserving privacy in the internet of connected vehicles. IEEE Trans. Intell. Transp. Syst. **22**(8), 5018–5027 (2021)
5. Liu, C.H., Lin, Q., Wen, S.: Blockchain-enabled data collection and sharing for industrial IoT with deep reinforcement learning. IEEE Trans. Ind. Inform. **15**(6), 3516–3526 (2019)
6. Bosri, R., Rahman, M.S., Bhuiyan, M.Z.A., et al.: Integrating blockchain with artificial intelligence for privacy-preserving recommender systems. IEEE Trans. Netw. Sci. Eng. **8**(2), 1009–1018 (2021)
7. Song, Y., Fu, Y., Yu, F.R., et al.: Blockchain-enabled internet of vehicles with cooperative positioning: a deep neural network approach. IEEE Internet Things J. **7**(4), 3485–3498 (2020)
8. Lin, P., Song, Q., Yu, F.R., et al.: Task offloading for wireless VR-enabled medical treatment with blockchain security using collective reinforcement learning. IEEE Internet Things J. **8**(21), 15749–15761 (2021)
9. Kang, J., Yu, R., Huang, X., et al.: Blockchain for secure and efficient data sharing in vehicular edge computing and networks. IEEE Internet Things J. **6**(3), 4660–4670 (2019)

10. Cui, J., Ouyang, F., Ying, Z., et al.: Secure and efficient data sharing among vehicles based on consortium blockchain. IEEE Trans. Intell. Transp. Syst. **23**(07), 8857–8867 (2022)
11. Xu, Y., Ren, J., Wang, G., et al.: A blockchain-based nonrepudiation network computing service scheme for industrial IoT. IEEE Trans. Ind. Inform. **15**(6), 3632–3641 (2019)
12. Lu, Y., Huang, X., Dai, Y., et al.: Blockchain and federated learning for privacy-preserved data sharing in industrial IoT. IEEE Trans. Ind. Inform. **16**(6), 4177–4186 (2019)

Economic Perspective of Cybersecurity: Principles and Strategies

Fei Xu[1] and Jing Xu[2(✉)]

[1] China Center for International Economic Exchanges, CCIEE, Beijing, China
[2] Beijing University of Science and Technology, Beijing, China
xj2018@ustb.edu.cn

Abstract. An economic perspective is essential but often neglected for understanding the state of cybersecurity, especially when security is increasingly viewed as a matter of national security. Analyze and learn the core economic principles of cybersecurity can help interpret many security phenomena and various challenges we are facing, as well as help to improve cybersecurity industry moving forward. In this paper, we will outline in greater detail the economic characteristics and principles plaguing cybersecurity: Invisibility of benefits, Trade-offs between security and other values, Asymmetries of defend and attack, Dynamic and uncertainty situations, social gains and losses. Then we discuss the pros and cons of the strategies that commonly used now to overcome these economic barriers in the cybersecurity context. Finally, we make several actionable policy recommendations for policy changes and market directions to improve cybersecurity.

Keywords: Cybersecurity · Economic · Public goods · Government intervention

1 Introduction

Today, our dependence on inter-networked computing systems means that virtually every move of daily life—whether personal or commercial, public or private, civilian or military—is intermediated by computer systems. But none of these systems are trustworthy and many are actively under real-time attack today [1]. Cyber threats are escalating in frequency, impact and sophistication [2]. Persistent and increasingly sophisticated malicious cyber campaigns are threatening the public sector, the private sector, and ultimately people's security and privacy [3]. While efforts and investment to improve cybersecurity continue to grow, security developments lag behind the pace of the malicious use of digital technologies. Although all parties are aware of the seriousness of the cybersecurity problem, it remains far from resolved.

Cybersecurity comes with the application of information technology. 'Cyber' is a constitutive elements of information societies, it is interwoven with the physical, economic, social and political elements, and its security it is essential to foster societal development, technological progress [4]. It is impossible to consider cybersecurity without information technology, and it is impossible to consider cybersecurity without the specific scenarios of information application. Cybersecurity has been considered as a

C. Su and K. Sakurai (Eds.): SciSec 2022 Workshops, CCIS 1680, pp. 119–130, 2022.
https://doi.org/10.1007/978-981-19-7769-5_9

very complex social issue, which integrates both science technology, sociology and jurisprudence.

There have been many discussions about the inherent nature of security itself and the characteristics. An economic perspective is essential for understanding the state of cybersecurity, especially when security is increasingly viewed as a matter of public and national security. However, most of the cybersecurity economic research is conducted from a microeconomic perspective. Many studies [5, 6] aiming to provide effective analytical models and frameworks for Cybersecurity Economics and Analysis (CEA), help to increase the economic and financial viability, effectiveness and value generation of cybersecurity solutions for organization's strategic, tactical and operational imperative. We will analyze cybersecurity from a macroeconomic perspective and agree with the idea that cybersecurity qualifies as "public affair", with can be better improved by government intervention and more participation of the public.

In this paper, we will outline in greater detail the economic characteristics and principles plaguing cybersecurity in the next section. Then we discuss the pros and cons of the strategies that commonly used for cybersecurity in Sect. 3. We make several principal policy recommendations for policy changes and market directions to improve cybersecurity in Sect. 4. Finally, we conclude this paper and give out future works in Sect. 5.

2 Economic Principles of Cybersecurity

Admittedly, cybersecurity investment has become an increasingly complex one, since information systems are typically subject to frequent attacks, whose arrival and impact fluctuate stochastically. Decisions are often made with imperfect knowledge, threats are persistent and adaptive, and rapidly changing technology is the norm. Methods to measure economic return in the cybersecurity domain are in their infancy. We now discuss the basic characteristics of cybersecurity from an economic perspective to better understand the causes of those dilemmas.

2.1 Invisibility of Benefits

Investment in cybersecurity is an important financial and operational decision for both governmental agencies and private enterprise. Typical business and government investments aim to create value or improve productivity, whereas cybersecurity investments aim to minimize loss incurred by cyber threats. As a result, cybersecurity is a market of insufficient motivation for investors inherently. To make things worse, due to the uncertainty of threats, the benefits of investing in cybersecurity is almost invisible. Which makes the efficiency and effectiveness of security investments can often be hardly determined due to the invisibility of their benefits.

When implementing IT-security measures, the predicted outcome, e.g. prevented losses, is uncertain in two ways. First of all, it is not certain that one measure and the corresponding investment will prevent a certain risk to occur in the future unless the risk turns out to be damages. Second, the seriousness and damage of the prevented incident is hard to calculate. People have difficulty reasoning about extremely low-probability events. Estimating the likelihood of a certain type of cyber attack is extremely uncertain and depends on unquantifiable psychological factors like dissuasion and deterrence. Were there some ways to analyze a system mechanically and obtain a quantity that indicates just how secure that system is, then we could have a basis for assessing what is gained from specific investments made in support of cybersecurity. But effective cybersecurity metrics do not exist even today. Quantities derived entirely from empirical observations also don't work for justifying investments. The absence of detected system compromises could indicate that investments in defenses worked, attacks haven't been attempted, or the compromise escaped notice. So whether or not prior security investments were well targeted is impossible to know, leaving security professionals to justify investments based solely on non-events.

Even if an organization already decided to invest in cybersecurity, the uncertainty of threats and invisibility of benefits makes it very hard to choose which type of security products and services to buy. They may not even be able to fully understand their organization's specific security demand, which makes demand-driven technology innovation and industrial development impossible. It is just not possible whether we want or not.

2.2 Trade-off Between Security and Other Values

Cybersecurity, like security in so many other contexts, involves tradeoffs with other values [10]. A tradeoff is a situation that involves losing one quality or aspect of something in return for gaining another quality or aspect. Conflicts is common and will have to be considered and resolved between public cybersecurity and other values or interests of specific individuals, entities, and society at large.

First of all, there is the trade-off between security and efficiency. Security is not perfect. There is a trade-off between ensuring system efficiency and improving cyber security. There is a natural tension between efficiency and resilience in the design of IT systems. Implementation of security products and methods consumes the resources of the system. Each system working with an optimal level of insecurity, where the benefits of efficient operation outweigh any reductions in risk brought about by additional security measures. Reconciling short-term incentives to reduce operating costs with long-term interest in reducing vulnerability is hard. Worse still, the party making the security-efficiency trade-off is not the one who loses out when attacks occur in most of the situations.

Second, there is the trade-off between security and individual rights. Surveillance of network traffic and online identity could be a powerful potential source of information about certain attacks and vulnerabilities. However, surveillance raises massive privacy concerns. There may be trade-offs: societal values as well as potential benefits for the collective versus constraints on activities by individuals and business. Systems' resilience hinges on a delicate trade-off between security and individual human rights. It poses serious risks of undermining and breaching users' privacy, users' exposure to extra risks, should data confidentiality be breached, and may have a mass-surveillance effect.

There are other trade-offs, such as security and technical innovation, etc. Even faced with so many trade-offs, there are really not much metrics and mechanisms suitable and be able for measuring them. Which makes the trade-off decision even more difficult, even if not possible.

2.3   Asymmetries of Attack and Defend

Cybersecurity is a confrontation between the attacker and defender which demonstrate a clear asymmetry characteristic. In the process of network attack and defense, the attacking party constantly innovates and always occupies the initiative in the confrontation process, while the defender falls into a passive situation of being tired of coping. The deterministic and static nature of the traditional network gives the attacker the advantage of time and space, and can repeatedly probe and analyze the vulnerability of the target system and conduct penetration tests, even social engineering, and then find a breakthrough path. The similarity of traditional networks and software structures gives attackers an advantage in attack costs, and the same attack methods can be applied to a large number of similar targets.

Defenders are reactive, attackers are proactive. Defenders must defend all places at all times, against all possible attacks, including those not known about by the defender; attackers need only find one vulnerability and one path. Also, they have the luxury of inventing and testing new attacks in private as well as selecting the place and time of attack at their convenience. New defenses are expensive, new attacks are cheap. Defenders have significant investments in their approaches and business models, while attackers have minimal sunk costs and thus can be quite agile. Besides, defenses can't be measured, but attacks can. Since we cannot currently measure how a given security technology or approach reduces risk from attack, there are few strong competitive pressures to improve these technical qualities. So vendors frequently compete on the basis of ancillary factors (e.g., speed, integration, brand development, etc.). Attackers can directly measure their return-on-investment and are strongly incentivized to improve their offerings.

Cyber spaces are consisting of virtual, agile, flexible, but brittle systems. This brittleness favors offence over defense, explaining in part the continued growth of cyber threats and the escalation of their impact. The more digital technologies become pervasive, the wider becomes the surface of attacks, and with it also number of successful attacks grows.

2.4   Dynamic and Uncertainty Situations

Information technology is evolving at a fast speed than we can imagine. Software development is inherently buggy, not to mention those fully functional complicated applications and platforms. Even responsible software companies that rigorously test for weaknesses couldn't find them all before a product ships. To expect all software to ship free of vulnerabilities is not realistic. For systems that incorporate humans as users and operators, we would need some way to prevent social engineering and intentional insider-malfeasance.

Also, the ability to attack will continue to increase along the time. We don't know which breaking technique will come out next minutes. Whenever new technology is introduced, it has the potential to change the system risks organizations face. The nature of risk and resulting harms is such that they can propagate through systems and supply chains. For example, quantum computing has been hailed as one of the next big revolutions. It is not just faster than traditional computing methods, but a fundamentally different approach to solve seemingly intractable problems. The mathematical operations that most traditional cryptographic algorithms rely on could be cracked with a sufficiently strong quantum computer [7].

Furthermore, cybersecurity measures and improvements, such as patches, become available at random points in time making investment decisions even more challenging [4]. Results indicate that greater uncertainty over the cost of cybersecurity attacks raises the value of an embedded option to invest in cybersecurity. Knowing that countermeasures effective against today's threats can be ineffective tomorrow, decision-makers need agile ways to assess the efficacies of investments in cybersecurity on assuring mission outcomes. Individuals and entities therefore can neither fully reap the benefit of their security investment nor entirely control their vulnerability through investments because of those dynamic and uncertainties [8].

2.5 Social Gains and Losses

The information technology sector already became a significant economic force. Computing, network and digitalization changed how people shopped, worked, communicated and socialized, greatly improved social efficiencies and the social value created is immeasurable. For instance, companies operating critical infrastructures have integrated control systems with the Internet to reduce near-term, measurable costs. Electricity companies have realized substantial efficiency gains by upgrading their control systems to run on the same IP infrastructure as their IT networks. Unfortunately, these changes in architecture leave systems more vulnerable to failures and attacks, and it is society that suffers most if an outage occurs. The control systems regulating power plants and chemical refineries are vulnerable to cyberattack, yet very little investment has been made to protect against these threats. While those raising the risk of catastrophic failure, whose losses will be primarily borne by society.

For example, a single compromised system anywhere in a network can serve as a launching point for attacks on other systems connected to that network. So local investment in defenses not only provides local benefits but also benefits others; and under-investment in defenses elsewhere in the network could facilitate local harms [9]. The society, organizations and individuals are enjoying the benefits of information technology, but neither party is willing to take responsibility of cybersecurity accordingly. Unfortunately, such a misalignment is inevitable for many information security decisions.

The lack of effective cybersecurity measures has a potential knock-on effect on the information revolution, and on the development of information societies around the globe. Its security it is essential to foster societal development, technological progress and also to harness the potential of digital technologies to deliver socially good outcomes.

3 Common Strategies for Cybersecurity

3.1 Laws and Regulations

Dan Assaf argues for greater government responsibility, saying that computer security is a public good. Since there's inadequate incentive for industry to fight cybercrime, perhaps there's a place for public action. In addition, national security today requires secure cyberinfrastructure; the absence of physical borders to defend makes the problem worse, not easier. Since only the government have the required capacity to deal with the sophisticated cybersecurity. What might government do?

Law could force system producers and/or purchasers to make the necessary investments on security. There are a host of laws and regulations directly and indirectly govern the various cybersecurity requirements for any given business. For example, the Federal Laws, Federal Regulations & Guidance, the State Laws, and International Laws for cybersecurity.

There are other cybersecurity frameworks that are not codified in law but rather are created and/or enforced by non-governmental entities. For example, the NIST or ISO 27001 cybersecurity frameworks are both widely used standards in many industries and government organizations [20]. Companies might be required to comply with these frameworks by industry dynamics or by organizational partnerships with government or other entities.

Government can also participate in standards—Regulation and liability. The adoption of mandatory standards can be seen as a way to support security. Some standards directly concern what functions an artifact must or must not support, some govern its internal structure, while others concern the process by which the artifact is constructed or maintained, and yet others govern qualifications of the personnel who are involved in creating the artifact. as well as security provisions in information privacy laws. Current market activity suggests that such mandates show value in some areas.

We could certainly use more research, especially on defense techniques. However, government agencies often limited their investments to problems with a short-term horizon. The number of projects supported is relatively small and the funding is often through special one time initiatives.

3.2 Industry Incentives

The cybersecurity market is expanding rapidly in recent years. It surpassed $150 billion in 2019 and is expected to exceed $400 billion and grow at over 15% Compound Annual Growth Rate (CAGR) between 2020 and 2026 [11]. The spike in the cybersecurity market is being seen in all parts of the world. Given the practical difficulties of teaching non-technical users and application sections the principles of adequate security, the logical plan should be to shift the cost to the industries that can do something about it. They might be encouraged to improve security via commercial pressure, regulation, or tort lawsuits. While the demand for cybersecurity is growing across the world, the market is getting increasingly competitive as new cybersecurity products launch, and more major providers form partnerships.

Deloitte reports that financial services companies spend 6 to 7 percent of their IT budget on security, but this is far from sufficient. Many companies probably still think that building in security is either too expensive or too inconvenient for users. Small companies might lack the resources to do security well [5]. Although the industry prefers neither regulation nor liability. Regulation tends to be slow to change, which poses difficulty in a rapidly changing world. Liability causes people to try to evade it and runs a risk that in the end the responsible party won't be able to pay damages. There is still the need for incentives to help accelerate the growing of cybersecurity market.

Aspects of industry incentives for cybersecurity may include: Cybersecurity Insurance, Grants, Process Preference, Liability Limitation, Streamline Regulations, Public Recognition and Cybersecurity Research, etc. It is important for the industry to promote cybersecurity practices and develop core security capabilities.

3.3 Technology Innovation

Confronted by a problem born of technology, the main focus of cybersecurity doctrine is on developing new detection and defense technologies at the beginning and still now. Government funded organizations and Scientists are investing heavily in technological means for improving cybersecurity. Intuitively this is the right and straight forward way to find the solution. However, Improved technology itself may not be able to solve problems that technology has created. Cybersecurity encompasses a wide set of practices, from risk assessment and penetration tests; disaster recovery; cryptography; access control and surveillance; architecture, software, and network security; to hack-back and security operations, and physical security. Each of these practices requires different techniques, which makes technology innovation even difficult.

Unfortunately, research in cybersecurity is not enough, and has been hamstrung on multiple fronts, therefore, has not been able to develop a much-needed science base to anchor cybersecurity innovations, nor has it been able to produce the range of solutions we require.

Despite the growing value of the cybersecurity market and the increasing efforts of companies and state actors to invest in technical innovation to improve the security of information systems and infrastructures, data on number and impact of cyber-attacks is still escalating. We can learn that technology innovation itself is inadequate to frame and govern cybersecurity.

4 Recommendations for Cybersecurity

4.1 Public Cybersecurity Doctrine

Cybersecurity comes along with information techniques. It is natural to consider cybersecurity as a technical problem and hopefully can be solved by developing security products. Cybersecurity is technical and business problem that has been presented as such in boardrooms for years. As cyberthreats becomes more sever and casing more significant damages, scholars and regulators began to think about the nature of cybersecurity, the cybersecurity doctrine.

Savage and Schneider discussed security is not a commodity in their work [1]. They pointed out that unlike computer and communications hardware and software, security is nota commodity.It cannot be scaled simply by doing more.In this respect, there is a mounting consensus on treating cybersecurity as a public good to be managed in the public interest. The management of a public good requires considering direct and indirect externalities, as well as medium and long-term consequences. This favor approaches to cybersecurity that focus on interdependencies among the security of different, but connected, technologies, their impact on the context of deployment and on the relevant public interest at stake.

Enhanced levels of cybersecurity can entail tensions involving cost, function, convenience, and societal values such as openness, privacy, freedom of expression, and innovation. Management of cybersecurity as a public good call for collaboration between the private and the public sectors to ensure that systems' robustness is designed to meet the public interest. It is up to the public sector to set standards, certification and testing and verification procedures capable of ensuring that a sufficient level of security is maintained. At the same time, the private sector bears responsibility for designing robust systems and developing and improving new cybersecurity methods for the services and products they offer, as well as for collaborating with the public sector around controlling and testing mechanisms. Envisaging systems' robustness as a public good also places some responsibility on the user in terms of their cyber hygiene practices.

4.2 Facing the "Right" Threats

Cyber threats are constantly changing and evolving with the development of information technology. For example, the frequency of identified Advanced Persistent Threats (APTs) has greatly increased recent years. APT's number one target were always organizations with high value assets and that's always the reason why those attacks are so persistent. In order to protect against this kind of threats, it is very important to understand the reasons and motivations behind these threats. Security is a trade-off, there is no perfect security. Since cybersecurity investments involve decision-making under uncertainty, it is more reasonable to think in terms of deploying defense as appropriate to the threat and to the value of what's being protected. We can't succeed by focusing our defenses on past attacks, and we must move from a reactive stance to a proactive one.

In addition to this, the range and scope of cyber-attacks create the need for organizations to prioritize the manner in which they defend themselves. With this in mind, each organization needs to consider the threats that they are most at risk from and act in such a way so as to reduce the vulnerability across as many relevant weaknesses as possible. So, based on the evaluation of the organization value itself, and understanding the different motivations of cyber threats, facing the right threats is very important. It is needed to define some agreed upon kinds and levels of cybersecurity, characterizing who is to be secured, at what costs (monetary, technical, convenience, and societal values), and against what kinds of threats. The goals might be absolute or they might specify a range of permissible trade-offs.

Basically, the defense of cybersecurity for an organization needs to be based on regulation compliance as the basic requirement of the passing line, and a high-line evaluation mechanism driven by the threat situation. At the same time, while information service provider is responsible for the security of their systems, it is needed for the government to provide the required techniques and supports for the service provider when facing extremely complicated threats, especially those well-organized and weaponized threats.

4.3 Reallocation of Responsibilities and Liabilities

One of the most significant characteristics of cybersecurity is ambiguous accountability. There are also capability gaps between the current cybersecurity approaches and defending ourselves against evolving threats. Investment incentives are missing when costs are borne by third parties, materialize only well after the breach occurs, and causation is difficult to discern much less prove.

In order to solve the problems of growing vulnerability and increasing cyber threats, policy and legislation must coherently allocate responsibilities and liabilities so that the parties in a position to fix problems have an incentive and ability to do so. In many circumstances cyber risks are allocated poorly. For example, it is very common now that the organizations that defend cybersecurity do not bear the full costs of failure. Also, it is unlikely that either vendors or users, left to their own devices, will solve the problems. Government must set the rules of the game; We can't rely on unintelligible and unread end user license agreements to be responsible for security breaches any more.

Enterprises should be fully responsible for their own security, bear most of the responsibility for their own security and the social governance security supported by themselves, and bear part of the responsibility for their own security and the public/national security associated with themselves. And to some point, defense of its citizens is a clear responsibility of government. Because in essence, responsibility is not simply a stipulation, responsibility means technical capabilities and the ability to invest. Those abilities are carried by the implementation of large projects, advanced technologies and products, and sophisticated teams. Cybersecurity for the State and public society is not something that can be achieved with enterprise-level investments, nor is it achieved through individual effort. It is not enough to only have the public attention or regulatory requirements. Reasonable reallocation of responsibilities and liabilities is the fundamental and starting point for ensuring cybersecurity.

4.4 Government Intervention and Policies

Conflicts and trade-offs will have to be resolved between public cybersecurity and other values or interests of specific individuals, entities, and society at large. This requires the government to make the overall adjustments due to the political nature of cybersecurity. Government policy interventions are required that incentivize responsibility allocation, accountability and collaboration on the part of both individuals, organizations and governments. Also, policy that incentivizes higher standards of care in regulation, technology and service delivery is needed.

Various government agencies themselves perform research and development, incident response, and forensic analysis in cybersecurity in many countries around the world. Although government funded projects seems to need massive financial investments, this is not a simple economic gain, but also involves political gain, and industrial driven gain. Yet it is difficult to calibrate the right nature and scale of investment in cybersecurity. Government leadership need to develop a set of policy actions that incentivize take-up of security solutions and that underpin greater trust and transparency between different components of the ecosystem. Possible solutions may include: government giving more finical support, clarifying issues of liability, reducing friction in current assurance and regulatory models, and addressing the security of new technology, invention and application scenarios changes. Clearly, some additional funding by the state is needed to help the state build a more effective, dynamic and elastic defense mechanism.

Besides, Government also needs to managing cyber risks in the face of the major technology trends taking place in the near future. However, security is not usually being considered as an integral component of technology innovations and as such, proper investment needed to be made into support (knowledge, guidance, research investment) and incentives (market forces, regulation) for developing emerging technologies securely [12].

4.5 Collaboration and Information Sharing

One future feature of cybersecurity is collaboration. The success of industry ISACs is indicative of a greater acceptance of the security community that collaboration is cheaper and more effective means of security than the alternative [13]. For example, NSA Cybersecurity Collaboration Center harnesses the power of industry partnerships to prevent and eradicate foreign cyber threats to National Security Systems [14]. The EU Information Sharing and Analysis Centers (ISACs) foster collaboration between the cybersecurity community in different sectors of the economy [15]. Cybersecurity collaboration also exists between nations. Such as, US-EU collaboration on cybersecurity and joint Statement of Intent Between the U.S. Department of Homeland Security and the Israel National Cyber Directorate [16]. When it comes to tackling these global cyberthreats, working with international partners can have benefits for resilience [17]. Particular attentions need to be taken of the needs of developing countries and the need for collective efforts to reduce cross-border cybercrime.

Cybersecurity defenses should reflect a proactive strategy that leverages from diverse areas of expertise and information. Information Sharing is increasingly important for addressing growing systemic risks. Sharing of information about vulnerabilities of different systems involved in the same supply chain, for example, will become essential for the private sector to guarantee system robustness and learn from peers. At the same time, the public sector may support this practice by including information sharing and collaboration as part of capabilities building initiatives and procedures. These practices can facilitate patching procedures and may reduce the zero-day and exploits market. In turn, this could slow down the cyber arms-race and weaponization dynamics of cyberspace.

Cyber threat information is any information that can help an organization identify, assess, monitor, and respond to cyber threats. Cyber threat information includes indicators of compromise; tactics, techniques, and procedures used by threat actors; suggested actions to detect, contain, or prevent attacks; and the findings from the analyses of incidents. Organizations that share cyber threat information can improve their own security postures as well as those of other organizations [18].

5   Conclusion

Society as a whole do not allocate sufficient attention, researches or resources to cybersecurity. Cybersecurity shows significant economic characteristics. Right understanding of public cybersecurity doctrine, appropriate architecture design and interventions that consider cybersecurity as a whole system and public affair can significantly improve our cybersecurity posture. Though cybersecurity problem resides in technologies, the solution requires concept changes, policies, interventions and collaboration. We believe that by partially alter the focus of cybersecurity from technical to economical will help to improve it moving forward. Our designed recommendations are to raise awareness to cybersecurity and assign responsibility for action within the society as a whole so that cyber risks to society may be mitigated.

References

1. Savage, S., Schneider, F.B.: Security is not a commodity: the road forward for cybersecurity research: a white paper prepared for the computing community consortium committee of the computing research association. http://cra.org/ccc/resources/ccc-led-whitepapers/
2. Taddeo, M., Bosco, F.: We must treat cybersecurity as a public good. Here's why. World Economic Forum, Centre for Cybersecurity (2019)
3. The White House. Executive Order on Improving the Nation's Cybersecurity (2021). https://www.whitehouse.gov/briefing-room/presidential-actions/2021/05/12/execut ive-order-on-improving-the-nations-cybersecurity/
4. Floridi, L.: The Fourth Revolution, How the Infosphere is Reshaping Human Reality. Oxford University Press, Oxford (2014)
5. Moore, T.: Introducing the economics of cybersecurity: principles and policy options. In: Proceedings Workshop Deterring Cyber Attacks: Informing Strategies and Developing Options for US Policy, Nat'l Academies Press (2010). www.cs.brown.edu/courses/csci1950-p/sou rces/lec27/Moore.pdf
6. Kobayashi, B.H.: An economic analysis of the private and social costs of the provision of cybersecurity and other public security goods. Supreme Court Econ. Rev. **14**, 261–280 (2006)
7. Subramanian, V.: Quantum and the Future of Cryptography. National defense magazine (2021)
8. Chronopoulos, M., Panaousis, E., Grossklags, J.: An options approach to cybersecurity investment. IEEE Access **6**, 12175–12186 (2018)
9. Lesk, M.: Cybersecurity and economics. IEEE Secur. Priv. **9**, 76–79 (2011)
10. Anderson, R., Moore, T.: The economics of information security. Science **314**(5799), 610–613 (2006)
11. Borchart, L.: The cybersecurity market is rapidly growing. highlights from a 2020 global market insights report on the growing cybersecurity market. https://techchannel.com/Trends/ 03/2021/cybersecurity-market-growing
12. World Economic Forum in collaboration with the University of Oxford. Future Series: Cybersecurity, emerging technology and systemic risk. https://www.weforum.org/reports/future-ser ies-cybersecurity-emerging-technology-and-systemic-risk
13. Nissenbaum, H.: Where computer security meets national security. Ethics Inf. Technol. **7**(2), 61–73 (2005). https://doi.org/10.1007/s10676-005-4582-3
14. Ford, K.: The future of cybersecurity is collaboration. https://www.cybergrx.com/resources/ research-and-insights/blog/the-future-of-cybersecurity-is-collaboration
15. NSA Cybersecurity Collaboration Center. National Security Agency/Central Security Service. https://www.nsa.gov/About/Cybersecurity-Collaboration-Center/
16. Cybersecurity Policies. Shaping Europe's digital future. European Commission. https://dig ital-strategy.ec.europa.eu/en/policies/cybersecurity-policies

17. Joint Statement of Intent Between the U.S. Department of Homeland Security and the Israel National Cyber Directorate. Homeland Security (2022). https://www.dhs.gov/news/2022/03/02/joint-statement-intent-between-us-department-homeland-security-and-israel-national

18. To counter cyber risks to critical sectors such as aviation we need international collaboration. World Economic Forum. https://www.weforum.org/agenda/2021/04/cybersecurity-aviation-international-regulation/

19. Johnson, C., Badger, L., Waltermire, D., Snyder, J., Skorupka, C.: Guide to cyber threat information sharing. NIST Special Publication 800-150

20. Baadsgaard, J.: Cybersecurity Laws & Regulations. https://www.ipohub.org/cybersecurity-laws-regulations/

21. Assaf, D.: Government intervention in information infrastructure protection. In: Goetz, E., Shenoi, S. (eds.) Critical Infrastructure Protection, vol. 253, pp. 29–39. Springer, Heidelberg (2008). https://doi.org/10.1007/978-0-387-75462-8_3

Towards a Dynamic Reputation Management Scheme for Cross-Chain Transactions

Lin-Fa Lee[1] and Kuo-Hui Yeh[1,2(✉)] (iD)

[1] National Dong Hwa University, Hualien 97401, Taiwan R.O.C.
{410635034,khyeh}@gms.ndhu.edu.tw
[2] National Sun Yat-Sen University, Kaohsiung, Taiwan R.O.C.

Abstract. Recently, research communities have dedicated their efforts to the development of versatile and innovative Blockchain-based application systems. These systems are usually independent and thus difficult to be integrated and cooperated with each other during cross-chain transactions in terms of the interoperability perspective. In addition, there may be potential risks once external malicious attackers desire to control or manipulate nodes in cross-chain systems. It is necessary to have a solution preventing users' misbehaviors during the process of information and value exchange among different blockchains. In this paper, we propose a dynamic reputation management scheme which can effectively detect misbehaviors and identify potential security risks during cross-chain transactions. Our scheme conducts a mechanism evaluating reputation and trustworthiness of nodes and chains, respectively, through their current state and transactions history. This characteristic can help any cross-chains system well-react and be resistant against ongoing-endangered behaviors within a reasonable computation time.

Keywords: Blockchain · Cross-chains · Reputation management · Interoperability

1 Introduction

Please note that the first paragraph of a section or subsection is not indented. The first Blockchain technology has become one of the most subversive innovative technologies after the bitcoin [1] system was proposed in 2008. Since then, Blockchain has been adopted and utilized in different applications, such as financial, medical and cryptocurrency, with its de-centralized property and immutability. However, the heterogeneity of current Blockchain platform technologies leaves it in a dilemma where it is difficult to integrate the value and information exchange processes of multiple blockchain platforms with versatile consensus protocol. The study [2] has proposed several critical issues for cross-chain transaction circumstances. For example, when one blockchain system tries to access the data from another blockchain system for cross-chain transactions, it is necessary to have a consensus on data access, processing and storage and, after that, to walk toward to a mechanism ensuring trustworthy and consistency on data/transactions exchanged among communicating entities from different blockchains. Nevertheless,

© The Author(s), under exclusive license to Springer Nature Singapore Pte Ltd. 2022
C. Su and K. Sakurai (Eds.): SciSec 2022 Workshops, CCIS 1680, pp. 131–134, 2022.
https://doi.org/10.1007/978-981-19-7769-5_10

once two application systems belong to separate organizations and each of them has its own blockchain system, the different architecture and consensus mechanism will lead to security issues when data exchange and data access across chain systems, i.e. denial of services (DoS) attacks [3], double-spending [4] and selfish-mining attack [5]. For this reason, it is necessary to design a secure method that can guarantee the trustworthiness of cross-chain interoperability process. Furthermore, the method must be universally suitable to heterogeneous blockchain systems in numerous application scenarios.

Hence, in this study we are devoted to develop a reputation management scheme to effectively detect and identify potential malicious attackers during cross-chain transactions. Our scheme focuses on evaluating the system trustworthiness in terms of nodes and chains. Moreover, to ensure the security of cross-chain interoperability, we adopt seven indicators resistant against existing known attacks as show in Table 1. These indicators will be considered as major evaluation criteria on rating the reputation of the nodes involved within cross-chains transactions.

Table 1. Reputation indicators and corresponding threats with condition judgement used in our proposed scheme.

Reputation Indicator	Initial Value	Condition Judgement	Pre-define weight	Corresponding Threat
(Node) *Node connect status*	None	$\begin{cases} \textit{if Async}, -1 \\ \textit{if sync}, 0 \end{cases}$	1	None
(Node) *Hardware usage*	Average GPU compute power of a period of time.	$\begin{cases} \textit{Increase or Decrease rapidly}, -1 \\ \textit{Slow or Constant}, 0 \end{cases}$	0.6	Selfish mining, Block withholding, Majority attack
(Node) *Average spending time of transaction*	Current time + Expect timeof block generation.	$\begin{cases} \textit{Overtime}, -1 \\ \textit{On time}, 0 \\ \textit{Less time consumption}, -1 \end{cases}$	0.4	Double-spending, Consensus delay
(Node) *Transaction consequence*	None	$\begin{cases} \textit{Success}, 1 \\ \textit{Failure}, -1 \end{cases}$	1	DDoS, Double-spending, Time-jacking attacks
(Chain) *Average network hashrate*	Average network hashing power of a period of time	$\begin{cases} \textit{Increase or Decrease rapidly}, -1 \\ \textit{Slow or Constant}, 0 \end{cases}$	0.6	Stale orphaned blocks, Selfish mining, Majority attack
(Chain) *The delay time in block propagation*	None	$\begin{cases} \textit{Delay } \frac{E(T)}{2} \textit{ time}, -1 \\ \textit{On time}, 0 \end{cases}$	1	Consensus delay, Selfish mining, Block withholding, Stale & Orphaned blocks, Time-jacking attacks
(Chain) *Average spending time of each transaction*	Expect time $E(T) = \frac{Difficulty\_value}{Hash\_rate}$	$\begin{cases} \textit{Overtime}, -1 \\ \textit{On time}, 0 \\ \textit{Less time consumption}, -1 \end{cases}$	0.4	Double-spending, Consensus delay

2 The Proposed Scheme

In this section, we introduce our proposed dynamic reputation management scheme in which three independently heterogeneous blockchain systems including one relay chain are involved with. The rely chain are responsible for the agreement of transaction and the corresponding consensus which will be uploaded and accepted by these three heterogeneous blockchain systems. As shown in Fig. 1, we have a major relaychain and two sub-chains in our system scenario. Each blockchain system and each node will have a specific reputation value as the degree of trust in the next interactions (and transactions). As the proposed system is used to prevent the misbehavior in heterogeneous blockchains, the analysis of the node and the chain's past normal transaction records is adopted to detect potential misbehaviors. In addition, the proposed system allows to dynamically modify indicator weights by nodes in the relaychain according to the frequency of current misbehaviors. Suppose that node Bj in *Blockchain_B* wants to exchange information with node Ai in *Blockchain_A*. The details of the phases are presented as follows.

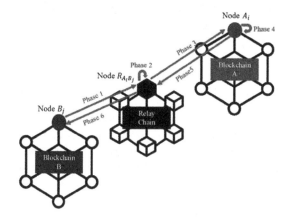

Fig. 1. The interoperation process for cross-chains transactions.

- Phase 1: Node Bj starts a request Rj to a bridge node RA_iB_j, which is responsible for transaction exchanging between nodes Ai and Bj, in the relay chain. The bridge node RA_iB_j will establish a secure channel to *Blockchain_A* and launch a cross-chain interoperation.
- Phase 2: Node RA_iB_j will judge the trustworthiness of *Blockchain_B* in terms of the reputation value through the three chain-level indicators, i.e. *average network hashrate, the delay time in block propagation* and *average spending time of each transaction*, as shown in Table 1. Meanwhile, node RA_iB_j will evaluate if the reputation of node Bj is satisfied through the four node-level indicators, i.e. *node connect status, hardware usage, average spending time of transaction* and *transaction consequence*, presented in Table 1. If one of these seven indicators does not pass a pre-defined threshold, node RB_j will be judged as a potentially misbehaved node. The incoming request Rj will be rejected and node RA_iB_j will send a message to node Bj as a termination commend. If all of these seven indicators are all passed, it will proceed to Phase 3.
- Phase 3: Node RA_iB_j then launches a request Rj' and sends Rj' to node Ai. At the same time, the trustworthiness of node Ai and *Blockchain_A* will be evaluated through the same steps in Phase 2. That is, the seven indicators presented in Table 1 will be adopted to examine whether node Ai and *Blockchain_A* is classified to misbehaved one or not.
- Phase 4: Similarly, based on the indicators, node Ai then evaluates if the reputation of node RA_iB_j is satisfied after obtaining the request Rj'. If it is not satisfied, node Ai will send a message to RA_iB_j to cancel the current transaction. Otherwise, node Ai will accept the request. Next, Ai will send a reply Pi to node RA_iB_j.
- Phase 5: Node RA_iB_j will then check whether node Ai has successfully completed the request after receiving Pi. In case of a normal transaction (which is successfully

completed), the reputation of node Ai will be adjusted and Pi will be sent back to node Bj through node RA_iB_j. Otherwise, the reputation of node Ai will be adjusted and the transaction will be terminated.

- Phase 6: Node Bj confirms Pi and the cross-chain transaction will be considered as a finished one. In case of a failed transaction, the reputation of Node RA_iB_j will be adjusted by node Bj. Afterwards, the information related to the failed transaction will be reported by node Bj.

3   Conclusion

In this study, we propose a reputation management scheme for communicating entities during cross-chain transactions. We summarize a list of indicators for reputation evaluation in which these indicators are against various Blockchain-relevant attacks. Then, our proposed scheme can utilize the evaluated reputation to detect and identify misbehaved node and chain.

Acknowledgement. This work was supported by the National Science and Technology Council, Taiwan under Grants NSTC 111-2221-E-259-006-MY3, NSTC 111-2218-E-011-012-MBK, NSTC 111-2926-I-259-501 and NSTC 110-2634-F-A49-004.

References

1. Nakamoto, S.: Bitcoin: a peer-to-peer electronic cash system (2008). https://bitcoin.org/bitcoin.pdf
2. Jin, H., Dai, X., Xiao, J.: Towards a novel architecture for enabling interoperability amongst multiple blockchains. In: The IEEE Conference on 38th International Conference on Distributed Computing Systems (ICDCS 2018), Vienna, Austria (2018)
3. Mirkin, M., Ji, Y., Pang, J., Klages-Mundt, A., Eyal, I., Juels, A.: BDoS: blockchain denial-of-service. In: The 2020 ACM SIGSAC Conference on Computer and Communications Security (ACM CCS'20), pp. 601–619 (2020)
4. Karame, G.O., Androulaki, E., Capkun, S.: Double-spending fast payments in bitcoin. In: The 2012 ACM Conference on Computer and Communications Security (ACM CCS'12), pp.906–917 (2012)
5. Sapirshtein, A., Sompolinsky, Y., Zohar, A.: Optimal selfish mining strategies in bitcoin. In: Grossklags, J., Preneel, B. (eds.) Financial Cryptography and Data Security. Lecture Notes in Computer Science, vol. 9603, pp. 515–532. Springer, Heidelberg (2017). https://doi.org/10.1007/978-3-662-54970-4_30

Mathematical Science of Quantum Safety and its Application Workshop (MathSci-Qsafe)

Revisiting Security of Symmetric-Key Encryption with Imperfect Randomness and Correlation Between Source and Keys

Bagus Santoso[✉]

The University of Electro-Communications, Tokyo, Japan
santoso.bagus@uec.ac.jp

Abstract. In the ideal environment, a secret key for a cryptosystem is generated with perfect randomness and is independent of other keys or sources. It is well-known that such an ideal condition gives the perfect security to many encryption schemes. However, in practice, it is not uncommon that due to limited resources, we can not always guarantee such ideal conditions. Thus, it is very important to know the amount of security we can guarantee under a non-ideal condition in practice.

In this paper, we are interested in investigating the security of symmetric encryption schemes under non-ideal conditions. Especially, we focus on a wide category of encryption schemes with the following property: *for any plaintext, there is no collision between ciphertexts generated from the encryption of the plaintext by different secret keys.* As the main contribution, we derive the sufficient and the necessary condition for guaranteeing the security of any such encryption scheme even in the non-ideal cases where: (1) the source (plaintext) and the secret key used in the encryption process are correlated, and (2) the secret key is not perfectly random.

1 Introduction

Ideally, a secret key for an encryption scheme is generated with perfect randomness and is independent of other keys or sources. It is a well-known fact given such an ideal condition, for many encryption schemes, including Shannon ciphers, we can prove the perfect security [12]. However, in the real-world practice, it is not uncommon that due to limitation in the implementation infrastructure or the amount of available resources, we can not guarantee that we can provide such ideal conditions.

The first issue is about the *randomness* of the secret key. As a practical example, when we target the implementation on lightweight devices, obtaining perfect randomness may require computing power more than the devices can provide. Therefore, as common practice, instead of generating true perfect random bits, we use pseudorandom generators which are lightweight enough to be implemented on the devices. Although a pseudorandom generator may generate a sequence of bits which is hard to distinguished from a sequence of true perfect random bits, in theory, it still can not guarantee the perfect security.

C. Su and K. Sakurai (Eds.): SciSec 2022 Workshops, CCIS 1680, pp. 137–149, 2022.
https://doi.org/10.1007/978-981-19-7769-5_11

Another issue is that the secret keys and the plaintexts may *correlate* to each other in practice. For instance, there are several practices which allow generation of random bits as paddings to the messages in order to keep the length of the plaintexts follow the format determined by the specification of the encryption scheme [1]. And the random bits for padding may be generated using the same random seed which is used for generating the secret key for the sake of efficiency in practice. This makes the secret keys and the plaintexts may correlate to each other and prevent us to guarantee the perfect security.

However, although we may not have a perfect security, it is still very important to know the amount of security we can guarantee when we have to deal with situations under such non-ideal conditions in practice.

Our Contributions

In this paper, we focus on a category of encryption schemes with the following property: *for any plaintext, there is no collision between ciphertexts generated from the encryption of the plaintext by different secret keys.* It turns out that this property is satisfied by many encryption schemes such as Shannon ciphers [12], e.g., one-time-pad encryption schemes.

As the main contribution, we derive the sufficient and the necessary condition for guaranteeing the security of any such encryption scheme even in the case where: (1) the source (plaintext) and the secret key used in the encryption process are correlated, and (2) the secret key is not perfectly random. To derive our results, we propose a new metric to represent the "amount of correlation" and we express the "amount of security loss" in the term of the amount of correlation between the plaintexts and ciphertexts. Thus, by converse, the "minimum amount of security" means the "maximum security loss" and the "maximum amount of security" means the "minimum security loss". In informal way, as our main theorems, we derive the followings:

(1) the minimum amount of security which can be guaranteed if the amount of correlation between the secret keys and the plaintexts and the amount of bias on the secret keys from the perfect randomness are limited to some extent, and

(2) the maximum amount of security which can be guaranteed under certain relation between the amount of bias on the secret keys from the perfect randomness and the amount of correlation between the secret keys and the plaintexts.

For simplicity and also as a limitation of current work, throughout this paper we only focus on *deterministic* encryption schemes. We consider the extension of this work into non-deterministic schemes as an open problem for further direction of future research.

Related Works

The security of cryptographic tasks using of different type of sources with imperfect randomness have been previously investigated in wide range by a series of works by Dodis et al. [3–5,8]. Also, there have been a series of works on generating or extracting good random bits from sources with imperfect randomness [2,6,7,11]. However these works only focus on the degree of randomness of the source used to generate the secret keys, and they do not take into account the correlation between plaintexts and the secret keys. Iwamoto et al. show comparison of different metrics for secrecy in [9]. However, it only considers about secrecy under ideal environment and does not cover the secrecy under non-ideal environment.

Roadmap. This paper is organized as follows. First, in Sect. 2 we show the basic notation and the formal definition of the symmetric-key encryption schemes. In Sect. 3 we introduce the formal definition of the class of symmetric-key encryption schemes we target in this paper. Then, in Sect. 4 we show the new metrics we propose to represent the amounts of correlation and bias. We also show the properties of the new proposed metrics. Next, in Sect. 5 we state the main theorems which are the main results of our research. And in Sect. 6 we show the proofs of our main theorems. We conclude this paper with a brief summary in Sect. 7.

2   Preliminaries

Unless noted otherwise, we assume that any random variable is randomly taken over its domain according to the uniform distribution. For any function $f : \mathcal{X} \times \mathcal{Y} \to \mathcal{Z}$ where $\mathcal{X}$, $\mathcal{Y}$, $\mathcal{Z}$ are arbitrary sets, $f(\mathcal{X}, \mathcal{Y})$ denotes the set $\{f(x', y')|x' \in \mathcal{X}, y' \in \mathcal{Y}\} \subseteq \mathcal{Z}$. Below, we show the definition of a symmetric-key encryption schemes

Definition 1 (Symmetric-key Encryption Scheme). *A symmetric-key encryption scheme $\mathcal{E} := (\mathsf{KG}, \mathsf{Enc}, \mathsf{Dec})$ is defined as a triplet of three algorithms: the key generation algorithm KG, the encryption algorithm Enc, the decryption algorithm Dec, and is associated with the system parameter $\lambda \in \mathbb{N}$ and the sets $\mathcal{K}, \mathcal{M}, \mathcal{C}$ which denote the set of secret keys, the set of plaintexts, and the set of ciphertexts respectively. The sizes of $\mathcal{K}$, $\mathcal{M}$, $\mathcal{C}$ are determined by λ. The algorithms KG, Enc, Dec are defined as follows.*

$\mathsf{KG}(\lambda) \to K$: *on input λ, KG generates the secret key $K \in \mathcal{K}$.*
$\mathsf{Enc}(K, M) \to C$: *on input the secret key $K \in \mathcal{K}$ and a plaintext $M \in \mathcal{M}$, Enc generates the ciphertext $C \in \mathcal{C}$.*
$\mathsf{Dec}(K, C) \to \widehat{M}$: *on input the secret key $K \in \mathcal{K}$ and a ciphertext $C \in \mathcal{C}$, Dec generates $\widehat{M} \in \mathcal{M}$.*

Definition 2 (Correctly Decryptable). *A symmetric-key encryption scheme $\mathcal{E} := (\mathsf{KG}, \mathsf{Enc}, \mathsf{Dec})$ associated with $\lambda \in \mathbb{N}$ and the sets $\mathcal{K}, \mathcal{M}, \mathcal{C}$ is said to be correctly decryptable if the following holds for any $m \in \mathcal{M}$ and $k \in \mathcal{K}$.*

$$\mathsf{Dec}(k, \mathsf{Enc}(k, m)) = m. \tag{1}$$

Unless under special circumstances, it is natural for a symmetric-key encryption scheme to be correctly decryptable. It is easy to see that the below lemma and corollary hold.

Lemma 1. *Let the symmetric-key encryption scheme $\mathcal{E} :=$ (KG, Enc, Dec) associated with $\lambda \in \mathbb{N}$ and the sets $\mathcal{K}, \mathcal{M}, \mathcal{C}$ be correctly decryptable. Thus, for any $m, m' \in \mathcal{M}$ such that $m \neq m'$, for any $k \in \mathcal{K}$, the following holds.*

$$\mathsf{Enc}(k, m)) \neq \mathsf{Enc}(k, m'). \tag{2}$$

Corollary 1. *Let the symmetric-key encryption scheme $\mathcal{E} :=$ (KG, Enc, Dec) associated with $\lambda \in \mathbb{N}$ and the sets $\mathcal{K}, \mathcal{M}, \mathcal{C}$ be correctly decryptable. For any $k \in \mathcal{K}$, we can define an injective function $\varphi_k : \mathcal{M} \to \mathcal{C}$ as follows.*

$$\varphi_k(m) := \mathsf{Enc}(k, m), \tag{3}$$

where $m \in \mathcal{M}$.

Remark 1. From above corollary, it is obvious that correctly decryptable symmetric-key encryption scheme requires $|\mathcal{C}| \geq |\mathcal{M}|$.

Below is the definition of perfect security for a symmetric-key encryption scheme. This definition is slightly modified from the original definition in [12] to accommodate a more general situation where $|\mathcal{C}| \neq |\mathcal{M}|$.

Definition 3 (Perfect Security). *A symmetric-key encryption scheme $\mathcal{E} :=$ (KG, Enc, Dec) associated with $\lambda \in \mathbb{N}$ and the sets $\mathcal{K}, \mathcal{M}, \mathcal{C}$ is said to satisfy perfect security if the following holds for any $m \in \mathcal{M}$ and any $c \in \mathsf{Enc}(\mathcal{K}, \mathcal{M})$.*

$$\Pr[M = m | C = c] = \Pr[M = m]. \tag{4}$$

3   Collision Free Symmetric-Key Encryption Schemes

Here we define a new class of symmetric-key encryption schemes where any scheme in the new class has a special property that we call as *collision free*. Informally, we say that a symmetric-key encryption scheme is collision free if all ciphertexts which are generated from *encrypting a single fixed plaintext using different keys* will will never collide to each other. One can see this property as a "dual" of the *correctly decryptable* property defined in the previous section: all ciphertexts which are generated from *encrypting different plaintexts using a single fixed secret key* will never collide to each other.

Definition 4 (Collision Free). *A symmetric-key encryption scheme $\mathcal{E} :=$ (KG, Enc, Dec) associated with $\lambda \in \mathbb{N}$ and the sets $\mathcal{K}, \mathcal{M}, \mathcal{C}$ is said to be collision-free if for any $M \in \mathcal{M}$, for any $K, K' \in \mathcal{K}$ such that $K \neq K'$, the following holds:*

$$\mathsf{Enc}(K, M) \neq \mathsf{Enc}(K', M).$$

One can easily see that the widely known the one-time-pad encryption scheme and its variants or the Shannon ciphers [12] are collision-free.

It is easy to see that the following lemma holds.[1]

Lemma 2. *Let the symmetric-key encryption scheme $\mathcal{E} := (\mathsf{KG}, \mathsf{Enc}, \mathsf{Dec})$ associated with $\lambda \in \mathbb{N}$ and the sets $\mathcal{K}, \mathcal{M}, \mathcal{C}$ be correctly decryptable and collision-free. Then, for any $c \in \mathsf{Enc}(\mathcal{K}, \mathcal{M})$, we can define an injective function $\phi_c : \mathcal{M} \to \mathcal{K}$ such that $\mathsf{Enc}(\phi_c(m'), m') = c$ holds for any $m' \in \mathcal{M}$.*

Remark 2. From Lemma 2, it is clear that one of necessary conditions for collision free symmetric-key encryption scheme is that $|\mathcal{K}| \geq |\mathcal{M}|$ holds.

One can also easily derive the following lemma on the perfect security of a symmetric-key encryption scheme which are both correctly decryptable and collision free.

Lemma 3. *Let the symmetric-key encryption scheme $\mathcal{E} := (\mathsf{KG}, \mathsf{Enc}, \mathsf{Dec})$ associated with $\lambda \in \mathbb{N}$ and the sets $\mathcal{K}, \mathcal{M}, \mathcal{C}$ be correctly decryptable and collision-free. Then, $\mathcal{E}$ achieves perfect security if only if:*

- *$|\mathcal{K}| = |\mathcal{M}| = |\mathcal{C}|$,*
- *K is generated randomly from the uniform distribution over $\mathcal{K}$,*
- *K and M are independent.*

4   New Metrics for Correlation and Randomness Bias

In this paper, in order to represent the amount of security and the amount of bias from perfect randomness, we propose new metrics. All our results are based on these metrics.

Definition 5 (Correlation Width). *For any two random variables X and Y taken over the sets $\mathcal{X}$ and $\mathcal{Y}$ respectively, let us defined the followings.*

$$\Delta_{\max}(X|Y) := \max_{x \in \mathcal{X}, y \in \mathcal{Y}} \left\{ \Pr_{X \leftarrow \mathcal{X}|y}[X = x|Y = y] - \Pr_{X \leftarrow \mathcal{X}}[X = x] \right\}, \quad (5)$$

$$\Delta_{\min}(X|Y) := - \min_{x \in \mathcal{X}, y \in \mathcal{Y}} \left\{ \Pr_{X \leftarrow \mathcal{X}|y}[X = x|Y = y] - \Pr_{X \leftarrow \mathcal{X}}[X = x] \right\}, \quad (6)$$

where $\mathcal{X}|y$ denote the subset of $\mathcal{X}$ such that all of its elements are available to select given $Y = y$. We define the correlation width of X and Y as follows.

$$\Delta_{\mathrm{corr}}(X|Y) := \Delta_{\max}(X|Y) + \Delta_{\min}(X|Y). \quad (7)$$

---

[1] One can easily derive the proof by following the detailed explanation on Shannon cipher in Sect. 2.4 of [10].

Definition 6. *Let X and Y be random variables taken over the sets $\mathcal{X}$ and $\mathcal{Y}$ respectively. Let us define the followings.*

$$P_{\max}(X|Y) := \max_{x \in \mathcal{X}, y \in \mathcal{Y}} \left\{ \Pr_{X \leftarrow \mathcal{X}|y}[X = x|Y = y] \right\}, \tag{8}$$

$$P_{\min}(X|Y) := - \min_{x \in \mathcal{X}, y \in \mathcal{Y}} \left\{ \Pr_{X \leftarrow \mathcal{X}|y}[X = x|Y = y] \right\}, \tag{9}$$

where $\mathcal{X}|y$ denote the subset of $\mathcal{X}$ such that all of its elements are available to select given $Y = y$.

Definition 7 (Randomness Bias Width). *For any random variable X taken over the set $\mathcal{X}$, we define the followings.*

$$\Delta_{\max}(X) := \max_{x \in \mathcal{X}} \left\{ \Pr_{X \leftarrow \mathcal{X}}[X = x] - \frac{1}{|\mathcal{X}|} \right\}, \tag{10}$$

$$\Delta_{\min}(X) := - \min_{x \in \mathcal{X}} \left\{ \Pr_{X \leftarrow \mathcal{X}}[X = x] - \frac{1}{|\mathcal{X}|} \right\}. \tag{11}$$

We define the randomness bias width of X as follows.

$$\Delta_{\mathrm{rnd}}(X) := \Delta_{\max}(X) + \Delta_{\min}(Y). \tag{12}$$

Definition 8. *Let X be a random variable taken over the set $\mathcal{X}$. Let us define the followings.*

$$P_{\max}(X) := \max_{x \in \mathcal{X}} \{ \Pr_{X \leftarrow \mathcal{X}}[X = x] \}, \tag{13}$$

$$P_{\min}(X) := \min_{x \in \mathcal{X}} \{ \Pr_{X \leftarrow \mathcal{X}}[X = x] \}. \tag{14}$$

4.1   Properties of Proposed Metrics

Here we list several properties which hold based on the definitions of the metrics above in the form of lemmas. Since it is easy to see that the lemmas hold, here we show them without proof.

Lemma 4. *For any two random variables X and Y taken over the sets $\mathcal{X}$ and $\mathcal{Y}$ respectively, $\Delta_{\mathrm{corr}}(X, Y) = 0$ if and only if X and Y are independent.*

Lemma 5. *Let X be a random variable taken over the set $\mathcal{X}$. Then, the followings hold.*

$$\Delta_{\min}(X) \geq 0. \tag{15}$$

Lemma 6. *Let X and Y be random variables taken over the set $\mathcal{X}$ and $\mathcal{Y}$ respectively. Then, the followings hold.*

$$\Delta_{\min}(X|Y) \geq 0. \tag{16}$$

Lemma 7. *Let X be a random variable taken over the set $\mathcal{X}$. Then, the followings hold.*

$$P_{\min}(X) = \frac{1}{|\mathcal{X}|} - \Delta_{\min}(X), \tag{17}$$

$$P_{\max}(X) = \frac{1}{|\mathcal{X}|} + \Delta_{\max}(X). \tag{18}$$

Lemma 8. *Let X and Y be random variables taken over the set $\mathcal{X}$ and $\mathcal{Y}$ respectively. Then, the followings hold.*

$$P_{\min}(X|Y) \geq P_{\min}(X) - \Delta_{\min}(X|Y), \tag{19}$$
$$P_{\max}(X|Y) \leq P_{\max}(X) + \Delta_{\max}(X|Y). \tag{20}$$

Lemma 9. *Let X be a random variable taken over the set $\mathcal{X}$. Then, for any $x \in \mathcal{X}$, the following holds.*

$$\frac{\Delta_{\mathrm{rnd}}(X)}{2} \leq \left| \Pr[X = x] - \frac{1}{|\mathcal{X}|} \right| \leq \Delta_{\mathrm{rnd}}(X). \tag{21}$$

Lemma 10. *Let X and Y be random variables taken over the set $\mathcal{X}$ and $\mathcal{Y}$ respectively. Then, for any $x \in \mathcal{X}$ and $y \in \mathcal{Y}$, the following holds.*

$$\frac{\Delta_{\mathrm{corr}}(X|Y)}{2} \leq \left| \Pr_{X \leftarrow \mathcal{X}|y}[X = x|Y = y] - \Pr_{X \leftarrow \mathcal{X}}[X = x] \right| \leq \Delta_{\mathrm{corr}}(X|Y), \tag{22}$$

where $\mathcal{X}|y$ denote the subset of $\mathcal{X}$ such that all of its elements are available to select given $Y = y$.

Remark 3. From here onwards, unless the domain of the random variables is not clear and hard to deduce, we abuse the notation of probability by omitting the writing of the domains of the random variables below the probability symbol $(\Pr[\cdot])$. Remind that unless noted otherwise, we always assume to use a uniform random distribution.

5   Main Theorems

In this section we state our main results.

Theorem 1 (Upper Bound of Security Loss). *Let the symmetric-key encryption scheme $\mathcal{E} := (\mathsf{KG}, \mathsf{Enc}, \mathsf{Dec})$ associated with $\lambda \in \mathbb{N}$ and the sets $\mathcal{K}, \mathcal{M}, \mathcal{C}$ be correctly decryptable and collision free. Let $K \in \mathcal{K}$, $M \in \mathcal{M}$, and $C \in \mathcal{C}$ be the random variables denoting the secret key, the plaintext, and the ciphertext respectively. Assume as follows.*

$$P_{\min}(K) > \Delta_{\min}(K|M). \tag{23}$$

Then, the following holds.

$$\Delta_{\mathrm{corr}}(M|C) \leq 2P_{\max}(M) \times \frac{\Delta_{\mathrm{rnd}}(K) + \Delta_{\mathrm{corr}}(K|M)}{P_{\min}(K) - \Delta_{\min}(K|M)}. \tag{24}$$

Remark 4. One can regard $\Delta_{\mathrm{corr}}(M|C)$ in Eq. (24) as the amount of security loss. Since the larger $\Delta_{\mathrm{corr}}(M|C)$, the larger the amount of correlation between ciphertexts and plaintexts is, and thus the larger the probability that an eavesdropper obtains some additional information on the plaintexts from the ciphertexts is.

Theorem 2 (Lower Bound of Security Loss). *Let the symmetric-key encryption scheme* $\mathcal{E} := (\mathsf{KG}, \mathsf{Enc}, \mathsf{Dec})$ *associated with* $\lambda \in \mathbb{N}$ *and the sets* $\mathcal{K}, \mathcal{M}, \mathcal{C}$ *be correctly decryptable and collision free. Let* $K \in \mathcal{K}$, $M \in \mathcal{M}$, *and* $C \in \mathcal{C}$ *be the random variables denoting the secret key, the plaintext, and the ciphertext respectively. If* $|\mathcal{K}| = |\mathcal{M}|$, *the following holds.*

$$\Delta_{\mathrm{corr}}(M|C) \geq P_{\min}(M) \times \left(\frac{\Delta_{\mathrm{rnd}}(K)}{2} - \Delta_{\mathrm{corr}}(K|M) \right). \tag{25}$$

6   Proofs of Main Theorem

In this section, we show the proofs of the main theorems stated above in Sect. 5.

6.1   Proof of Theorem 1

First, let us consider a fixed plaintext $m \in \mathcal{M}$ and a fixed ciphertext $c \in \mathsf{Enc}(\mathcal{K}, m)$. By applying Bayes theorem, we have the following equation.

$$\Pr[M = m | C = c] = \frac{\Pr[C = c | M = m] \Pr[M = m]}{\Pr[C = c]}. \tag{26}$$

From Lemma 2, we can define an injective function $\phi_c : \mathcal{M} \to \mathcal{K}$ such that $\mathsf{Enc}(\phi_c(m'), m') = c$ holds for any $m' \in \mathcal{M}$. Thus, we can rewrite Eq. (26) as follows.

$$\Pr[M = m | C = c] = \frac{\Pr[K = \phi_c(m) | M = m] \Pr[M = m]}{\sum_{m' \in \mathcal{M}} \Pr[K = \phi_c(m') | M = m'] \Pr[M = m']} \tag{27}$$

Then we can rewrite Eq. (27) as follows.

$$\Pr[K = \phi_c(m) | M = m] \Pr[M = m]$$
$$= \Pr[M = m | C = c] \times \sum_{m' \in \mathcal{M}} \Pr[K = \phi_c(m') | M = m'] \Pr[M = m'] \tag{28}$$

By applying Eq. (19) and Eq. (20) from Lemma 8 into Eq. (28), it is easy to see that we can obtain the following two inequations.

$$(P_{\min}(K) - \Delta_{\min}(K|M)) \Pr[M = m]$$
$$\leq \Pr[M = m|C = c] (P_{\max}(K) + \Delta_{\max}(K|M)), \quad (29)$$
$$(P_{\max}(K) + \Delta_{\max}(K|M)) \Pr[M = m]$$
$$\geq \Pr[M = m|C = c] (P_{\min}(K) - \Delta_{\min}(K|M)). \quad (30)$$

By applying the assumption $P_{\min}(K) > \Delta_{\min}(K|M)$ on Eq. (30) and by arranging both sides of Eq. (29) and Eq. (30), we obtain as follows.

$$\frac{P_{\min}(K) - \Delta_{\min}(K|M)}{P_{\max}(K) + \Delta_{\max}(K|M)} \Pr[M = m] \leq \Pr[M = m|C = c], \quad (31)$$

$$\frac{P_{\max}(K) + \Delta_{\max}(K|M)}{P_{\min}(K) - \Delta_{\min}(K|M)} \Pr[M = m] \geq \Pr[M = m|C = c]. \quad (32)$$

By subtracting both sides of above inequations by $\Pr[M = m]$, we obtain as follows.

$$\left(\frac{P_{\min}(K) - \Delta_{\min}(K|M)}{P_{\max}(K) + \Delta_{\max}(K|M)} - 1 \right) \Pr[M = m]$$
$$\leq \Pr[M = m|C = c] - \Pr[M = m], \quad (33)$$

$$\left(\frac{P_{\max}(K) + \Delta_{\max}(K|M)}{P_{\min}(K) - \Delta_{\min}(K|M)} - 1 \right) \Pr[M = m]$$
$$\geq \Pr[M = m|C = c] - \Pr[M = m]. \quad (34)$$

By computing and simplifying the terms inside the parentheses, and also by applying Lemma 7, we obtain as follows.

$$-\frac{\Delta_{\mathrm{rnd}}(K) + \Delta_{\mathrm{corr}}(K|M)}{P_{\max}(K) + \Delta_{\max}(K|M)} \Pr[M = m]$$
$$\leq \Pr[M = m|C = c] - \Pr[M = m], \quad (35)$$

$$\frac{\Delta_{\mathrm{rnd}}(K) + \Delta_{\mathrm{corr}}(K|M)}{P_{\min}(K) - \Delta_{\min}(K|M)} \Pr[M = m]$$
$$\geq \Pr[M = m|C = c] - \Pr[M = m]. \quad (36)$$

Now, notice that by definition, the followings hold.

$$P_{\max}(K) + \Delta_{\max}(K|M) \geq P_{\min}(K) - \Delta_{\min}(K|M). \quad (37)$$

Notice that Eq. (35) and Eq. (36) hold for any $m \in \mathcal{M}$ and $c \in \mathsf{Enc}(\mathcal{K}, m)$. Applying Eq. (37), we can set the followings.

$$\Delta_{\min}(M|C) \leq P_{\max}(M) \frac{\Delta_{\mathrm{rnd}}(K) + \Delta_{\mathrm{corr}}(K|M)}{P_{\min}(K) - \Delta_{\min}(K|M)},$$

$$\Delta_{\max}(M|C) = P_{\max}(M) \frac{\Delta_{\mathrm{rnd}}(K) + \Delta_{\mathrm{corr}}(K|M)}{P_{\min}(K) - \Delta_{\min}(K|M)}. \quad (38)$$

and by applying Eq. (7), we can easily obtain the Eq. (24). This ends the proof of Theorem 1. □

6.2   Proof of Theorem 2

First, let us consider a fixed plaintext $m \in \mathcal{M}$ and a fixed ciphertext $c \in$ $\mathsf{Enc}(\mathcal{K}, m)$.

Similar to the proof of Theorem 1, from Lemma 2, we can define an injective function $\phi_c : \mathcal{M} \to \mathcal{K}$ such that $\mathsf{Enc}(\phi_c(m'), m') = c$ holds for any $m' \in \mathcal{M}$. Thus, we can rewrite Eq. (26) as follows.

$$\Pr[M = m | C = c] \Pr[C = c] = \Pr[K = \phi_c(m) | M = m] \Pr[M = m]. \qquad (39)$$

Notice that by definition, the followings hold.

$$-\Delta_{\min}(M|C) \le \Pr[M = m | C = c] - \Pr[M = m] \le \Delta_{\max}(M|C), \qquad (40)$$
$$-\Delta_{\min}(K|M) \le \Pr[K = \phi_c(m) | M = m] - \Pr[K = \phi_c(m)] \le \Delta_{\max}(K|M), \qquad (41)$$

Applying Eq. (40) and Eq. (41) into Eq. (39), we obtain the followings.

$$(\Pr[M = m] - \Delta_{\min}(M|C)) \Pr[C = c]$$
$$\le (\Pr[K = \phi_c(m)] + \Delta_{\max}(K|M)) \Pr[M = m], \qquad (42)$$
$$(\Pr[M = m] + \Delta_{\max}(M|C)) \Pr[C = c]$$
$$\ge (\Pr[K = \phi_c(m)] - \Delta_{\min}(K|M)) \Pr[M = m]. \qquad (43)$$

By rearranging the terms in inequations above, we obtain as follows.

$$-\Delta_{\min}(M|C) \Pr[C = c]$$
$$\le \Pr[M = m] (\Pr[K = \phi_c(m)] + \Delta_{\max}(K|M) - \Pr[C = c]), \qquad (44)$$
$$\Delta_{\max}(M|C) \Pr[C = c]$$
$$\ge \Pr[M = m] (\Pr[K = \phi_c(m)] - \Delta_{\min}(K|M) - \Pr[C = c]). \qquad (45)$$

Furthermore, above inequations imply the followings.

$$-\Delta_{\min}(M|C) \Pr[C = c]$$
$$\le P_{\max}(M) (\Pr[K = \phi_c(m)] + \Delta_{\max}(K|M) - \Pr[C = c]) \qquad (46)$$
$$\Delta_{\max}(M|C) \Pr[C = c]$$
$$\ge P_{\min}(M) (\Pr[K = \phi_c(m)] - \Delta_{\min}(K|M) - \Pr[C = c]) \qquad (47)$$

By arranging the terms in inequations above, we obtain as follows.

$$-\left(\frac{\Delta_{\min}(M|C)}{P_{\max}(M)}\Pr[C=c]+\Delta_{\max}(K|M)\right)+\Pr[C=c]\le\Pr[K=\phi_c(m)],\tag{48}$$

$$\left(\frac{\Delta_{\max}(M|C)}{P_{\min}(M)}\Pr[C=c]+\Delta_{\min}(K|M)\right)+\Pr[C=c]\ge\Pr[K=\phi_c(m)].\tag{49}$$

Since $P_{\min}(M)\le P_{\max}(M)$ and $\Pr[C=c]\le 1$, above inequations imply the followings.

$$-\left(\frac{\Delta_{\min}(M|C)}{P_{\min}(M)}+\Delta_{\max}(K|M)\right)+\Pr[C=c]\le\Pr[K=\phi_c(m)],$$
$$\left(\frac{\Delta_{\max}(M|C)}{P_{\min}(M)}+\Delta_{\min}(K|M)\right)+\Pr[C=c]\ge\Pr[K=\phi_c(m)].\tag{50}$$

Note that Eq. (50) applies to any $m\in\mathcal{M}$. Also remind that due to the injective property of ϕ_c, $\sum_{m'\in\mathcal{M}}\Pr[K=\phi_c(m')]=1$ holds. Based on these, summing up the inequations in Eq. (50) over all $m\in\mathcal{M}$, using the assumption that $|\mathcal{K}|=|\mathcal{M}|$, we obtain as follows.

$$-\left(\frac{\Delta_{\min}(M|C)}{P_{\min}(M)}+\Delta_{\max}(K|M)\right)+\Pr[C=c]\le\frac{1}{|\mathcal{K}|},$$
$$\left(\frac{\Delta_{\max}(M|C)}{P_{\min}(M)}+\Delta_{\min}(K|M)\right)+\Pr[C=c]\ge\frac{1}{|\mathcal{K}|}.\tag{51}$$

Then, combining Eq. (50) and Eq. (51), the following holds for any $m\in\mathcal{M}$.

$$\Pr[K=\phi_c(m)]-\frac{1}{|\mathcal{K}|}\ge-\frac{\Delta_{\mathrm{corr}}(M|C)}{P_{\min}(M)}-\Delta_{\mathrm{corr}}(K|M),$$
$$\Pr[K=\phi_c(m)]-\frac{1}{|\mathcal{K}|}\le\frac{\Delta_{\mathrm{corr}}(M|C)}{P_{\min}(M)}+\Delta_{\mathrm{corr}}(K|M).\tag{52}$$

By definition of Δ_{corr}, we can write above inequations as follows.

$$\frac{\Delta_{\mathrm{rnd}}(K)}{2}\le\frac{\Delta_{\mathrm{corr}}(M|C)}{P_{\min}(M)}+\Delta_{\mathrm{corr}}(K|M).\tag{53}$$

This ends the proof of Theorem 2.   □

7   Conclusion

In this paper, we have formulated the upper bound and the lower bound of the security loss for encryption schemes which are both correctly decryptable and collision free when they are implemented in a non-ideal environment where: (1) secret keys are correlated with the plaintexts up to certain amount, and (2) the secret keys are not perfectly random up to certain degree. We have concretely showed the conditions for the encryption schemes to have a proper upper bound and the lower bound. As a further research direction, we plan to apply the formulation into the non-deterministic encryption schemes and public key encryption schemes.

Acknowledgement. This work is supported by JSPS KAKENHI Kiban JP18H01438 and JPSPS KAKENHI JP18K11292.

References

1. ANSI X9.23 and IBM 4700: z/OS cryptographic services icsf application programmer's guide SA22-7522-16. Technical report, IBM Corporation (2014). https://www.ibm.com/docs/en/zos/2.1.0?topic=rules-ansi-x923-4700
2. Barak, B., et al.: Leftover hash lemma, revisited. In: Rogaway, P. (ed.) CRYPTO 2011. LNCS, vol. 6841, pp. 1–20. Springer, Heidelberg (2011). https://doi.org/10.1007/978-3-642-22792-9_1
3. Dodis, Y.: New imperfect random source with applications to coin-flipping. In: Orejas, F., Spirakis, P.G., van Leeuwen, J. (eds.) ICALP 2001. LNCS, vol. 2076, pp. 297–309. Springer, Heidelberg (2001). https://doi.org/10.1007/3-540-48224-5_25
4. Dodis, Y., López-Alt, A., Mironov, I., Vadhan, S.: Differential privacy with imperfect randomness. In: Safavi-Naini, R., Canetti, R. (eds.) CRYPTO 2012. LNCS, vol. 7417, pp. 497–516. Springer, Heidelberg (2012). https://doi.org/10.1007/978-3-642-32009-5_29
5. Dodis, Y., Ong, S.J., Prabhakaran, M., Sahai, A.: On the (Im)possibility of cryptography with imperfect randomness. In: FOCS 2004, pp. 196–205. IEEE Computer Society (2004)
6. Dodis, Y., Reyzin, L., Smith, A.: Fuzzy extractors: how to generate strong keys from biometrics and other noisy data. In: Cachin, C., Camenisch, J.L. (eds.) EUROCRYPT 2004. LNCS, vol. 3027, pp. 523–540. Springer, Heidelberg (2004). https://doi.org/10.1007/978-3-540-24676-3_31
7. Dodis, Y., Vaikuntanathan, V., Wichs, D.: Extracting randomness from extractor-dependent sources. In: Canteaut, A., Ishai, Y. (eds.) EUROCRYPT 2020. LNCS, vol. 12105, pp. 313–342. Springer, Cham (2020). https://doi.org/10.1007/978-3-030-45721-1_12
8. Dodis, Y., Yao, Y.: Privacy with imperfect randomness. In: Gennaro, R., Robshaw, M. (eds.) CRYPTO 2015. LNCS, vol. 9216, pp. 463–482. Springer, Heidelberg (2015). https://doi.org/10.1007/978-3-662-48000-7_23
9. Iwamoto, M., Ohta, K., Shikata, J.: Security formalizations and their relationships for encryption and key agreement in information-theoretic cryptography. IEEE Trans. Inf. Theory **64**(1), 654–685 (2018)
10. Katz, J., Lindell, Y.: Introduction to Modern Cryptography, vol. 6, 2nd edn. CRC Press, Boca Raton (2014)

11. Matsuda, T., Takahashi, K., Murakami, T., Hanaoka, G.: Improved security evaluation techniques for imperfect randomness from arbitrary distributions. In: Lin, D., Sako, K. (eds.) PKC 2019. LNCS, vol. 11442, pp. 549–580. Springer, Cham (2019). https://doi.org/10.1007/978-3-030-17253-4_19
12. Shannon, C.E.: Communication theory of secrecy systems. Bell Syst. Tech. J. **28**(4), 656–715 (1949)

A Secure Image-Video Retrieval Scheme with Attribute-Based Encryption and Multi-feature Fusion in Smart Grid

Qian Dang[1(✉)], Bo Zhao[2], Biying Sun[1], Yu Qiu[1], and Chunhui Du[1]

[1] State Grid Gansu Information & Telecommunications Company,
Lanzhou 730050, China
54295925@qq.com
[2] State Grid Gansu Electric Power Company, Lanzhou 730000, China

Abstract. With the continuous development of smart grid, massive sensitive videos of power grid are stored in semi-trusted cloud servers, which leads to various security threats. And the existing secure video retrieval solutions are difficult to achieve both high retrieval rate and accuracy. We propose a novel secure video retrieval scheme in smart grid based on image content, by utilizing symmetric searchable encryption technology with attribute-based encryption and multi-feature fusion. Fine-grained access control is achieved for sensitive video data to eliminate illegal authorized access. This scheme converts the video into a keyframe set and transforms the difficult video secure retrieval problem to the more mature image secure retrieval region, which can effectively reduce the overhead of video secure retrieval and improve the retrieval accuracy. Security analysis demonstrates that the proposed scheme can preserve the privacy of data, resist known ciphertext attacks, known background attacks and collusion attacks. The experimental results indicate that the proposed scheme has the best balance between retrieval efficiency and retrieval accuracy among the three comparison schemes. The proposed scheme is feasible in the smart grid application scenario.

Keywords: Smart grid · Ciphertext-policy attribute-based encryption · Image content-based video retrieval · Locality-sensitive hash · Multi-feature fusion

1 Introduction

With the continuous and in-depth application of cloud computing technology, artificial intelligence and big data technology in the field of electric power, the smart grid generates a large amount of sensitive multimedia data every day [1], including monitoring videos of substations and construction sites, and personal privacy videos of grid users. In the remote monitoring of lower-level power plants and substations , the transmitted video data by the power grid monitoring center is usually in plaintext and can be easily stolen, altered or even replaced, which

C. Su and K. Sakurai (Eds.): SciSec 2022 Workshops, CCIS 1680, pp. 150–166, 2022.
https://doi.org/10.1007/978-981-19-7769-5_12

puts the security of the power grid at risk. In addition, with the explosive growth of data and the rapid development of information technology, most of the smart grid data are stored on cloud servers, but most of cloud storage servers are "honest but curious", i.e., cloud servers can correctly execute objective protocols and functions, but would actively detect the sensitive data stored on them. Video data often contains personal privacy information of power grid users. Once it is leaked, it will bring incalculable losses to power grid and users. Therefore, in order to protect the security and data privacy of smart grid, sensitive videos need to be encrypted before uploaded to the cloud [2]. The encrypted video data no longer has the property of being retrievable in plaintext, and surveillance video of the power grid is usually long, so how to retrieve video content with high similarity among the encrypted video data while ensuring efficiency and accuracy of retrieval becomes a pressing challenge.

Secure image retrieval enables image-based querying of image databases while preserving privacy. And it is easier to handle than secure video retrieval. The video is composed of continuous images. A feasible approach to convert secure video retrieval into secure image retrieval is to extract key frame image sets for videos and search directly on the image sets. In the information retrieval, features extraction is an essential aspects. Traditional methods generally extract and mix various features such as color histogram [3], texture [4], and shape [5], which are simple and easy to implement, but cannot be effectively used in similarity matching for all types of images and have low accuracy. In recent years, many researchers believe that deep learning methods such as CNN [6] can be used to extract more reliable and effective image features. Liu [7] propose an effective image retrieval method by combining the high-level features of CNN and the low-level features of point spread block truncation coding. Chen [8] used Faster R-CNN model [9] to extract feature vectors and keyword sets of image sets with a coarse-then-fine classification retrieval model, but the computational consumption is large. Besides, the existing secure retrieval schemes are not fully applicable to video retrieval in smart grid. The access to sensitive information in smart grid is hierarchical, and the ciphertext policy attribute-based encryption mechanism [10] allows data owners to formulate access policies, which can be combined with searchable encryption mechanism to achieve fine-grained access control on ciphertext retrieval results.

Related Work. We present research works related to secure video retrieval, including secure retrieval in smart grids, content-based secure image retrieval and video retrieval.

Secure retrieval in smart grid. Li [11] constructed a searchable symmetric encryption scheme for smart grid, which achieved easy data updating by allowing a little information leakage. Eltayieb [12] proposed an attribute-based online/offline searchable encryption scheme, which divided the encryption algorithm and trapdoor algorithm into two phases, and achieves better results in cloud smart grid results. However, secure retrieval schemes in smart grid are mainly for structured data.

Content-based secure image retrieval and video retrieval. The common techniques used to construct secure image retrieval schemes are order-preserving encryption [23] and homomorphic encryption [24]. However, the security of the former is difficult to guarantee, and the latter has high computational complexity. Secure image content-based retrieval schemes [17–22] mainly used computer vision to describe the image content. Zhu [25] proposed a ciphertext image retrieval scheme based on secure similarity operation and proved the security and effectiveness of the scheme. Yuan [21] classified image sets through K-means algorithm and constructed a tree-based image index with optimized retrieval speed, but the retrieval results were not accurate enough. Li [26] constructed an encrypted image retrieval scheme based on secure nearest neighbor, locally sensitive hash and proxy re-encryption techniques in an edge computing environment. Xia [27] proposed a retrieval scheme based on encrypted images without leaking sensitive information to cloud servers. Shen [29] supported simultaneously protecting the privacy of image owners, encrypting image features by using secure multi-party computation technique. Xia [30] constructed pre-filter tables by locality-sensitive hashing to increase content-based image retrieval efficiency and proposed a watermark-based protocol to deter illegal distributions. Zhang [13] combined convolutional neural networks and visual word-wrapping to design a model for searching large-scale videos. Song [14] proposed a general framework for scalable image and video retrieval by using a quantization-based hashing approach. Josef [15] proposed a method to automatically obtain object representations from video footage. Andre [16] proposed an asymmetric comparison technique for fisher vectors of video clips and used different aggregation techniques to retrieve relevant scenes.

Our Contribution. To address the security threats of sensitive videos and the shortcomings of existing secure video retrieval schemes, we propose a secure image-video retrieval scheme(SIVR) in smart grid. Our contributions are summarized as follows.

- We convert difficult secure video retrieval problems into easier and more sophisticated secure image retrieval problems, and propose a secure image-video retrieval scheme with attribute-based encryption and multi-feature fusion in smart grid.
- We combine deep image features with traditional image features to enhance the representation of the final feature vector.The combination of ciphertext policy attribute base encryption mechanism and searchable encryption achieves fine-grained access control on ciphertext retrieval results and eliminates illegal authorized access.
- We analyze and evaluate the security and performance of the proposed scheme, and the results show that our scheme is secure and feasible in the smart grid application scenario.

Organization. The rest of this paper is organized as follows. Section 2 introduces some basic skills used in this paper. Section 3 illustrates the system model, threat model, and design objectives. Section 4 describes the proposed scheme in detail. Section 5.1 evaluates the performance of the proposed scheme and compares it with other related schemes. Section 6 is conclusion.

2 Preliminaries

Bilinear Mapping. Let G_0 and G_1 be two multiplicative cyclic groups over a finite field Z_p with order p a large safe prime, then the bilinear map $f : G_0 \times G_0 \to G_1$ has the following properties. (1) Bilinear. $\forall m, n \in Z_p$ and $\forall x, y \in G_0$, $f(x^m, y^n) = f^{mn}(x, y)$; $\forall x_1, x_2, y \in G_0$, $f(x_1 x_2, y) = f(x_1, y)f(x_2, y)$. (2) Non-degeneracy. $\forall x, y \in G_0$, such that $f(x, y) \neq 1$, where 1 is the unit element of G_1. (3) Computability. $\forall x, y \in G_0$, there exists an effective polynomial-time algorithm to compute $f(x, y)$.

ρ-Stable Locally Sensitive Hash Function. ρ-Stable LSH is one of the locally sensitive hash functions that can be used in Euclidean spaces. It maps the l-dimensional feature vector V to a number and constructs inverted indexes for feature vectors with high dimensionality. It downscales features and reduces the associated computational effort effectively.

Access Control Tree. Suppose the participants are a set $U = \{U_1, U_2, \cdots, U_n\}$ and if there exists a monotonic access structure $S \subseteq 2^{\{U_1, U_2, \cdots, U_n\}}$, for any K_1, K_2, if $K_1 \subseteq S$ and $K_2 \subseteq K_1$, that is, there is $K_2 \subseteq S$. A monotonic access structure S is a non-empty monotonic set S, called an authorized set, otherwise it is a non-authorized set. The data access policy utilized by the proposed scheme is implemented by constructing an access control tree Γ consisting of a set of non-leaf nodes (logical threshold gates) and leaf nodes (user attributes). When the set of attributes of a user satisfies the logical rules of the access control tree Γ, the user can access the corresponding content.

3 System Model

3.1 The Model of Sensitive Video Retrievable Encryption Scheme in Smart Grid

The system structure of the proposed scheme are shown in Fig. 1.The model includes four entities: a. Trusted Authorization Authority (TA), which is responsible for system initialization, generation and distribution of user-related keys; b. Cloud Server (CS), which stores a large number of video and image files and provides most of the computing resources for retrieval; c. Data Owner (DO), grid enterprises or individual users who store video and image files on the cloud server, needs to encrypt the video set, keyframe set, encryption key and construct the security index; d. Data User (DU), the grid enterprises or individual users who want to query video data in the cloud server, decrypts the ciphertext retrieval result returned by CS using the attribute private key.

3.2 Design Objectives

To guarantee the privacy of data owners and the feasibility of secure video retrieval in the smart grid, this paper designs the security and performance objectives as follows.

1) Retrievability of ciphertext video. A large number of ciphertext images and ciphertext videos of smart grid are stored in CS, and DU can retrieve the video files corresponding to similar images in CS using the existing plaintext images.
2) Accurate retrieval and access. The depth features of keyframes of videos are fused and downscaled with traditional features to improve the retrieval accuracy, while the ciphertext policy attribute encryption mechanism is combined to eliminate illegal authorized access.
3) Privacy protection of data.CS and other attackers cannot detect the plaintext information of ciphertext video set, ciphertext keyframe set, ciphertext feature vector, secure index and search trapdoor, while CS cannot infer the value of plaintext vector inner product from the result of ciphertext vector inner product calculation.

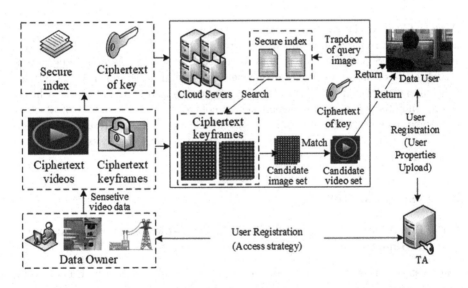

Fig. 1. System structure diagram

3.3 Threat Model

In this paper, we consider CS as semi-trustworthy, which honestly and correctly executes requests sent by DO and DU, but also actively probe the stored contents and mine more information through associative reasoning. The system attack models can be summarized into the following three types.

1) Known ciphertext attack model. CS only knows the encrypted video set from the DO, the encrypted keyframe set, the security index, and the search trapdoor from the DU.
2) Known context attack model. Besides the ciphertext video set, ciphertext keyframe set and search trapdoor, CS can get more background knowledge, such as some plaintext videos, the plaintext corresponding to the search trapdoor, etc.
3) User collusion attack model. DUs that do not conform to the access policy, share their own attribute private keys and symmetric encryption keys among each other in order to access the search results of the system.

4   The Proposed Scheme

Here is the whole process of the proposed scheme. Firstly, TA initializes the system and generates attribute private keys for DO and DU. Secondly, DO extracts frames from the video by feature value comparison method to get the keyframe set, and extracts CNN features, BOW features and HOG features of keyframe set respectively, and uses PCA and ρ-Stable LSH functions to reduce the dimensionality of the fused feature vector and generates a security index. Finally, CS performs similarity matching in the security index based on the search trap to obtain the candidate keyframe set, and returns the video set corresponding to the candidate keyframe set to DU. If and only if the set of user attributes of DU satisfies the access policy of DO, DU can decrypt the ciphertext video and get the plaintext video.

4.1   Keyframes Extraction

For frequently queried cloud-based videos, it takes a lot of time and computing resources for each retrieval. Using key frames instead of video to be retrieved can save resources significantly, and frames in the same clip are similar. Therefore, in this paper, We adopt the feature value comparison method to extract keyframes from videos, which reduces the time space for retrieval. At first, load the video and extract frames at 1 frame per second as the image set. Then, compute and compare SIFT features values of any two continuous images in the image set. If the comparison result is smaller than the threshold value we set, only one of the two comparison images is kept, otherwise both images are kept. Finally, get the keyframe set. The method could filter frames with very high similarity well.

4.2   Multi-feature Extraction and Fusion

Three main types of features are extracted in this scheme, which are CNN features, Bow features and HOG features. Each input of DenseNet [28] is related to the output of each previous layer, which can maximize the use of the features of each layer and save computation, so this paper extracts 1,024-dimensional CNN features from the keyframe set through DenseNet network.Bow features are bag-of-words semantic representations of the scale-invariant image feature transform features, and 120-dimensional BOW features can be obtained through the K-means algorithm. HOG features are a global image feature descriptor used to detect the presence of image objects by segmenting an image region into multiple connected local regions, calculating the edge or gradient direction histogram of each local region, and then performing statistics and normalization. Finally, the 3,780-dimensional HOG features are obtained.

After extracting the three features, feature fusion is performed. Then the PCA algorithm is used to reduce the correlation between the three features and the dimensionality of the fused features. The main steps are as follows.

1) Let the feature matrix of the keyframe set be $V = [V_1, V_2, \cdots, V_n]^T$ and the feature vector of the ith image be $V_i = [v_{i1}, v_{i2}, \cdots, v_{ie}]$. where is the number of images in the image set and is the dimensionality of the feature vector. Centering the feature matrix V to obtain $\widehat{V}$, we get

$$\widehat{V} = \left[V_1 - \overline{V_1}, \cdots, V_i - \overline{V_i}, \cdots, V_n - \overline{V_n} \right]^T \tag{1}$$

$$\overline{V_i} = \sum_{j=1}^{e} \frac{v_{ij}}{e}, 1 \leq i \leq n \tag{2}$$

2) Calculate the covariance of $\widehat{V}$ with the formula

$$cov(\widehat{V}) = E\left(\left[\widehat{V} - E(\widehat{V}) \right] \left[\widehat{V} - E(\widehat{V}) \right] \right)^T \tag{3}$$

3) Singular value decomposition of the covariance $cov(\widehat{V})$, which in turn yields the eigenvalue matrix $\boldsymbol{\lambda}$ and the eigenvector matrix $\boldsymbol{\zeta}$

$$[\boldsymbol{\lambda}, \boldsymbol{\zeta}] = SVD(cov(\widehat{V})) \tag{4}$$

where: $\boldsymbol{\lambda} = [\lambda_1, \lambda_2, \cdots, \lambda_l]$; $\boldsymbol{\zeta} = [\zeta_1, \zeta_2, \cdots, \zeta_l]$, l represents the number of feature sets, ζ_i represents the feature vector corresponding to the feature value λ_i; SVD represents the singular value decomposition function.

4) The elements of eigenvalue matrix $\boldsymbol{\lambda}$ are sorted in descending order, and then the elements' positions of the eigenvector matrix $\boldsymbol{\zeta}$ are swapped according to the descending eigenvalue matrix, and the projection matrix $\zeta' = [\zeta_1, \zeta_2, \cdots, \zeta_d]$ is obtained by selecting first d eigenvectors.

5) The reduced dimensional feature matrix V' is obtained from the projection matrix ζ' and the feature matrix V

$$V' = \zeta'^T V = [V_1', \cdots, V_i', \cdots, V_n']^T \tag{5}$$

where: $V_i' = [v_{i1}', v_{i2}', \cdots, v_{id}']$ is the fused feature vector of image i after dimensionality reduction, and d is the dimensionality of the feature.

4.3 Ciphertext Image-Video Retrieval Algorithm Based on CP-ABE

Initialization. $Setup(1^\epsilon) \to K_S, K_P$. Input safety factor ϵ, define G_0 and G_1 as two multiplicative cyclic groups on the wired domain Z_p, g is the generating element of G_0, and order p is a large safety prime, bilinear mapping $f : G_0 \times G_0 \to G_1$, γ set of collision-resistant hash functions $H = \{h_1, h_2, \cdots, h_\gamma\}$. Set d as the final feature vector dimension of keyframes and μ is a random positive integer, then randomly select the $(d + \mu + 1)$-dimensional binary vector U, $(d + \mu + 1)(d + \mu + 1)$-dimensional invertible matrices A_1 and A_2. TA randomly select $\alpha, \beta \leftarrow Z_p$ as the system master private key $K_S = [\alpha, \beta]$, master public key $K_P = [G_0, G_1, p, g, f^\alpha(g, g), g^\beta, H, U, A_1, A_2]$ are the system public parameters.

User Registration. $URegist(K_P, K_S, S) \to K_U$. When a new user U requests registration from the system, TA randomly selects $r \leftarrow Z_p$, $r_s \leftarrow Z_p$, and calculates its corresponding attribute private key K_U according to the attribute set S of that user as

$$K_U = \left[L = g^{\frac{\alpha+r}{\beta}}, L_s = g^r h(s)^{r_s}, L_s' = g^{r_s} \right], \forall s \in S \tag{6}$$

Encryption. $ENC(K_P, D, \Gamma, K) \to C, C_K$. Suppose DO has plaintext image set $D = \{D_1, D_2, \cdots, D_n\}$ to be stored.

$PEnc(D, K) \to C$. The image set is encrypted with the feature vector. k-dimensional binary vector K is randomly generated by DO as the symmetric encryption key for the plaintext image set D, which is encrypted to obtain the ciphertext image set $C = \{C_1, C_2, \cdots, C_n\}$, and sent to CS.

$KEnc(K_P, D, \Gamma, K) \to C_K$. The DO defines the access tree structure Γ according to the access policy and generates a polynomial q_o for each node o starting from the root node r. Let k_o be the threshold value of node o and the order $deg(q_o) = k_o - 1$ of the polynomial q_o. For the root node r, the DO randomly selects $deg(q_r)$ coefficients from Z_p and a constant δ (as the value of $q_r(0)$) to generate the polynomial q_r; as for the generation of polynomial q_o for any other non-root node o, $deg(q_o)$ coefficients are also randomly selected from Z_p, and the constant term $q_o(0) = q_{par(o)}(id(o))$, where $par(o)$ is the parent of node o and $id(o)$ is the identification value given to node o by the parent of node o. For easy understanding, assume that node o is the 2nd child of its parent node o_f, then the constant term $q_o(0) = q_{(o_f)}(2)$ of the polynomial q_o of node o, where the function $q_{(o_f)}$ is the polynomial of the parent node of. DO calculates the ciphertext C_K after the encryption key K as

$$C_K = \left[\Gamma, \overline{C} = f^{\alpha\delta}(g, g), C = g^{\delta\beta}, C_t = g^{q_t(0)}, C_t{}' = h(at(t))^{q_t(0)} \right], \forall t \in T \tag{7}$$

where: T is all leaf nodes in tree Γ; $at(t)$ denotes the attribute value associated with leaf node t; $q_t(0)$ is the constant term in the polynomial of leaf node t.

Index Generation. $IndexGen(\boldsymbol{K}_P, D) \rightarrow \boldsymbol{I}'$. DO extract, fuse and reduce the dimension of multiple features of the keyframe set D according to Subsect. 4.1 and 4.2 to obtain the plaintext feature set $\boldsymbol{V}' = [\boldsymbol{V}_1', \cdots, \boldsymbol{V}_i', \cdots, \boldsymbol{V}_n']^T$, and then construct the plaintext index $\boldsymbol{I}$ by using the ρ-Stable LSH function, followed by the single hash function and the secure nearest neighbor algorithm to obtain the secure index $\boldsymbol{I}'$.

$IndexGen(\boldsymbol{K}_P, D) \rightarrow \boldsymbol{V}', \boldsymbol{I}$. The unencrypted index is generated. For each image D_i, DO performs a hashing operation on its feature vector $\boldsymbol{V}_i'$ to obtain $H(\boldsymbol{V}_i') = [h_1(\boldsymbol{V}_i'), h_2(\boldsymbol{V}_i'), \cdots, h_r(\boldsymbol{V}_i')]$ by using the set of collision-resistant hash functions $H = \{h_1, h_2, \cdots, h_r\}$. Repeat σ times to obtain σ hash tables to reduce the error rate. $\boldsymbol{H}_t(\boldsymbol{V}_i')$ is the set of bucket values of the hash table obtained from the tth hash operation, where $t \in [1, \sigma]$ and N_t denotes the number of buckets in the tth hash table, and similar images will be placed in the same hash bucket. The feature vector $\boldsymbol{V}_i'$, the identity P_i of image D_i are stored together in the hash table, i.e., in index $\boldsymbol{I}$.

$IndexEnc(\boldsymbol{K}_P, \boldsymbol{V}', \boldsymbol{I}) \rightarrow \boldsymbol{I}'$. Secure index generation. For each image D_i, the d-dimensional feature vector $\boldsymbol{V}_i'$ is expanded into a $(d + \mu + 1)$-dimensional vector $\boldsymbol{M}_i = \left[\boldsymbol{V}_i', \| \boldsymbol{V}_i' \|^2, \vartheta\right]$, and ϑ is a μ-dimensional random binary vector, and then $\boldsymbol{M}_i$ is split into two parts $\boldsymbol{M}_i^1$ and $\boldsymbol{M}_i^2$ according to the splitting rule and the random binary vector $\boldsymbol{U}$. Next, the random invertible matrices $\boldsymbol{A}_1^T$ and $\boldsymbol{A}_2^{-1}$ are multiplied by $\boldsymbol{M}_i^{1T}$ and $\boldsymbol{M}_i^{2T}$, respectively, to obtain the encrypted eigenvector $\boldsymbol{F}_i' = \left[\boldsymbol{A}_1^T \boldsymbol{M}_i^{1T}, \boldsymbol{A}_2^{-1} \boldsymbol{M}_i^{2T}\right]$, and the bucket values of σ hash tables are encrypted with the monomial hash function $\varphi(\cdot)$.

Trapdoor Generation. $TrapdoorGen(\boldsymbol{K}_P, m) \rightarrow \boldsymbol{T}_m$. DU first calculates the fused feature vector $\boldsymbol{V}_m' = [v_{m1}', v_{m2}', \cdots, v_{md}']$ of the image m. Then the hash is calculated using the set of functions $H = \{h_1, h_2, \cdots, h_r\}$ to get $H(\boldsymbol{V}_m') = [h_1(\boldsymbol{V}_m'), h_2(\boldsymbol{V}_m'), \cdots, h_r(\boldsymbol{V}_m')]$, repeating σ times to obtain σ hash tables, and $\boldsymbol{H}_t(\boldsymbol{V}_m')$ is the set of bucket values of the hash table obtained by the tth hashing operation, where $t \in [1, \sigma]$. Then, encrypting it by the monomial hash function $\varphi(\cdot)$ yields $\psi_m = [\varphi(\boldsymbol{H}_1(\boldsymbol{V}_m')), \cdots, \varphi(\boldsymbol{H}_\sigma(\boldsymbol{V}_m'))]$. Set $\omega = [\omega_1, \omega_2, \cdots, \omega_\mu]$, expand $\boldsymbol{V}_m'$ to $\boldsymbol{M}_m = [-2\boldsymbol{V}_m', 1, \omega]$, and then split $\boldsymbol{M}_m$ into two parts $\boldsymbol{M}_m^1$ and $\boldsymbol{M}_m^2$. Then randomly select a positive integer τ and multiply $\boldsymbol{A}_1^{-1}$ and $\boldsymbol{A}_2^T$ by $\boldsymbol{M}_m^{1T}$ and $\boldsymbol{M}_m^{2T}$ respectively to obtain the cryptographic query vector $\boldsymbol{F}_m' = \left[\tau \boldsymbol{A}_1^{-1} \boldsymbol{M}_m^{1T}, \tau \boldsymbol{A}_2^T \boldsymbol{M}_m^{2T}\right]$. Finally, the search trap $\boldsymbol{T}_m$ consisting of $\boldsymbol{F}_m'$ and ψ_m is sent to CS.

Search. $Search(\boldsymbol{I}', \boldsymbol{T}_m) \rightarrow C_m, \boldsymbol{C}_K$. The cloud server CS receives the ciphertext image set security index $\boldsymbol{I}'$, search token $\boldsymbol{T}_m$, and first finds the same hash bucket as ψ_m, and then calculates the inner product of feature vectors of all images in that bucket with the feature vectors of the query image, and measures the similarity of the two images based on the magnitude of the values, with the following formula

$$\boldsymbol{F'_m}^T \boldsymbol{F'_i} = (\tau \boldsymbol{A}_1^{-1} \boldsymbol{M_m}^{1T})^T \boldsymbol{A}_1^T \boldsymbol{M_i}^{1T} + (\tau \boldsymbol{A}_2^T \boldsymbol{M_m}^{2T})^T \boldsymbol{A}_2^{-1} \boldsymbol{M_i}^{2T} = \tau \boldsymbol{M_m} \boldsymbol{M_i}^T$$

$$= \tau(\| \boldsymbol{V'_i} \|^2 - 2\boldsymbol{V'_i}^T \boldsymbol{V'_m} + \boldsymbol{\omega}\boldsymbol{\vartheta}^T) = \tau(\| \boldsymbol{V'_m} - \boldsymbol{V'_i} \|^2 - \| \boldsymbol{V'_m} \|^2 + \boldsymbol{\omega}\boldsymbol{\vartheta}^T) \tag{8}$$

The set of ciphertext images $C_m = \{C_1, \cdots, C_j\}$ with the top j similarity ranked according to the inner product value size and the key ciphertext $\boldsymbol{C_K}$ containing the corresponding image access policy are output.

Decryption. $Dec(\boldsymbol{K_U}, \boldsymbol{C_K}, C_m) \rightarrow D_m/\varnothing$. The image data requester DU needs to input the attribute private key $\boldsymbol{K_U}$, the retrieval result C_m returned by the cloud server CS and the key cipher $\boldsymbol{C_K}$ containing the corresponding image access policy, and locally verify whether it has the decryption authority.

$Test(\boldsymbol{K_U}, \boldsymbol{C_K}) \rightarrow \boldsymbol{K}/\varnothing$. Verify the key. After DU receives $\boldsymbol{C_K}$, check whether the attribute private key $\boldsymbol{K_U}$ and the access policy Γ match, if not match return $\varnothing$, otherwise use recursive algorithm to get $B = f^{r\delta}(g,g)$. the formula for DU to recover the symmetric key is

$$\boldsymbol{K} = \frac{\overline{C}}{B^{-1}f(C,L)} = \frac{\boldsymbol{K}f^{\alpha\delta}(g,g)f(g^{\delta\beta}, g^{\frac{\alpha+r}{\beta}})}{f^{r\delta}(g,g)} = \frac{\boldsymbol{K}f^{\alpha\delta}(g,g)f^{r\delta}(g,g)}{f^{\delta(\alpha+r)}(g,g)} \tag{9}$$

$Dec(\boldsymbol{K}, C_m) \rightarrow D_m$. User decryption. The retrieval result $C_m = \{C_1, C_2, \cdots, C_j\}$ is decrypted using the symmetric key $\boldsymbol{K}$ from the decryption to obtain the plaintext image set $D_m = \{D_1, D_2, \cdots, D_j\}$.

5   Performance and Analysis

5.1   Security Analysis

In the scheme proposed in this paper, the method of encrypting video sets and key frame sets is a traditional symmetric encryption algorithm, which can strongly protect the privacy of images. Among them, the ciphertext feature vectors stored in the secure index table are subject to higher strength privacy protection due to operations such as random matrix multiplication and adding redundant terms in the secure nearest neighbor algorithm. If the cloud server CS wants to get the plaintext feature vectors, it first needs to obtain the vector $\boldsymbol{U}$ and matrices $\boldsymbol{A}_1$ and $\boldsymbol{A}_2$. However, since the vector $\boldsymbol{U}$ and matrices $\boldsymbol{A}_1$ and $\boldsymbol{A}_2$ are randomly generated, it is almost impossible for the cloud server CS to get the exact data of this information, i.e., it cannot decrypt the ciphertext feature vectors in the secure index table. The privacy security of the search trapdoor also relies on whether the data of the random vector $\boldsymbol{U}$ and the random matrices $\boldsymbol{A}_1$, $\boldsymbol{A}_2$ can be stolen. Besides, the random number τ makes the generation of search trapdoors random, so CS cannot reason about the association of search trapdoors with query images.

Whether a system user or an external attacker, who wants to obtain the plaintext video, has to decrypt the ciphertext $\boldsymbol{C_K}$ of the symmetric encryption key K first. From equation $\overline{C} = K f^{\alpha\delta}(g,g)$, to get K, it must first calculate $f^{\alpha\delta}(g,g)$, which can be obtained only when the user's access structure tree property is satisfied. In order to be able to access the retrieval results normally in the system, users who do not satisfy the access policy may conspire to gather their different attributes together in order to satisfy the rules of the access structure tree. A malicious user can calculate $f^{\delta(\alpha+r)}(g,g)$ based on $C = g^{\beta\delta}$ in his own key ciphertext C_K and $L = g^{\frac{\alpha+r}{\beta}}$ in his own attribute private key K_U. To get $f^{\alpha\delta}(g,g)$ the malicious user needs to get $f^{r\delta}(g,g)$ first. The r of each user in the system is randomly generated by TA and hidden from the user, and the user does not know the r. In addition, the other components of the user's attribute private key $L_s = g^r h(s)^{r_s}$ and $L'_s = g^{r_s}$ are also affected by the random number r. Therefore, even if multiple malicious users share their respective attribute keys or symmetric encryption keys, the respective components are not the same and K cannot be obtained. The proposed scheme can resist collusion attacks among users in the system.

With a known background attack model, inner product computation secures the ciphertext feature vector and search trapdoor in polynomial time. The adversary is able to detect the set of ciphertext images, the set of secure index tables and search trapdoors, and even other background knowledge. Suppose adversary A has access to a set of plain ciphertext pairs $[V', F']$ of feature vectors, a set of plain ciphertext pairs $[V'_{td}, F'_{td}]$ of feature vectors in trapdoors, the set $E' = [F'_1, F'_2, \cdots, F'_j]$ of encrypted feature vectors, and the set $E = [V'_1, V'_2, \cdots, V'_j]$ of unencrypted feature vectors. The set of query vectors $T'_{td} = [F'_{m1}, F'_{m2}, \cdots, F'_{ms}]$ in the trapdoor. In the known ciphertext model, the image content is secure. However, for images, the image feature vectors are able to leak the image content, and the search trapdoor is similar to the generation process of ciphertext feature vectors, so the privacy of image feature vectors is mainly discussed.

The similarity between image vectors is measured by Eq. 9. Adversary A substitutes $[V', F']$ and $[V'_{td}, F'_{td}]$ into Eq. 9 to obtain ${F'_{td}}^T F' = \tau(\| V' \|^2 - 2V'V'_{td} + \omega\vartheta^T)$. Where both τ and $\omega\vartheta^T$ are unknown and the ciphertext feature vector cannot leak information related to the plaintext feature vector. Even if the set of plaintext feature vectors E is known, the adversary cannot violently crack the ciphertext feature vectors in polynomial time. Therefore, under the known background attack model, the polynomial-time adversary cannot obtain the encrypted dataset and search for the plaintext of the trapdoor.

5.2   Comparison of Theoretical Analysis

Table 1 gives the theoretical computational overhead analysis of three comparison schemes ref [25], ref [29] and the scheme SIVR proposed in this paper, comparing the more costly cryptographic operations in the schemes. In the Table 1, Q_G is group exponential operation, Q_{Z_p} is group exponential operation, Q_E is bilinear pair operation, Q_H is hash operation, Q_M is matrix operation, w is the number of image owners, n is the number of keyframes d is the plaintext feature vector dimension, d' is the ciphertext feature vector dimension, r is the number of hash functions, σ is the number of hash tables, $|T|$ is the number of leaf nodes of the access tree.

Table 1. Theoretical comparison of computational expenses.

Scheme	Key generation	Index generation	Video retrieval
[25]	$2dwQ_{Z_p}$	$2nQ_M$	$2d^2n^2$
[29]	$(2+3d)wQ_{Z_p}$	$ndqQ_{Z_p}$	$2nQ_{Z_p}$
SIVR	$2|T|wQ_G + wQ_{Z_p} + 2d'^2$	$n(r\sigma Q_H + 2Q_M)$	$2nd'^2 + Q_E$

As can be seen from Table 1, in the key generation stage, the key generation time of SIVR increases with the increase of the number of leaf nodes in the access tree and feature vector dimensions , and in order to strengthen the security of inner product calculation, redundant terms are added to the ciphertext feature vector in the secure nearest neighbor algorithm. In the index generation phase, the index generation time of all three schemes is positively correlated with the total number of keyframes. In the search trapdoor generation stage, the trapdoor generation time of the 3 schemes is mainly affected by the feature vector dimension, hash calculation and matrix multiplication, which is omitted by considering it as the index establishment for the number of keyframes as 1. In the image retrieval phase, the number of keyframes and feature vector dimensions have a significant impact on the computational overhead. The computational overhead of key generation in the SIVR scheme is large, mainly because of the generation of attribute private keys, but this can be traded for fine-grained access control of the retrieval results. The index establishment in the ref [25] is fast, but it only encrypts the feature vectors using image encryption keys and does not achieve the real sense of privacy. Therefore, in the image retrieval stage, it needs to calculate the inner product of ciphertext feature vectors of all ciphertext images according to the search trapdoor, and then compare them two by two to get the final result, so it has a large computational overhead when the number of images is large. The group index operation has an impact on the computational overhead of all stages of ref [29], while SIVR has only two stages related with it.

5.3   Experimental Performance Analysis and Comparison

The experimental environment consists of 12th Gen Intel(R) Core(TM) i7-12700K @3.60 GHz, Win10 and 64G RAM, and the experimental tools are python 3.7. The dataset used in the experiment consists of 500 videos collected from smart grid, including 400 surveillance videos and 100 field operation videos. Set the number of hash tables as 4, each hash table needs to utilize 4 hash functions, set the dimension of fused features as 120, and the number of leaf nodes of access tree Γ as 10.

The simulation results of the computational overhead are shown in Table 2. In the image retrieval phase, the comparison object is the average time of retrieval among 500 videos from the three schemes. The ciphertext generation time and index generation time of the ref [25] are shorter, 56 and 62 ms, respectively, but the use of traversing the inner product to calculate and compare the ciphertext features of the images leads to too long average time for image retrieval, about 212.2 s. The ref [29] adopts a clustering approach, and the ciphertext image retrieval time is the shortest among the three compared schemes, about 36 ms, but the index generation time is longer, about 126.6 s. Since SIVR needs to generate attribute private keys for users, the key generation time is 565 ms, which is higher compared with ref [25] and ref [29], but it is a one-time process, which is acceptable. The index generation time and image retrieval time of SIVR are not the shortest, they are not much higher than the shortest time but much shorter than the longest time in Table 2. In the experiments, the features used in all three schemes are 3 features fused together. It should be noted that due to the long feature extraction and fusion times, the index generation times in Table 2 do not include these times for the sake of comparison. At this time, the dimensionality of the fused features after PCA dimensionality reduction is 120 dimensions and the time spent is 380.5 s.

Table 2. Simulation comparison of computational cost.

Scheme	Time/ms		
	Key generation	Index generation	Video retrieval
[25]	56	62	212158
[29]	42	126587	36
SIVR	565	72	235

The retrieval accuracy rate of each scheme is calculated by using the formula $P_r = s'/s$. Where, s indicates the number of videos related to keyframes returned by retrieval, and s' indicates the number of videos related to keyframes returned by retrieval of the same category as the query image. The number of retrieval results returned is 25. The comparison results of the retrieval accuracy rate of the three schemes are average accuracy of 10 queries, shown in Fig. 2. It can be seen that: ref [25] exchanges a higher retrieval accuracy rate at the cost of time overhead; ref [29] simplifies the Euclidean distance calculation method by giving up the retrieval accuracy to get a higher retrieval efficiency, and the practicality of both schemes was seriously affected; when feature extraction was performed on the image set, only three traditional features were processed. When the number of video sets to be retrieved is 100, the scheme SIVR -CNN features, the accuracy rate at this time is 88.0%, which is comparable to that of the ref [25]; when CNN features are taken into consideration, the accuracy rates of both the ref [25] and the ref [29] are also improved to some extent, by 1.6% and 4.0%, respectively;

the retrieval accuracy rate of the scheme SIVR in this paper is weaker than that of the enhanced ref [25], but the CNN features improve the retrieval accuracy by 2.4%, which illustrates the effectiveness of combining CNN depth features with traditional features.

The ciphertext image retrieval time is shown in Fig. 3. SIVR uses the key-value pair-based method to construct a secure index, so even if the number of keyframes and videos to be retrieved keep increasing, the retrieval efficiency remains at the same level, and the average test retrieval time is 240.8 ms. The locally sensitive hash function effectively shortens the retrieval time.

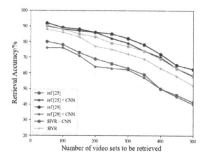 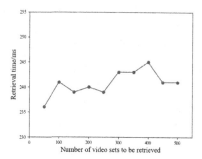

Fig. 2. Comparison results of secure video retrieval accuracy

Fig. 3. Encrypted video retrieval time comparison chart

In the experiments, 1,024-dimensional CNN features, 3,780-dimensional HOG features, and 120-dimensional BOW features are extracted from the dataset, and the fused features of 80, 100, 120, and 140 dimensions after dimensionality reduction by PCA are experimented according to the SIVR scheme, and the experimental results are shown in Table 3. The number of video set to be retrieved is 100, which is randomly selected from the whole dataset, and the comparison results of the retrieval accuracy are average accuracy of 10 queries. It can be seen that: when the dimensionality of the fused features after dimensionality reduction is in a suitable range, the higher the feature dimensionality, the longer the retrieval time, but due to the structure of the index, the retrieval time is very similar; when the feature dimensionality is controlled at 120 dimensions, the retrieval accuracy rate is the highest; the feature dimensionality of the fused features has a greater impact on the retrieval accuracy rate, and the dimensionality is too low or too high, which will cause the missing or redundant image feature information, and then reduce the The retrieval accuracy of cryptographic images will be reduced if the dimensionality is too low or too high.

Table 3. Comparison results of fusion features with different reduced dimensionality.

Dimensionality	Retrieval time/ms	Retrieval accuracy rate/%
80	235	76.8
100	238	80.8
120	240	90.4
140	250	86.0

6   Conclusion

In this paper, we propose a multi-feature fusion and image-based retrievable scheme for sensitive video data in smart grid, which combines symmetric searchable encryption with ciphertext policy attribute-based encryption to achieve efficient and secure retrieval. Among the three comparison schemes in this paper, the proposed scheme achieves the best balance between efficiency and accuracy, and is feasible and effective for practical application in smart grid scenarios. The use of locally sensitive hash function and secure nearest neighbor algorithm with added redundant terms can effectively shorten the retrieval time while enhancing security. The combination of deep image features and traditional image features enhances the expressiveness of the final feature vector, which in turn improves the accuracy of video retrieval based on ciphertext images. However, the proposed video retrieval model only allows searching video by image. The next research work will be carried out for the keyword query video function.

Acknowledgements. This work was supported by the Science and Technology Project of State Grid Gansu Province Electric Power Company (No. 522723191004).

References

1. Feng, G., Gu, M., Ji, X.: Research and implementation of unstructured data management platform for power grid enterprises. South. Energy Constr. **2**(S1), 222–225 (2015)
2. Shi, J., Jiao, H., Zhao, Q., et al.: Research on multi-tenant privacy preservation in public cloud environment. Comput. Eng. Appl. **52**(20), 138–144 (2016)
3. Nazir, A., Ashraf, R., Hamdant, T., et al.: Content based image retrieval system by using HSV color histogram, discrete wavelet transform and edge histogram descriptor. In: iCoMET, pp. 1–6. IEEE, Sukkur (2018). https://doi.org/10.1109/ICOMET.2018.8346343
4. Yang, T., Shi, G., Yang, N., et al.: Combining multiple feature for texture image classification. In: CISP-BMEI, pp. 1–5. IEEE, Shanghai (2017). https://doi.org/10.1109/CISP-BMEI.2017.8301967
5. Ahmfd, K.T., Ummfsaft, S., Iqbai, A.: Content based image retrieval using image features information fusion. Inf Fusion **51**, 76–99 (2019)
6. Husatn, S.S., Bobfr, M.: REMAP: multi-layer entropy-guided pooling of dense CNN features for image retrieval. IEEE Trans. Image Process. **28**(10), 5201–5213 (2019)

7. Liu, P., Guo, J., Wu, C., et al.: Fusion of deep learning and compressed domain features for content-based image retrieval. IEEE Trans. Image Process. **26**(12), 5706–5717 (2017)

8. Chen, X., He, H., Li, P., et al.: Ciphertext image retrieval scheme based on target detection in cloud environment. Comput. Eng. Appl. **56**(11), 75–82 (2020)

9. Ren, S., He, K., Girshick, R., et al.: Faster R-CNN: towards real-time object detection with region proposal networks. IEEE Trans. Pattern Anal. Mach. Intell. **39**(6), 1137–1149 (2017)

10. Miao, Y., Ma, J., Liu, X., et al.: Attribute-based keyword search over hierarchical data in cloud computing. IEEE Trans. Serv. Comput. **13**(6), 985–998 (2020)

11. Li, J., Niu, X., Sun, J.: A practical searchable symmetric encryption scheme for smart grid data. In: ICC, pp. 1–6. IEEE, Shanghai (2019). https://doi.org/10.1109/ICC.2019.8761599

12. Eltayieb, N., Elhabob, R., Hassan, A., et al.: An efficient attribute-based online/offline searchable encryption and its application in cloud-based reliable smart grid. J. Syst. Softw. **98**, 165–172 (2019)

13. Zhang, C., Lin, Y., Zhu, L., et al.: CNN-VWII: an efficient approach for large-scale video retrieval by image queries. Pattern Recognit. Lett. **123**, 82–88 (2019)

14. Song, J., Gao, L., Liu, L., et al.: Quantizationbased hashing: a general framework for scalable image and video retrieval. Pattern Recognit. **75**, 175–187 (2018)

15. Josef, S., Frederik, S., Andrew, Z.: Object level grouping for video shots. Int. J. Comput. Vis. **67**(2), 189–210 (2006)

16. Andre, A., Bernd, G.: Large-scale video retrieval using image queries. IEEE Trans. Circuits Syst. Video Technol. **28**(6), 1406–1420 (2017)

17. Liu, Y., Zhang, D., Lu, G., et al.: A survey of content based image retrieval with high-level semantics. Pattern Recognit. **40**(1), 262–282 (2007)

18. Dharant, T., Aroqutaraj, I.: A survey on content based image retrieval. In: ICPRME, pp. 485–490. IEEE, Salem (2013). https://doi.org/10.1109/ICPRIME.2013.6496719

19. Qtn, Z., Yan, J., Ren, K., et al.: Towards efficient privacy-preserving image feature extraction in cloud computing. In: ACM MM, pp. 497–506. ACM, New York (2014). https://doi.org/10.1145/2647868.2654941

20. Wand, Q., Hu, S., Wang, J., et al.: Secure surfing: privacy-preserving speeded-up robust feature extractor. In: ICDCS, pp. 700–710. IEEE, Nara (2016). https://doi.org/10.1109/ICDCS.2016.84

21. Yuan, J., Yu, S., Guo, L.: SEISA: secure and efficient encrypted image search with access control. In: INFOCOM, pp. 2083–2091. IEEE, Hong Kong (2015). https://doi.org/10.1109/INFOCOM.2015.7218593

22. Yan, H., Chen, Z., Jia, C.: SSIR: secure similarity image retrieval in IoT. Inf. Sci. **479**, 153–163 (2019)

23. Rakesh, A., Jerry, K., Ramakrishan, S., et al.: Order preserving encryption for numeric data. In: ACM SIGMOD, pp. 563–574. ACM, New York (2004). https://doi.org/10.1145/1007568.1007632

24. Gentry, C., Boneh, D.: A Fully Homomorphic Encryption Scheme. Stanford University Publication, Redwood City (2009)

25. Zhu, X., Li, H., Guo, Z.: Privacy-preserving query over the encrypted image in cloud computing. J. Xidian Univ. **41**(2), 151–158 (2014)

26. Li, Y., Ma, J., Miao, Y.: Encrypted image retrieval in multi-key settings based on edge computing. J. Commun. **41**(4), 14–26 (2020)

27. Xia, Z., Xiong, N., Vastiakos, A., et al.: EPCBIR: an efficient and privacy-preserving content-based image retrieval scheme in cloud computing. Inf. Sci. **387**, 195–204 (2017)
28. Huang, G., Liu, Z., Van, D., et al.: Densely connected convolutional networks. In: CVPR, pp. 2261–2269. IEEE, Honolulu (2017). https://doi.org/10.1109/CVPR.2017.243
29. Shen, M., Cheng, G., Zhu, L., et al.: Content-based multi-source encrypted image retrieval in clouds with privacy preservation. Future Gener. Comput. Syst. **109**, 621–632 (2020)
30. Xia, Z., Wang, X., Zhang, L., et al.: A privacy-preserving and copy-deterrence content-based image retrieval scheme in cloud computing. IEEE Trans. Inf. Forensics Secur. **11**(11), 2594–2608 (2016)

A Survey on Privacy Preserving Synthetic Data Generation and a Discussion on a Privacy-Utility Trade-off Problem

Debolina Ghatak[1]([⊠]) and Kouichi Sakurai[2]

[1] TCG CREST, Kolkata, India
deboghatak@gmail.com
[2] Kyushu University, Fukuoka, Japan

Abstract. Sharing microdata is a very important part of the present day world, but when they contain sensitive information, privacy to individuals needs to be guaranteed before release of data. One idea is to study the distributional properties of a data-set and generate synthetic data which has similar properties but unlike the original data comes with a privacy guarantee. In this review paper, we describe in detail, some advanced privacy guarantees that needs to be checked before release of such information. Also, we discuss some utility metrics to measure the remaining utility of released data. Very few mechanisms have been developed to ensure utility to synthetic data, provided a very strong privacy guarantee is maintained. We discuss some existing methodologies on privacy preserving synthetic data generation and discuss a privacy utility tradeoff problem.

Keywords: Data obfuscation · Differential privacy · Synthetic data · Privacy utility tradeoff

1 Introduction

The uses of statistical data and knowledge of their distributional properties is enormous in today's world. Medical data-sets are required to carry medical, biotechnological, public health research. Economic and business data-sets are collected and analyzed by business analysts to benefit in their endeavours. Artificial intelligence has given rise to computer applications and various machines whose performance depends highly on the data they receive. But, sometimes these data may carry some sensitive information, especially in case of microdata, i.e., if the data is based on information corressponding to certain individuals. Release of microdata for various industrial and research purposes may hurt the privacy of the individuals. For example, in a medical database, it may show that a person is schizophrenic. This information, when released publicly might hurt the individual sentiment. Or, in a bank database, the income of a person might be publicly visible which can be sensitive to the individual. Also, there might be

C. Su and K. Sakurai (Eds.): SciSec 2022 Workshops, CCIS 1680, pp. 167–180, 2022.
https://doi.org/10.1007/978-981-19-7769-5_13

some intruder who is trying to guess the individual data-value to harm him or hurt his sentiment in some way. Any publicly released information thus must be free from all such sensitive information and this calls for privacy measures to ensure a privacy guarantee to a particular data-release mechanism.

The problem of privacy protection to ensure data security was studied in statistical literature from 1960's which may be found in articles such as, Steinberg and Pritzker (1967) [42], Bachi and Banon (1969) [1], DeGroot (1970) [8], Dalenius (1974) [6] Cassel (1976) [4], Frank (1978, 1979, 1982) [14–16], Mugge (1983) [35], Duncan and Lambert (1986,1989) [10,11] etc. At first, the problem was viewed as an uncertainity problem. If the function $U(\cdot)$ defines the uncertainity of an intruder for any target value in the released database, then larger the values of $U(\cdot)$, higher the privacy guarantee of the data-release mechanism. The study of randomized response techniques in statistical literature [38,46] is also quite similar to this problem. However, with time, advanced techniques and privacy measures started developing. Due to the increasing privacy concerns in the present-day world of big data, e-data; this problem has gained a significant attention now-a-days from the computer science researchers as well. Bakshy et al. [3] Beagrow et al. [2] discuss some present day privacy issues faced in social network platforms. There are a lot of unsolved issues in this field of research and many proposed mechanisms lack sufficient mathematical and statistical analysis.

Various government websites including NIST (under United States Government), GSS (under United Kingdom Government) share the importance of statistical data sharing in various departments such as Office of National Statistics, department of Education, departments of Culture, Media and Sports. However, due to the increasing privacy issues, it becomes hard to release the data in its raw form. This calls for the requirement of robust, efficient, trustworthy methods to generate data that ensures individual privacy along with being useful to make meaningful statistical inferences.

To give a clear view to the problems, let us discuss a simple example. We consider a certain hypothetical bank data-set containing information corresponding to customers.

The attributes corresponding to each individual consists of customer id, age, gender, pincode, occupation, income, account balance. Here, customer id may be considered as an identifying attribute as knowledge of it would help an intruder to exactly guess the row of his target individual in the raw data-set. Some other common examples of identifying attributes are name, enrollment number, or some other identity number. These attributes usually contribute less to the utility of the data and hence can be removed. But removal of identifying attributes may not be sufficient to protect the identity disclosure of the individual. The intruder may have some prior knowledge about his target individual, i.e., he may have some idea that the person he is trying to target is an old lady and is a doctor who lives near New-Alipore Kolkata. From this knowledge, he can clearly identify the corresponding row to his target individual from the given Table 1.

Table 1. Identification of individual information from data-set with multiple attributes

I.D.	Gender	Age	Pin code	Occupation	M.Income (in 1000)	Account balance
10101	"M"	43	700012	Worker	35	612342
10102	"M"	55	700043	Officer	90	5534567
10103	"F"	50	700003	Officer	70	3965478
10104	"F"	28	700082	Scholar	40	800432
10105	"F"	47	700055	Officer	120	1020045
10106	"M"	22	700100	Student	10	200654
10107	"F"	42	700049	Officer	60	1530128
10108	"F"	36	700082	Worker	25	983071
10109	"M"	34	700039	Worker	30	856313
10110	**"F"**	**60**	**700053**	**Doctor**	**70**	**1708349**
10111	"F"	29	700076	Scholar	25	481496
⋮	⋮	⋮	⋮	⋮	⋮	⋮

Any raw data released cannot be ensured, in general, to be protected from such privacy threats. In traditional statistical practices, a lot of methods were proposed to protect data privacy and utilize it for further statistical inferences. Some of the classical methods of obfuscation may be found in the surveys of [19,29]. For categorical data, the general practice was to either use a randomised response technique of multiplicative noise [38,46], or the post randomisation method (PRAM) [20,50] was used for data perturbation (a method of obfuscation where the obfuscated data values can be treated as original data values while making statistical inferences). For numerical or continuous data, methods like topcoding, grouping, data swapping, rank swapping, addition or multiplication of noise were used [7,17,34]. Later on, Muralidhar (1999) [36] proposed the method of General Additive Perturbation Method for data perturbation of continuous data (GADP).

In 1993, Rubin [39] proposed the idea of synthetic data generation to achieve data privacy. The idea was to generate synthetic or false numeric values that might be a good representation for the original data distribution. The idea has gained a huge importance in the present day research world of data security. To generate synthetic data-sets, one needs to, at first, study the data distribution from the original data and release such information with modifications to achieve some privacy guarantees to the released information. Then this information is used to generate false samples to represent original data. However, the more diverged the distributions of the original and synthetic data-sets are, the less accurate is any inference one is making from the released data.

In this review paper, we discuss some theoretical privacy measures and some statistical techniques used in the practice of synthetic data generation from microdata. In Sect. 2, we discuss the privacy measures to ensure how well the released data is protected from any possible intruder. In Sect. 3, we discuss some utility metrics used in the analysis of information loss due to security. In Sect. 4, we describe some relevant works on statistical models and masking techniques that are developed to help achieve data security. In Sect. 5, we discuss a privacy utility tradeoff problem. In Sect. 6, we will illustrate how the existing techniques work on a real-life data-set. Finally, we would conclude in Sect. 7 with some open problems in this field of work. It is to be noted that the aim of this review paper is not to go into the mathematical details of the privacy guarantee metrics or the utility metrics but is to discuss the standard tools for generation of synthetic data from microdata under data privacy.

2   A Discussion on Privacy Measures

Although research on privacy measures had started long ago, a few notable widely recognised works on microdata protection may include the works of k-anonymity, l-diversity, and t-closeness guarantee to a released data-set [24, 27, 43]. However, the one that has probably been a pioneer work in this field of work is the one by Dwork et al. (2006) [12] where they introduced the idea of α-differential privacy guarantee to a released information.

α-*Differential Privacy:* The basic problem deals with a situation where we have a data-set, say D, which has n samples and m attributes. We wish to release an information $f(D)$ from it. Now, can we guarantee that $f(D)$, if released publicly, is free from any previous threat? The notion of differential privacy aims to achieve a theoretical guarantee to any released information from a given data-set. Let $\mathcal{D}$ ($D \in \mathcal{D}$) be the set of all possible data-sets of a given type. A mechanism $\mathcal{M}$ defined on a dataset is said to be α-differentially private ($\alpha > 0$) if given any two datasets D and D' that differ in at most one row (denoted usually by $D \sim D'$),

$$e^{-\alpha} \leq \frac{P[\mathcal{M}(D) \in \mathcal{S}]}{P[\mathcal{M}(D') \in \mathcal{S}]} \leq e^{\alpha}$$

for any $S \subset \mathcal{S}$ where $\mathcal{S}$ is the range set of $\mathcal{M}$. If the value of α is small ($\leq$ 0.1 usually), the value of e^{α} is slightly more than 1 and the value of $e^{-\alpha}$ is slightly less than 1 and thus for any possible range set the probability of the output value of the mechanism to belong to that set is more or less same for the datasets D and D'. Now since this is true for any range set $\mathcal{S}$, it signifies that looking at the output value of the mechanism, it will be hard to guess if the information is coming from D or D', or more precisely, it would be hard to guess if a particular individual belongs to the underlying true data-set or not. Thus, one can ensure privacy protection to an individual. Dwork et al. (2006) [12] in the same paper showed that it is practically possible to achieve this theoretical guarantee through Laplace Noise Addition to true output $f(D)$ if the output has finite range. The scsle parameter of the noise must be chosen as $\dfrac{\nabla f}{\alpha}$ where ∇f denotes the range of output $f(D)$. However, later on, some other methods were developed to achieve similar results with minor improvements. Some notable works may include Gaussian Mechanism [9], Exponential Mechanism [32], K-norm Mechanism [22].

After the discovery of the differential privacy guarantee, several variants of it were proposed with similar sense but minor changes. These works may include Approximate Differential Privacy [48], Rényi Differential Privacy [33], Random Differential Privacy [21], Local Differential Privacy [28], etc.

The proposed criterion is a theoretical guarantee and not much can be said about its practical usefulness. There is no proper attack till date on this guarantee, however it is not free from disadvantages. First of all, differential privacy is not known to work if the output range is unknown. Second, the choice of α is very vital to ensure differential privacy. It is very clear from the definition that if α is not very close to 0 then the definition makes no sense. However, to get useful synthetic data, most organizations choose α as 1 or more which might make the data prone to severe attacks. In 2022, NIST declared a challenge on the selection of privacy parameter to achieve differential privacy. They claim that different organizations give different choices of α. Apple's differential privacy system uses it to be between 2 and 16. The US Census Bureau and Google's Community mobile reports have their choices as 19.61 and 16.4 respectively (URL: https://www.nist.gov/blogs/cybersecurity-insights/differential-privacy-future-work-open-challenges). Such large values of α is infeasible in case of microdata protection and hence choice of a proper α, if exists, is very debatable.

3 A Short Note on Differentially Private Techniques of Synthetic Data Generation

Microdata contains attributes mainly of two types, either categorical or continuous. Although categorical variables can be both ordinal (i.e., order of values are important; eg. Rating, Educational Qualification etc.) or nominal (i.e., order of values are not important; eg. Gender, Nationality etc.) but very less attention has been given to this part of analysis as per our knowledge. Usually the problem is thought of in discrete and continuous cases. Although there has been several algorithms and designs to generate synthetic data-sets for both types; it is often hard to say, in general, which method is useful for a particular problem. In 2018, NIST conducted the differentially private synthetic data challenge in which McKenna et al. (2021) [30] won the contest by modelling a discrete data distribution with Gaussian graphical model. Some other useful models that earned good attention in the contest were PrivSyn, PrivBayes, Differentially private Wasserstein GAN. In this section, we discuss some basic problems related to discrete and continuous data in the first two subsections. In the last subsection, we discuss the advanced high-dimensional models.

3.1 Discrete Data Distribution

The input data is assumed to be a set of vectors $\{x_1, x_2, \cdots, x_n\}$ each of dimension d which is the number of attributes in the data-set. Each attribute $\{\chi_i, i = 1, 2 \cdots, d\}$ is categorical and can take values in $\{i = 1, 2, \cdots, \nu_i\}$ $(1 < \nu_i < \infty)$. Set of all possible values of the data is a set of cardinality $\nu = \prod_{i=1}^{d} \nu_i$ and the probability vector $\mathbf{p}$ is a vector in $[0,1]^{\nu} \subset \mathbb{R}^{\nu}$ and the index set of $\mathbf{p}$ has lexicographical ordering of attributes. It gives the frequency of data points falling into a given category in d-dimensions. Considering $\mathbf{p}$ as the desired output from the database, one can easily generate a differentially private version of it, say $\mathbf{p}'$, using either Laplace, Gaussian, or Exponential Mechanism. Then $\mathbf{p}'$ is used to generate false representations of true data. The choice of the mechanism used to obtain differential privacy depends on the model and ease of computation. The comparison of different mechanisms as obfuscation tools studying the degree of security or utility guarantees they provide is a hard problem in general. In our experimental study, we used the Laplace Mechanism as the same is used in the proposed PGM. However, for 10 attributes in a data-set with 25 categories each, the probability vector has 25^{10} elements. In practice, data-sets can be much more complex than that. If the number of estimable parameters exceeds the sample size, we face the curse of dimensionality. One obvious question here is that how to deal with such situations? There have been several designs developed to deal with such circumstances. A brief discussion on the same is given in Subsect. 3.3.

3.2 Continuous Data Distribution

When the data is continuous it is usually assumed to belong to a known bounded region scaled to $[0,1]$ for each variable. If there are d such attributes, each data point is a point in $[0,1]^d$. To develop a synthetic data-set of such data type, if a methodology is applied similar to the discrete case, one would break the data region $[0,1]^d$ into equal sized small histogram bins and release the differentially private histogram counts for each such bin. Synthetic data can be generated from the perturbed histogram.

The first mechanism was proposed by Dwork (2006) [12]. For a histogram with bins $\{B_1, B_2, \cdots, B_m\}$, if the counts are denoted by $\{C_j, j = 1, 2, \cdots, m\}$,

$$D_j = C_j + \vartheta_j \ , \ \vartheta_j \sim \text{Laplace}(0, \tfrac{2}{\alpha})$$

is released which makes the released information differentially private. If $\tilde{D}_j = \max(D_j, 0)$ and $\tilde{q}_j = \frac{\tilde{D}_j}{\sum_{s=1}^{m} \tilde{D}_s}$ then a random sample $\{Z_1, Z_2, \cdots, Z_k\}$ drawn from the histogram given by,

$$\tilde{f}(x) = h^{-r} \sum_{j=1}^{m} \tilde{q}_j \mathbb{I}(x \in B_j)$$

is also differentially private. Wasserman and Zhou (2010) [47] calculates the theoretical error for the convergence of the estimated density of released data to the true density and it is shown to be $O(n^{-2/2+d})$ for $L2$ Error and $O(\min(\frac{\log n}{n^{2/2+d}}, \sqrt{\frac{\log n}{n}}))$ for expected Kolmogorov-Smirnov distance maintaining $k \geq n$ and $m \approx n^{\frac{d}{2+d}}$. The paper of Wasserman and Zhou (2010) [47] also studies the convergence rate to be $O(n^{-1/3})$ for perturbed histogram counts due to applying Exponential Mechanism. This study uses the expected Kolmogrov-Smirnov distance between the empirical cdfs of true and synthetic data.

Similar to discrete case, here also with the increase in dimension of data, the number of bins may become too large to handle and hence a few remedies to the curse of dimensionality are prescribed in the following subsection.

3.3 Dealing with High Dimensional Data

Several designs have been made to overcome the challenge of dealing with the curse of dimensionality in this problem. As it is not possible to discuss every such algorithm, we choose to mention the strategies of a few, mainly the winners of the NIST 2018 challenge. This might give an idea to the types of modelling that has been observed to be highly effective for high dimensional synthetic data generation.

Probability Graphical Models: This model [31] won the NIST challenge by assuming a graphical model for data distribution. They assumed a parametric model for the joint data distribution over the set of measurements that are cliques of the graph. They use MARGINAL-ORACLE to compute clique marginals μ of the graphical model. The parameters are estimated to be the ones that maximize the entropy among all with marginals μ and then sufficient noise is added to them to generate their private values. Synthetic data is simulated from the estimated data distribution. Thus, this model is highly dependent on the choice of the graphical model of data and is usually very useful when the cliques of the graphs are correctly guessed. It ensures $\alpha - \delta$-differential privacy to released synthetic data-set.

PrivSyn: They propose [51] a measure named 'Indif' that stands for independent difference and measures the pairwise correlation among attributes. Given the Indif values of all pairs of attributes, they propose a greedy algorithm to search for 2-way marginals that need to be taken account of. Then they add noise to the marginals to release differentially private query outputs. Synthetic data-sets are generated from noisy marginals using sampling algorithms. It is to be noted here that the PrivSyn algorithm considers only two way marginals and conditional dependence among 3 or more attributes is not taken into consideration here.

PrivBayes: This design [49] assumes a Bayesian network $\mathcal{N}$ for the data that provides a succinct model of the correlations among the attributes in the dataset. Using a set of low dimensional noisy marginals and the assumed network model, one can compute differentially private distribution function of true data and then synthesize a data-set from the modified probability values. This model is highly dependent on the choice of the model, exactly like PGM.

DPCopula: This method was proposed by Li et al. (2014) [23] and is used for high dimensional continuous data-sets. The histogram mechanism incur a lot of inaccuracy when there are a lot of attributes. DPCopula mechanism performs well even in such situations with comparatively less computational complexity. It assumes a Gaussian copula structure for the data distribution and computes differentially private correlation parameters and marginal histograms. Once the differentially private parameters are computed the true data distribution can be estimated from it and synthetic data can be generated accordingly.

DP-WGAN: Another way to generate synthetic data-sets is by using generative networks [44]. Once we have a data-set we can train a generative model G that behaves like the data distribution using GAN. To make it differentially private a laplace noise is added in the stochastic gradient step of the generative algorithm and then synthetic data-sets can be generated from the differentially private version of G. The idea of using a Wasserstein GAN instead of GAN is that a WGAN minimizes the Wasserstein distance, or Earth Mover's Distance among noise and data distribution instead of the general Jensen-Shannon divergence. This metric is usually more useful in case of microdata.

While PGM, PrivSyn, PrivBayes methodologies deal with categorical variables, DPCopula and DPWGAN are for continuous attributes. Since, in practice, data is usually composed of continuous and categorical variables, DPCopula or DPWGAN fails in presence of categorical variables. The discrete models can be applied to mixed type data by considering the histogram bins as a category and the variable as an ordinal variable.

4   Some Common Utility Metrics

For a synthetic data-set, it is not hard to understand the meaning of utility of data. The more close the joint distribution of the synthetic attributes is with the true data distribution, the better utilization is expected from the synthetic data. Traditionally, to measure distance between the true and estimated distribution curve, metrics like Kolomogorov-Smirnov distance, L1 or L2 distances were studied. Some papers also study divergence functions like Kullback-Leibler, Jensen-Shannon for the same purpose. However, these traditional statistical techniques fail to capture the semantic meaning of distances among attribute distributions quite often. NIST in 2021 awarded the work of Li et al. [25] as the best utility metric for checking utility of synthetic data-sets. The authors propose to compute the Marginal Difference (MGD) between true and synthetic data sets as a measure of utility that takes into account both categorical and continuous variables. It uses the Approximate Earth Movers Distance to compute the distances between the marginal data distributions and computes an average over all to return the MGD value. The utility assesment is done considering the ordinal and nominal features of attributes. In this section, we describe the metric in detail.

Let us denote the true and synthetic datasets by D_T and D_S respectively. The MGD metric is computed based on a selected set of marginals Φ from the dataset. The metric, at first, computes a distance named AEMD between two one dimensional discrete distributions and then computes their weighted average based on specified weights given to each marginal to get the final score value.

The AEMD distance is based on the Earth Mover's distance (EMD) between two distributions studied in statistical literature. If two data distributions are considered as two piles of sands on different locations, the EMD between these two distributions P and Q is the minimum cost of moving the pile from one location to the other. The cost function is given by summarizing the product of the amount of mass moved multiplied by the distance between the original and transformed point.

In our case, M denotes the $\chi_i \times \chi_i$ matrix where the j, k^{th} cell denotes the distance between j^{th} and k^{th} bin or category. Clearly all the diagonal elements of the matrix are 0 and each element is in $[0, 1] \cup \infty$ where an infinite distance signifies no possible path between the bins. Also, here $\infty \cdot 0 = 0$. If X_{jk} denotes the cost of moving from j^{th} to k^{th} bin, the AEMD between the marginals P and Q is given by,

$$AEMD_{M,\triangle}(P,Q) = \frac{1}{\parallel Q \parallel_1} \min_X \sum_{j,k} X_{jk} M_{jk} + \sum_k \max\{|\sum_j X_{jk} - Q_k| - \triangle, 0\}$$

such that $\sum_k X_{jk} = P_j$ for every $j \in \chi_i$. Here $\parallel Q \parallel_1$ denotes the L_1 norm of the marginal Q and $\triangle$ is a parameter of relaxation such that if the Kolmogorov-Smirnov distance between P and Q is less than $\triangle$, AEMD returns a score value 0.

5   A Privacy-Utility Tradeoff Problem

Privacy guarantee to individuals is important but a data-set is of no use if the inference made from it are far from reality. Guaranteeing privacy is hard and so is finding ideal utility metrics, but what is probably the biggest challenge is to find a tradeoff between privacy and utility. It is not counter intuitive that as the level of privacy protection increases, utility of data reduces.

The research on the privacy utility tradeoff problem started long ago and a few earlier works like Cox et al. (2011) [5] Fienberg et al. (2010) [13] can be taken account of. Some other works such as Sankar et al. (2013) [41] Ghatak and Roy (2019) [18] discuss the same paradigm. However, the privacy guarantees mentioned by these are not as strong as differential privacy. Muralidhar et al. (2020) [37] argues that differential privacy is not a very good privacy measure to choose for this type of problem as the parameter ϵ is neither a measure of the level of privacy guarantee nor of utility. Hence it gives no idea to the amount of information lost due to privacy protection. Thus the tradeoff problem cannot be approached with differential privacy.

Recently, Salamation et al. (2020) [40] discusses a privacy utility tradeoff problem with a different framework than the previous ones. In their set-up, the curator keeps the sensitive data to himself while transfering only the non-sensitive data to the public, but distorting it because much information about the sensitive data gets revealed with it. They define an optimization algorithm to find an ideal mechanism for the generation of obfuscated synthetic data inspired by the information bottleneck optimization problem used in machine learning. In this section, we briefly discuss this privacy-utility tradeoff problem.

Let us denote the sensitive data by S, the nonsensitive data by X and the shared data as Y. The curator has X and S in hand and wants to protect S. But since X and S are correlated, X carries information about S. Thus X is transformed to Y before release but in a way such that Y carries the maximum information about X. The authors make an assumption that $S \to X \to Y$ satisfy the Markov property, i.e., the distribution of $\{Y \mid X, S\}$ is dependent only on X given the information on both X and S. Measuring the information contained in a data by its entropy $H(X) = -E[\log(p_X(X))]$, and the mutual information shared between any X and Y by $I(X,Y) = E[\log \dfrac{p_{XY}(X,Y)}{p_X(X)p_Y(Y)}]$, they propose to solve an optimization algorithm, termed as *Privacy Funnel* given by,

$$\text{Minimize } I(S,Y)$$

$$p_{Y \mid X} : I(X,Y) \geq t$$

for a given utility level t, i.e., among all the possible transformations for which $I(X,Y) \geq t$, the *Privacy Funnel* chooses the one that minimizes $I(S,Y)$.

A few more similar works were discussed by Zwakenberg et al. (2020) [26] Wang et al. (2017) [45].

6   A Real Life Example

To practically validate the use of the existing algorithms, we wished to test the procedures on a real-life data-set. For the given purpose, we chose the "Insurance" Data Set, which is publicly available online. We noted that in the given data-set there was a security threat. The data-set consisted of 1338 individual information corresponding to 7 attributes like age, sex, bmi, number of children, smoking habit, residential region and charges paid for insurance. If an intruder knows that his target individual is a male senior citizen residing in southeast region and having 3 children, then looking at the data he will find that there is only one row corresponding to this information. Thus he will know about the bmi, smoking habit and charges of the individual. Thus the released data is not secure.

Since there are 7 attributes in the dataset consisting of continuous variables like bmi, charges, categorical attributes like sex, residence and smoking habit and also the discrete ordinal variables age and number of children. We grouped the data into m bins where $m \approx n^{1/3} \approx 11$. The contingency table formed of resulting attributes consisted of $p = 12776$ unknown distinct parameters to be estimated. As $p >> 1338$, we faced the curse of dimensionality. Taking $\alpha = 0.1$, the laplace noise has scale parameter 20 while each cell consisted of either 0 members or small number (≤ 5) of members. This would raise a huge question on the remaining utility of data as most of it becomes noise. So we must choose a high dimensional remedy like PGM in this case.

For our validation, we run the program in Python 3.10 and chose two marginal queries to check whether the true and synthetic data are giving similar results. The marginals we chose were the contingency tables formed of 'sex' and 'smoker' and 'children' and 'bmi'. For the first contingency table, four parameters were to be estimated and for the second one sixty six. Choosing both the security parameters to be 1, for the first table the errors were given by $(0.02256, -0.02171, -0.00865, 0.00781)$. The second table resulted in error values $(-0.00051, 0.01162 \cdots)$. The maximum absolute values for each were given by 0.02256 and 0.0170 respectively.

7 Conclusion and Remarks

Although the last decade has witnessed serious attention to privacy preserving protocols to microdata and generation of synthetic data from it, yet perhaps there is a lot more to be done in this field. The protocols, although proven to be feasible lack proper analysis over different metric spaces of data structures. Dwork et al. (2006) [12] shows that when noise is added to histogram counts instead of raw data, the noise parameter involved is free of data range. However, in case large amounts of data are not available at present for each cell, like the case in our data-set, dealing with small samples and large noises are still hard which affects the utility of synthetic data produced.

Moreover, in case of continuous attributes, differential privacy assumes the data range for the attributes to be known and finite. However, that is not the case in general and the scaling is done based on minimum and maximum of the available values. Proper analysis is not given to the ideal choice of data range from given data.

Other than all the struggles to develop useful protocols for inferencing, the choice of privacy parameter in α differential privacy is perhaps the most vital issue currently as most organizations are keeping $\alpha \geq 1$ to maintain data utility which is harmful for security assurance to individuals.

Acknowledgments. We are grateful to the reviewers of SciSec 2022 for their thorough proof-reading and valuable comments on our paper.

References

1. Bachi, R., Baron, R.: Confidentiality problems related to data banks. Bull. Int. Stat. Inst. **43**, 225–241 (1969)
2. Bagrow, J.P., Liu, X., Mitchell, L.: Information flow reveals prediction limits in online social activity. Nat. Hum. Behav. (2019). https://doi.org/10.1038/s41562-018-0510-5
3. Bakshy, E., Rosenn, I., Marlow, C., Adamic, L.: The role of social networks in information diffusion. In: Proceedings of the 21st Annual Conference on World Wide Web (2012). https://doi.org/10.1145/2187836.2187907

4. Cassel, C.: Probability based disclosures in personal integrity and the need for data in the social sciences, pp. 189–193. Stockholm Swedish council for the social sciences (1976)

5. Cox, L.H., et al.: Risk-utility paradigms for statistical disclosure limitation: how to think, but not how to act [with discussions]. International Statistical Review/Revue Internationale de Statistique **79**(2), 160–199 (2011). https://www.jstor.org/stable/41305021

6. Dalenius, T.: The invasion of privacy problem and statistics production-an overview. Statistisk Tidskrzft **12**, 213–225 (1974)

7. Dalenius, T., Reiss, S.P.: Data-swapping: a technique for disclosure control. J. Stat. Plann. Infer. **6**, 73–85 (1982)

8. DeGroot, M.H.: Optimal Statistical Decisions. Mc-Graw-Hill, New York (1970)

9. Dong, J., Roth, A., Su, W.J.: Gaussian differential privacy (2019)

10. Duncan, G., Lambert, D.: Disclosure-limited data dissemination. J. Am. Stat. Assoc. **81**, 10–28 (1986)

11. Duncan, G., Lambert, D.: The risk of disclosure for microdata. J. Bus. Econ. Stat. **7**, 207–217 (1989)

12. Dwork, C., McSherry, F., Nissim, K., Smith, A.: Calibrating noise to sensitivity in private data analysis. In: Halevi, S., Rabin, T. (eds.) TCC 2006. LNCS, vol. 3876, pp. 265–284. Springer, Heidelberg (2006). https://doi.org/10.1007/11681878_14

13. Fienberg, S.E., Rinaldo, A., Yang, X.: Differential privacy and the risk-utility tradeoff for multi-dimensional contingency tables. In: Domingo-Ferrer, J., Magkos, E. (eds.) PSD 2010. LNCS, vol. 6344, pp. 187–199. Springer, Heidelberg (2010). https://doi.org/10.1007/978-3-642-15838-4_17

14. Frank, O.: An application of information theory to the problem of statistical disclosure. J. Stat. Plann. Infer. **2**, 143–152 (1978)

15. Frank, O.: Inferring individual information from released statistics. paper presented at the 42nd Session of the Intemational Statistical Institute Subcommittee on Disclosure Avoidance Techniques Federal Committee on Manila Philippines (1979)

16. Frank, O.: Statistical disclosure control. Technical report 108, University of California, Riverside (1982)

17. Fuller, W.A.: Masking procedures for microdata disclosure limitation. J. Official Stat. **9**, 383–406 (1993)

18. Ghatak, D., Roy, B.: Estimation of true quantiles from quantitative data obfuscated with additive noise. J. Official Stat. **34**, 671–694 (2018)

19. Ghatak, D.: Data obfuscation. Thesis submitted to ISI Kolkata (2019)

20. Gouweleeuw, J., Kooimann, P., L.Willenberg, Dewolf, P.: Post randomization for statistical disclosure control; theory and implementation. J. Official Stat. **14**(4), 463–478 (1998)

21. Hall, R., Rinaldo, A., Wasserman, L.: Random differential privacy. J. Priv. Confidentiality, **4**–**2**, 43–59 (2012)

22. Hardt, M., Talwar, K.: On the geometry of differential privacy. vol. 705:714. STOC 10: In: Proceedings of the forty-second ACM symposium on Theory of computing (2010). https://doi.org/10.1145/1806689.1806786

23. Li, H., Xiong, L., Jiang, X.: Differentially private synthesization of multi-dimensionaldata using copula functions. In: 17th International Conference on Extending Database Technology (2014). https://doi.org/10.5441/002/edbt.2014.43

24. Li, N., Li, T., Venkatasubramanian, S.: t-closeness: privacy beyond k-anonymity and l-diversity. In: IEEE 23rd International Conference on Data Engineering, Istanbul, pp. 106–115 (2007). https://doi.org/10.1109/ICDE.2007.367856

25. Li, Z., Dang, T., Wang, T., Li, N.: MGD: a utility metric for private data publication, pp. 106–119 (2021). https://doi.org/10.1145/3491371.3491385

26. Lopuhaä-Zwakenberg, M., Tong, H., Škorić, B.: Data sanitisation protocols for the privacy funnel with differential privacy guarantees. Int. J. Adv. Secur. **13**(3–4), 162–174 (2021). https://arxiv.org/abs/2008.13151

27. Machanavajjhala, A., Gehrke, J., Kifer, D., Venkitasubramaniam, M.: L-diversity: privacy beyond k-anonymity. In: 22nd International Conference on Data Engineering (ICDE 2006), Atlanta, GA, USA (2006). https://doi.org/10.1109/ICDE.2006.1

28. Mahawaga Arachchige, P.C., Bertok, P., Khalil, I., Liu, D., Camtepe, S., Atiquzzaman, M.: Local differential privacy for deep learning. IEEE Internet Things J. **7**, 5827–5842 (2020)

29. Matthews, G., Harel, O.: Data confidentiality: a review of methods for statistical disclosure limitation and methods for assessing privacy. Stat. Surv. **5**, 1–29 (2011). https://doi.org/10.1214/11-SS074

30. McKenna, R., Miklau, G., Hay, M., Machanavajjhala, A.: Optimizing error of high-dimensional statistical queries under differential privacy. In: Proceedings of the VLDB Endowment, vol. 11(10) (2018). https://doi.org/10.14778/3231751.3231769

31. McKenna, R., Sheldon, D., Miklau, G.: Graphical-model based estimation and inference for differential privacy abs/1901.09136 (2019). https://proceedings.mlr.press/v97/mckenna19a.html

32. McSherry, F., Talwar, K.: Mechanism design via differential privacy. In: Proceedings - Annual IEEE Symposium on Foundations of Computer Science, FOCS, pp. 94–103 (2007). https://doi.org/10.1109/FOCS.2007.66

33. Mironov, I.: Rényi differential privacy. In: IEEE 30th Computer Security Foundations Symposium (CSF), pp. 263–275 (2017). https://doi.org/10.1109/CSF.2017.11

34. Moore, R.A.: Controlled data swapping techniques for masking use microdata sets. US Bureau of the Census, Statistical Research Division (1996). https://www.census.gov/srd/www/byyear.html2

35. Mugge, R.: Issues in protecting confidentiality in national health statistics. In: Proceedings of the Section on Survey Research Methods, American Statistical Association, pp. 592–594 (1983)

36. Muralidhar, K., Parsa, R., Sarathy, R.: A general additive data perturbation method for database security. Manage. Sci. **45**, 1399–1415 (1999)

37. Muralidhar, K., Domingo-Ferrer, J., Martínez, S.: epsilon-differential privacy for microdata releases does not guarantee confidentiality (let alone utility). In: Book: Privacy in Statistical Databases, UNESCO Chair in Data Privacy, International Conference, PSD 2020, Tarragona, Spain, 23–25 September 2020, Proceedings (2020). https://doi.org/10.1007/978-3-030-57521-2_2

38. Poole, W.K.: Estimation of the distribution function of a continuous type random variable through randomized response. J. Am. Stat. Assoc. **69**(348), 1002–1005. Taylor and Francis (1974)

39. Rubin, D.B.: Discussion statistical disclosure limitation. J. Official Stat. **461–468**, 461–468 (1993)

40. Salamatian, S., Calmon, F., Fawaz, N., Makhdoumi, A., Médard, M.: Privacy-utility tradeoff and privacy funnel (2020)

41. Sankar, L., Rajagopalan, S.R., Poor, H.V.: Utility-privacy tradeoffs in databases: an information-theoretic approach. IEEE Trans. Inform. Forensics Secur. **8**(6), 838–852 (2013). https://doi.org/10.1109/TIFS.2013.2253320

42. Steinberg, J., Pritzker, L.: Some experiences with and reflections on data linkage in the united states. Bull. Int. Stat. Inst. 786–808 (1967)

43. Sweeney, L.: k-anonymity: A model for protecting privacy. Int. J. Uncertainty, Fuzziness Knowl. Based Syst. 10(5), 557–570 (2002)

44. Torkzadehmahani, R., Kairouz, P., Paten, B.: DP-CGAN: differentially private synthetic data and label generation. In: Proceedings of the IEEE Conference on Computer Vision and Pattern Recognition Workshops (2019)

45. Wang, W., Ying, L., Zhang, J.: On the relation between identifiability, differential privacy, and mutual-information privacy. IEEE Trans. Inf. Theory 62(9), 5018–5029 (2016). https://doi.org/10.1109/TIT.2016.2584610

46. Warner, S.L.: Randomized response: a survey technique for eliminating evasive answer bias. J. Am. Stat. Assoc. 60, 63–69 (1965)

47. Wasserman, L., Zhou, S.: A statistical framework for differential privacy. J. Am. Stat. Assoc. 105(489), 375–389 (2010). https://doi.org/10.1198/jasa.2009.tm08651

48. Winograd-Cort, D., Haeberlen, A., Roth, A., Pierce, B.C.: A framework for adaptive differential privacy. Proc. ACM Program. Lang. (2017). https://doi.org/10.1145/3110254

49. Zhang, J., Cormode, G., Procopiuc, C.M., Srivastava, D., Xiao, X.: PrivBayes: Private data release via Bayesian networks. ACM Trans. Database Syst. 42(4), 1–41 (2017). https://doi.org/10.1145/3134428

50. Zhang, T.K.N.C., You, J.: Measuring identification risk in microdata release and its control by post-randomization. Center for Disclosure Avoidance Research U.S. Census Bureau Washington DC 20233 (2016)

51. Zhang, Z., et al.: PrivSyn: differentially private data synthesis. arXiv:2012.15128 (2021)

Multi-client Private Decision Tree Classification Using Threshold Fully Homomorphic Encryption

Bo Pang[1,2]([✉]) and Mingsheng Wang[1]

[1] State Key Laboratory of Information Security, Institute of Information Engineering, Chinese Academy of Sciences, Beijing, China
`pangbo215@gmail.com`
[2] School of Cyber Security, University of Chinese Academy of Sciences, Beijing, China

Abstract. Decision tree is a widely-used machine-learning classifier known for its simplicity and effectiveness. Recent works mainly focus on how to privately evaluate a decision tree in a two-party setting where the sensitive data of the client or the decision tree model of the server is kept secret from another party. However, collaboration among mutually untrusted clients for machine learning tasks is needed more and more.

In this paper, we consider a mutli-client private decision tree classification protocol, in which one server holds the decision tree and multiple clients provide secret data. At the end of the protocol, either the clients or the server could learn the classification result while protect privacy of each individual input. More importantly, we would also minimize the interaction with each client. To reach the goal, we make use of the threshold fully homomorphic encryption. Our protocols are proven secure against "honest-but-lazy" adversaries. Furthermore, we try to improve the computation overhead and ciphertext size, making our construction much more efficient.

Keywords: Private decision tree classification · Threshold fully homomorphic encryption · Multi-party computation

1 Introduction

Machine learning classification algorithms can make the predication when given new data as a query, which are widely applicable, used to recommendation systems, spam filtering and disease diagnosis, etc. In order to provide accurate predication, they often need to access to sensitive information that clients may not want to reveal. Leakage of sensitive data, like health records in remote diagnosis, would be a life-or-death problem. On the other hand, the classification model could be a valuable asset that the server prefer not to share, as the result of dedicated research effort which spent a considerable amount of resources. Moreover, making the model public may leak information about the sensitive training data [17], even violating laws and regulations.

C. Su and K. Sakurai (Eds.): SciSec 2022 Workshops, CCIS 1680, pp. 181–195, 2022.
https://doi.org/10.1007/978-981-19-7769-5_14

Ideally, privacy-preserving machine learning classification protects the privacy of both the client and the model owner. In this paper, we focus on decision-tree classifier [9], which is well-known for its simplicity, effectiveness and low training cost [20]. The evaluation process starts from the root node as the first decision node of the tree. It compares the node-specific threshold value in the model with one of the input variables in the client query. The boolean results of comparison decide which child node to traverse. The process iterates across each level and eventually leads to a leaf node, representing a classification label as a tree classification result.

Recently, many efficient privacy-preserving solutions for decision tree evaluation in a two-party setting has been proposed [6,16,19,24–27]. For example, Tai et al. propose a private decision-tree evaluation protocol purely based on additive homomorphic encryption, without introducing dummy nodes for hiding the tree structure, therefore it works well for sparse trees, which are abundant in practice. However, in many relevant scenarios, collaboration among multiple mutually untrusted clients becomes a commonplace, as it provides more precise classification. For instance, multiple hospitals, holding different health records of one patient, collaborate to offer a better disease diagnosis, while this can only happen if the privacy of each individual input is guaranteed.

Multi-client Private Decision Tree Classification. To capture the above exemplary collaboration scenario, we provide multi-client private decision tree classification protocols in which sensitive input variables from multiple clients might be sent to a server for collaborative classification. Specifically, we wish to have a 3-round protocol, that multiple clients initializes the protocol with a first round message, then the server does the node evaluation and path evaluation locally and sends out the second round message, and then multiple clients and the server jointly recover the classification label as the evaluation result. The security requirement is that either the server or multiple clients can learn the final classification result and nothing more. Inherently, the server could derive the corresponding tree path of clients' input query from the received classification label, since it holds the tree model. More importantly, we would like to minimize the cost of clients since they might be weak IoT devices: (1) both the computation and communication cost of each client are independent of the tree size; (2) and allowing the clients to go offline after the first round if they are not interested in receiving the final result, or might lose connectivity and hence be unable to continue the protocol, what are called "honest but lazy" parties [2].

Overview of Our Construction. Motivated by the 3-round multi-client private decision tree classification evaluation protocol while keeping the minimal cost of clients, we make use of a low-depth threshold fully homomorphic encryption (TFHE).

The basic idea is: (1) Each client posts a component-wise encryption of her secret input variables, and then the server does a comparison of the encrypted clients' input variable and his own encrypted threshold value of each decision node with homomorphic operations. Then the server stores the encrypted result bit of all node's comparisons at their child nodes. For a decision node $d \in \mathcal{D}$, let the encrypted comparison bit be given by $\mathsf{Enc}(b) \leftarrow \mathsf{Enc}(x_{d.index} \geq d.threshold)$, then store $\mathsf{Enc}(b)$ at the right child node and $\mathsf{Enc}(1-b)$ at the left child node. In order to find the correct traversing path with corresponding classification label in the tree, all path should be considered. All path can be securely evaluated by combining the comparison bits of all decision nodes on that path. In particular, the server could homomorphically multiply the comparison bits per path, only the correct path will have a encrypted value $\ell.cmp$ equal to 1, otherwise equal to 0. The corresponding leaf node $\ell \in \mathcal{L}$ holds the correct classification label ℓ_{label}. (2) The server broadcasts the encryption of correct classification label by homomorphically adding $\sum_{\ell \in \mathcal{L}} \mathsf{Enc}(\ell.cmp) \cdot \mathsf{Enc}(\ell_{label})$. (3) As long as a threshold number of clients and the server are available to publish a partial decryption (say t out of n), the correct classification label will reveal even if several weak clients are already offline. Moreover, the compactness property of TFHE scheme ensures depth-proportional communication complexity, independent of the tree size.

Certainly, the above basic solution based on TFHE succeeds to bring down the overhead for multiple clients. However, the computation overhead for the server is too high to restrict its usage in practice. Tuneo et al. showed that it needs several seconds of a single execution to output the classification result for a tree with 50–500 decision nodes, even in a two-party setting [25]. It is well-known that homomorphic multiplication causes a larger noise growth than homomorphic addition. Namely, lowing the multiplicative depth of path evaluation could significantly save on computational costs, also the ciphertext size. Therefore, we turn to Tai et al's approach of path evaluation, which only invokes homomorphic additions [24]. Specifically, their approach stores $\mathsf{Enc}(1-b)$ at the right child node, while $\mathsf{Enc}(b)$ at the left child node. The paths are evaluated by adding up the encrypted comparison bits of all nodes on that path homomorphically. This summation is called the path cost. Now, only if the path cost equal to 0, the corresponding leaf node holds the correct classification label.

In contrary to the above basic solution, to correctly output the final classification label, we let the threshold number of parties jointly decrypt all path costs. Then they can find the exact path, whose cost is equal to 0, and the corresponding leaf node's classification label can be sent by adding the label to the path cost homomorphically. To avoid any more information about non-selected paths and classification labels being leakage, [24] multiply the path costs with random non-zero elements r_0, r_1.

Remarkably, in our $n-1$ clients and one server scenario, since we assume that the collusion might happen among some clients and the server, the two random non-zero values r_0, r_1 must be chosen independently and privately. Otherwise, either $r_0 = 0$ or $r_1 = 0$ will violate the correctness of the protocol or the privacy of the server's tree model. Most importantly, the leakage of r_0 will directly leak non-selected path costs, violating the privacy of both the clients and the server. If r_0 and r_1 are not chosen independently, the non-selected classification labels might be revealed. Therefore, in our multi-client private decision tree classification protocol, we require n clients and the server provide their own contribution r_i^j in the first round by broadcasting its encryption, where $i = 0, 1$, such that $r_i = r_i^1 + \cdots + r_i^{n+1}$, assuming these parties are semi-honest or relying on non-interactive zero-knowledge proof of knowledge to against malicious adversaries. Additionally, we still require the server to do random shuffle of the leaf nodes, which was introduced in [24], in order to prevent the clients from getting knowledge about the location of the output leaf node within the tree.

For threshold FHE decryption by applying Shamir t-out-of-n secret sharing to the secret key sk, as pointed out by Asharov et al. [1], we need each decryptor i to add additional smudging noise to the partial decryption, preventing the leakage of information about her secret key share sk_i. Surprisingly, all other works [1,5] use a comparatively less efficient method, where each party adds independent noise to the partial decryption before broadcasting it. However, this method will not work for our case. In our reconstruction procedure, these noise values are blown up by $\mathcal{O}((n!)^2)$, when the partial decryptions are multiplied by Lagrange coefficients. To solve this problem, we take the technique of [18]: let each decryptor i secret share some small noise e_i into $(e_i^1, \cdots, e_i^n)$ and send the shares the other parties. Then each decryptor i locally adds $\sum_j e_j^i$ to its partial decryption. Since the Shamir secret sharing scheme is linear, this is equivalent to add $e_1 + \cdots + e_n$ to the original reconstructed output value, significantly reducing the noise growth and thus improving the overall performance of our TFHE construction.

1.1 Additional Related Works

2-Party Private Decision Tree Evaluation. The existing two-party private decision tree evaluation protocols can be divided into three categories based on the underlying techniques, including homomorphic encryption, garbled circuit and secret sharing.

Bost et al. [6] treated the decision tree as a high-degree polynomial, with the classification result as the output, then use fully homomorphic encryption (FHE) to evaluate it. Wu et al. [27] got rid of FHE by adding dummy node to form a complete binary-tree for hiding the tree structure. But in many real cases, the decision tree is deep-but-sparse, and padding such a tree into a complete one results in huge waste in communication and computation. Tai et al. [24] did not introduce dummy nodes to complete tree transformation, and proposed a more efficient protocol with their novel concept of "path cost", to execute path evaluation via purely additive homomorphic encryption. In 2018, Joye and Salehi [19] reduced the amount of secure comparisons in [27] to $d - 1$, where d is the tree depth and each comparison takes 2 rounds at each tree level. Thus the total number of rounds is linear in d. Unlike [24], this protocol still requires the server to add dummy nodes for hiding the tree structure. Lately, Tueno et al. [25] introduced a non-interactive decision tree evaluation protocol by evaluating the tree on ciphertext encrypted under the client's public key homomorphically.

Concurrent to [19], Tueno et al. [26] proposed a sub-linear decision-tree protocol by representing the trees as arrays and implementing oblivious array indexing (OAI) with garbled circuit (GC). Earlier, both Brinckell et al. [9] and Barni et al. [3] proposed privacy-preserving decision tree evaluation solutions based on GC, which were outperformed by the above approach.

Cock et al. [16] proposed an information theoretically secure decision tree evaluation protocol based on secret sharing and utilize commodity-based cryptography [4] to reduce the number of interactions. Their protocol performs better than all other protocols for especially small trees. But their protocol is less efficient for large trees, since it is still linear in the tree size. In 2019, Damgard et al. [15] used a new secret-sharing based protocol [14], that works over rings instead of fields, to significantly improve efficiency of implementations, although with a slightly more communication cost.

Threhosld Fully Homomorphic Encryption. A TFHE scheme allows evaluation on encrypted data as well as threshold decryption of ciphertexts, where a threshold number of key-holders must come together to decrypt any ciphertext.

In 2012, Asharov et al. [1] extended the FHE constructions of [7] with n-out-of n threshold decryption procedure to enable multiparty computation with low communication (independent of the function being computed), low interaction and cloud-assisted computation (the bulk of the computation can be efficiently outsourced to a cloud service). Their protocol is 3 rounds of interaction in the common random string (CRS) model and 2 rounds when the Setup could be reused. By assuming that non-interactive zero-knowledge arguments (NIZKs) exit, the construction is secure under (ring) learn with errors (LWE) assumption, against fully malicious attackers.

Multi-Key FHE [8,11,13,21,23] could dynamically extend a ciphertext encrypted under one key to a concatenation of keys from all parties. López-Alt et al. [21] firstly proposed an Multi-Key FHE scheme based on the NTRU assumption. Clear and McGoldrich [13] introduced an LWE-based construction. In 2016, Mukherjee and Wichs [22] proposed the first 2 rounds general multi-party computation (MPC) protocol in the CRS model under standard assumptions without obfuscation, by significantly simplifying the construction of [13]. These schemes are single-hop for keys where the list of parties has to be known before the computation starts. In the same year, both Peikert-Shiehian [23] and Brakershi-Pelman [8] tried to solve this issue. Chen et al. [11] constructed a multi-hop scheme which can encrypt a ring element, instead of a single bit. Unfortunately, all previous schemes are impractical and can not be implemented. Recently, Chen et al. [10] proposed the first attempt to implement an multi-hop Multi-Key FHE scheme.

In 2018, Boneh et al. [5] designed a new primitive named the universal thresholdizer, which is constructed from the relatively heavy threshold fully homomorphic encryption (TFHE), supporting t-out-of-n threshold access structure. In 2020, Badrinarayanan et al. [2] introduced the new notion called threshold mult-key FHE (TMFHE), to handle arbitrary access patterns that can reconstruct the output. However, the above two schemes are impractical due to the method of dealing with the noise blow up. In particular, Boneh et al. [5] firstly proved that $\{0,1\}$-LSSS class is sufficient to express t-out-of-n threshold access structure. Then they used a different linear secret sharing scheme where the reconstruction coefficients are always binary, instead of multiplying with the Lagrange coefficients. But the transformation from threshold access structure to $\{0,1\}$-LSSS is really expensive and impractical.

2 Preliminaries

2.1 Decision-Tree Classifiers

In this work, we consider that multiple clients contribute their individual input variables and one server provides the tree model. Intuitively, the decision tree classification on an input query x means traversing the decision tree; at each decision node, the corresponding input entry is compared to the node-specific threshold value. Based on the comparison result, either the right or left child node is picked as the next node. The traversal ends at a certain leaf node, which tells the unique classification label of the input query according to the tree.

Let the input x_i of the client i be a k_i-dimension positive integer vector over Z, then the total input query is $x = (x_1, \cdots, x_{n-1}) \in Z^k$, where $k = k_1 + \cdots + k_{n-1}$. Let T be a decision tree, including a set of decision nodes $\mathcal{D}$ and a set of leaf nodes $\mathcal{L}$. Then the decision tree evaluation on input $x = (x_1, \cdots, x_{n-1})$ is given by $\ell_{label} = T(x)$ with $T : Z^k \to \{\ell^1_{label}, \cdots, \ell^m_{label}\}$, in which m is the number of leaf nodes. This function starts from the root node and then does a comparison at each decision node. Let j be the index of a decision node and f be the function that mapping the decision node index j to the corresponding input entry's index $f(j)$. Besides, let t_j be the threshold value of decision node j. Then if $x_{f(j)} \geq t_j$ holds for node j, the right child is chosen as the next decision node, otherwise the left child node. At the end, the function outputs the classification label ℓ_{label} of the final leaf node.

2.2 Threshold Fully Homomorphic Encryption

In this work, we provide two efficient mutli-client private decision tree classification protocols relying on a low-depth threshold fully homomorphic encryption (TFHE). Here, we review the standard syntax and security definitions of TFHE.

Definition 1 (Threshold Fully Homomorphic Encryption [5]). *Let $P = \{P_1, \cdots, P_n\}$ be a set of parties and let $\mathbb{S}$ be a class of efficient access structure on P. A threshold fully homomorphic encryption scheme for $\mathbb{S}$ is a tuple of PPT algorithms $TFHE = (TFHE.Setup, TFHE.Enc, TFHE.Eval, TFHE.PartDec, TFHE.FinDec)$ with the following properties:*

- *$TFHE.Setup(1^\lambda, 1^d, \mathbb{A}) \to (pk, sk_1, \cdots, sk_n)$: On input the security parameter λ, a depth bound d and an access structure $\mathbb{A}$, it outputs a public key pk, and a set of secret key shares $sk_1, \cdots, sk_n$.*
- *$TFHE.Enc(pk, \mu) \to ct$: On input a public key pk, and a plaintext $\mu \in \mathbb{F}_2^N$ for $N = poly(\lambda)$, it outputs a ciphertext ct.*
- *$TFHE.Eval(pk, C, ct_1, \cdots, ct_l) \to ct_C$: On input a public key pk, circuit $C : \mathbb{F}_2^{N \times l} \to \mathbb{F}_2^N$ of depth at most d, and a set of ciphertexts $ct_1, \cdots, ct_l$, it outputs a ciphertext ct_C.*
- *$TFHE.PartDec(pk, ct, sk_i) \to p_i$: On input a public key pk, a ciphertext ct, and a secret key share sk_i, it outputs a partial decryption p_i related to the party P_i.*

– $TFHE.FinDec(pk, ct, B) \rightarrow \mu$: *On input a public key pk, a ciphertext ct and a set $B = \{p_i\}_{i \in S}$ for some $S \subseteq \{P_1, \cdots, P_n\}$, it outputs a plaintext $\mu \in \mathbb{F}_2^N \cup \perp$.*

In order for a TFHE to be considered secure for our purposes, it must satisfy the compactness, correctness, semantic security and simulation security.

Definition 2 (Compactness [5]**).** *We say that a TFHE scheme is compact if there exists polynomials $poly_1(\cdot)$ and $poly_2(\cdot)$ such that for all security parameter λ, depth bound d, circuit $C : \mathbb{F}_2^{N \times l} \rightarrow \mathbb{F}_2^N$ of depth at most d, access structure $\mathbb{A}$, and $\mu \in \mathbb{F}_2^N$, the following holds. For $(pk, sk_1, \cdots, sk_n) \leftarrow TFHE.Setup(1^\lambda, 1^d, \mathbb{A})$, $ct_i \leftarrow TFHE.Enc(pk, \mu_i)$ for $i \in [l]$, $ct_C \leftarrow TFHE.Eval\ (pk, C, ct_1, \cdots, ct_l)$, $p_j \leftarrow TFHE.PartDec(pk, ct_C, sk_j)$ for $j \in [n]$, we have that: $|ct_C| \leq poly_1(\lambda, d)$ and $|p_j| \leq poly_2(\lambda, d, n)$.*

Definition 3 (Evaluation Correctness [5]**).** *We say that a TFHE scheme satisfies evaluation correctness if for all security parameter λ, depth bound d, circuit $C : \mathbb{F}_2^{N \times l} \rightarrow \mathbb{F}_2^N$ of depth at most d, subset $S \in \mathbb{A}$, and $\mu_i \in \mathbb{F}_2^N$ for $i \in [l]$, the following holds. For $(pk, sk_1, \cdots, sk_n) \leftarrow TFHE.Setup(1^\lambda, 1^d, \mathbb{A})$, $ct_i \leftarrow TFHE.Enc(pk, \mu_i)$ for $i \in [l]$, $ct_C \leftarrow TFHE.Eval(pk, C, ct_1, \cdots, ct_l)$, we have that:*
$$\Pr[TFHE.FinDec(pk, ct, \{TFHE.PartDec(pk, ct, sk_i)\}_{i \in S} = C(\mu_1, \cdots, \mu_l))]$$
$$\geq 1 - negl(\lambda).$$

Definition 4 (Semantic Security [5]**).** *We say that a TFHE scheme satisfies semantic security if for all security parameter λ, and depth bound d, the following holds. For any PPT adversary $\mathcal{A}$, the following experiment $Expt_\mathcal{A}^{sem}(1^\lambda, 1^d)$ defined in Fig. 1 outputs 1 with negligible probability.*

$$Expt_\mathcal{A}^{sem}(1^\lambda, 1^d)$$

1. On input the security parameter 1^λ and a circuit depth 1^d, the adversary $\mathcal{A}$ outputs $\mathbb{A} \in \mathbb{S}$.
2. The challenger runs $(pk, sk_1, \cdots, sk_n) \leftarrow TFHE.Setup(1^\lambda, 1^d, \mathbb{A})$ and provides pk to $\mathcal{A}$.
3. $\mathcal{A}$ outputs a set $S \subseteq \{P_1, \cdots, P_n\}$ such that $S \notin \mathbb{A}$ as well as messages $m_0, m_1 \in \mathbb{F}_2^N$.
4. The challenger provides $\{sk_i\}_{i \in S}$ along with $TFHE.Enc(pk, m_b)$ for $m_b \leftarrow \{m_0, m_1\}$ to $\mathcal{A}$.
5. $\mathcal{A}$ outputs a guess m'. The experiment outputs 1 if $m' = m_b$.

Fig. 1. Semantic security experiment for TFHE

Definition 5 (Simulation Security [5]**).** *We say that a TFHE scheme satisfies simulation security if for all security parameter* λ, *depth bound* d, *and access structure* $\mathbb{A}$, *the following holds. There exists a stateful PPT algorithm* $Sim = (Sim_1, Sim_2)$ *such that for any PPT adversary* $\mathcal{A}$, *the follwing experiments* $Expt_{\mathcal{A}}^{Real}(1^\lambda, 1^d)$ *defined in Fig. 2 and* $Expt_{\mathcal{A}}^{Ideal}(1^\lambda, 1^d)$ *defined in Fig. 3 are indistinguishable.*

$$Expt_{\mathcal{A}}^{Real}(1^\lambda, 1^d)$$

1. On input the security parameter 1^λ and a circuit depth 1^d, the adversary $\mathcal{A}$ outputs $\mathbb{A} \in \mathbb{S}$.
2. The challenger runs $(pk, sk_1, \cdots, sk_n) \leftarrow TFHE.Setup(1^\lambda, 1^d, \mathbb{A})$ and provides pk to $\mathcal{A}$.
3. $\mathcal{A}$ outputs a maximal invalid set $S^* \subseteq \{P_1, \cdots, P_n\}$ and messages $\mu_1, \cdots, \mu_l \in \mathbb{F}_2^N$.
4. The challenger provides the keys $\{sk_i\}_{i \in S^*}$ and $\{TFHE.Enc(pk, \mu_i)\}_{i \in [l]}$ to $\mathcal{A}$.
5. $\mathcal{A}$ issues a polynomial number of adaptive queries of the form $(S \subseteq \{P_1, \cdots, P_n\}, C)$ for circuits $C : \mathbb{F}_2^{N \times l} \to \mathbb{F}_2^N$ of depth at most d. For each query, the challenger computes $ct_C \leftarrow TFHE.Eval(pk, C, ct_1, \cdots, ct_l)$ and provides the set $\{TFHE.ParDec(pk, ct_C, sk_i)\}_{i \in S}$ to $\mathcal{A}$.
6. At the end of the experiment, $\mathcal{A}$ outputs a distinguishing bit b.

Fig. 2. Real world SIM-based security experiment for TFHE

$$Expt_{\mathcal{A}}^{Ideal}(1^\lambda, 1^d)$$

1. On input the security parameter 1^λ and a circuit depth 1^d, the adversary $\mathcal{A}$ outputs $\mathbb{A} \in \mathbb{S}$.
2. The challenger runs $(pk, sk_1, \cdots, sk_n, st) \leftarrow Sim_1(1^\lambda, 1^d, \mathbb{A})$ and provides pk to $\mathcal{A}$.
3. $\mathcal{A}$ outputs a maximal invalid set $S^* \subseteq \{P_1, \cdots, P_n\}$ and messages $\mu_1, \cdots, \mu_l \in \mathbb{F}_2^N$.
4. The challenger provides the keys $\{sk_i\}_{i \in S^*}$ and $\{TFHE.Enc(pk, \mu_i)\}_{i \in [l]}$ to $\mathcal{A}$.
5. $\mathcal{A}$ issues a polynomial number of adaptive queries of the form $(S \subseteq \{P_1, \cdots, P_n\}, C)$ for circuits $C : \mathbb{F}_2^{N \times l} \to \mathbb{F}_2^N$ of depth at most d. For each query, the challenger runs the simulator $\{p_i\}_{i \in S} \leftarrow Sim_2(C, \{ct_1, \cdots, ct_l\}, C(\mu_1, \cdots, \mu_l), S, st)$ and sends $\{p_i\}_{i \in S}$ to $\mathcal{A}$.
6. At the end of the experiment, $\mathcal{A}$ outputs a distinguishing bit b.

Fig. 3. Ideal world SIM-based security experiment for TFHE

To conclude, the simulation security definition says that no information abut the secret key shares $sk_1, \cdots, sk_n$ or the messages $\mu_1, \cdots, \mu_l$ should be leaked by the partial or final decryptions, other than what can be directly derived from the result of homomorphic evaluation $C(\mu_1, \cdots, \mu_l)$.

2.3   Additional Building Blocks

In this paper, we divide our decision tree evaluation into secure node evaluation and path evaluation. Here, we recall methods used by Tueno et al. [25] and Tai et al. [24].

Node Data Structure. We make use of the notation and node data structure in [25]. For each node $\nu \in \mathcal{T}$, the following information is stored:

- $\nu.left$: pointer to the left child node.
- $\nu.right$: pointer to the right child node.
- $\nu.cmp$: stores b if ν is the right child node, otherwise $1 - b$, where b is the boolean result of comparison at the parent node. (for the root node, this value is fixed to 1).

And for each decision node $d \in \mathcal{D}$, the following information is stored:

- $d.index$: the index of the corresponding input entry, in the multiple clients' query vector x, for the decision node d.
- $d.threshold$: the threshold value of the decision node d.

Beside, for each leaf node $\ell \in \mathcal{L}$, the following information is stored:

- ℓ_{label}: the corresponding classification label of the leaf node ℓ.

Node Evaluation. For the node evaluation, we need a bit-wise comparison method of the corresponding encrypted input entry and the encrypted node-specific threshold value.

Following the idea of Tuneo et al. [25], we choose the secure comparision protocol proposed by Cheon et al. [12]. Then Tuneo et al. [25] store the encrypted results of all nodes' comparisons at their child nodes. Specifically, for a decision node $d \in \mathcal{D}$, let the encrypted comparison bit result be given by $\mathsf{Enc}(b) \leftarrow \mathsf{Enc}(x_{d.index} \geq d.threshold)$, in which x is the whole input integer vector from multiple clients. Finally, they store $\mathsf{Enc}(b)$ at the right child node, and $\mathsf{Enc}(1-b)$ at the left child node.

Path Evaluation. To be able to output the correct classification label of the clients' input vector, traversing the unique correct path, all paths should be considered. Each path can be evaluated by combining stored comparison bits of all decision nodes on that path.

In the two-party setting, Tueno et al. [25] use the idea that by homomorphically multiplying these comparison bit results per path, only the correct path will have an encrypted value equal to 1, else 0. The corresponding leaf node holds the correct classification label. Finally, they came up with algorithm *Evaluation* as defined in Fig. 4.

Evaluation

1. On input $PathEval(\mathcal{T}, \mathsf{Enc}(x))$.
2. For all $d \in \mathcal{D}$, computes $\mathsf{Enc}(b) \leftarrow \mathsf{Enc}(x_{d.index} \geq d.threshold)$, $\mathsf{Enc}(\nu.right.cmp) \leftarrow \mathsf{Enc}(b)$, and $\mathsf{Enc}(\nu.left.cmp) \leftarrow \mathsf{Enc}(1-b)$.
3. Let Q be a queue, and $Q.enqueue(root)$. While $Q.empty(\cdot) = false$, runs $\nu \leftarrow Q.dequeue(\cdot)$, $\mathsf{Enc}(\nu.right.cmp) \leftarrow \mathsf{Enc}(\nu.right.cmp) \otimes \mathsf{Enc}(\nu.cmp)$, $\mathsf{Enc}(\nu.left.cmp) \leftarrow \mathsf{Enc}(\nu.left.cmp) \otimes \mathsf{Enc}(\nu.cmp)$, if $\nu.right \in \mathcal{D}$, then $Q.enqueue(\nu.right)$, and if $\nu.left \in \mathcal{D}$, then $Q.enqueue(\nu.left)$.
4. Let $\mathsf{Enc}(result) = \mathsf{Enc}(0)$, outputs $\mathsf{Enc}(result) \leftarrow \mathsf{Enc}(result) \oplus \sum_{\ell \in \mathcal{L}}(\mathsf{Enc}(\ell.cmp) \otimes \mathsf{Enc}(\ell_{label}))$.

Fig. 4. Evalation algorithm in [25]

Additionally, Tai et al. [24] proposed another method for path evaluation, purely based on homomorphic addition. They store $\mathsf{Enc}(1-b)$ at the right child node and $\mathsf{Enc}(b)$ at the left child node, in which b is the comparison bit at the parent decision node. Then each path can be evaluated by adding up the encrypted comparison bits of all notes on that path homomorphically. This summation is called the path cost. And only if the encrypted path cost is equal to 0, this path corresponds to the correct leaf node, holding the correct classification label. In their method, *root.cmp* should be set to 0.

3 Our Construction

Multi-client Private Decision Tree Classification. In this section, we present our multi-client private decision tree classification protocol, to capture the scenario in which multiple clients provide secret data and a single server owns the decision tree model. Particularly, we requires at most the server and clients could gain the knowledge of the classification result and nothing more about other parties individual input. Our protocol is secure against "honest-but-lazy" parties, allowing several clients to go offline after participating in the first round.

Obviously, by using TFHE techniques suggested by [5], instead of evaluating the tree on ciphertext under a single client's public key, we can generalize the construction in [25] to obtain a multi-client private decision tree classification scheme. However, there are two efficiency issues that we need to tackle.

Firstly, as pointed out by Tuneo et al. [25] themselves, the computation overhead for the server still very high, restricting its usage in practice. To reduce the overall computation overhead, we ultilize the fact that the homomorphic multiplication brings much more noise growth than homomorphic encryption. Namely, we need a low multiplicative depth tree evaluation circuit, in order to save on computational costs and ciphertext size. Then we turn to the novel concept called "path cost", proposed by Tai et al [24]. By combining the node evaluation of [25] and the path evaluation of [24], we propose the following *Evaluation** algorithm as defined in Fig. 5.

Evaluation*

1. On input $PathEval(\mathcal{T}, \mathsf{Enc}(x))$.
2. For all $d \in \mathcal{D}$, computes $\mathsf{Enc}(b) \leftarrow \mathsf{Enc}(x_{d.index} \geq d.threshold)$, $\mathsf{Enc}(\nu.right.cmp) \leftarrow \mathsf{Enc}(1 - b)$, and $\mathsf{Enc}(\nu.left.cmp) \leftarrow \mathsf{Enc}(b)$.
3. Let Q be a queue, and $Q.enqueue(root)$. While $Q.empty(\cdot) = false$, runs $\nu \leftarrow Q.dequeue(\cdot)$, $\mathsf{Enc}(\nu.right.cmp) \leftarrow \mathsf{Enc}(\nu.right.cmp) \oplus \mathsf{Enc}(\nu.cmp)$, $\mathsf{Enc}(\nu.left.cmp) \leftarrow \mathsf{Enc}(\nu.left.cmp) \oplus \mathsf{Enc}(\nu.cmp)$, if $\nu.left \in \mathcal{D}$, then $Q.enqueue(\nu.left)$, and if $\nu.right \in \mathcal{D}$, then $Q.enqueue(\nu.right)$.
4. For all $\ell \in \mathcal{L}$, computes the encryption of two uniformly non-zero random value r_0^ℓ, r_1^ℓ and outputs $(\mathsf{Enc}(cost_\ell), \mathsf{Enc}(result_\ell)) = (\mathsf{Enc}(r_0^\ell) \otimes \mathsf{Enc}(\ell.cmp), \mathsf{Enc}(r_1^\ell) \otimes \mathsf{Enc}(\ell.cmp) \oplus \mathsf{Enc}(\ell_{label})$ for all $\ell \in \mathcal{L}$.

Fig. 5. Our *Evaluation** algorithm

Then, to guarantee the output of final classification result, we let the threshold number of parties to jointly decrypt all returned ciphertext pairs by *Evaluation**. As in our $n - 1$ clients ($n \geq 3$) and single server application scenario, the collusion might happen among some clients and the server, we need to generate these random values $\{r_0^\ell, r_1^\ell\}$ fairly and privately. Intuitively, the leakage of $\{r_0^\ell\}$ will directly leak other path costs, breaking the privacy of the clients and the server. If $\{r_0^\ell, r_1^\ell\}$ are chosen maliciously, the non-selected classification labels might be revealed, hurting the privacy of the server's tree model. Therefore, we let $n - 1$ clients and the server to provide their contribution $\{r_{i,j}^\ell\}$, where $i \in \{0, 1\}, j \in [n]$, to these values $\{r_0^\ell, r_1^\ell\}$, in the first round by broadcast its corresponding encryption.

Secondly, for threshold FHE supporting t-out-of-n access structure, the general smudging noise techniques introduce in [1,5] are impractical. Indeed, to ensure that no information about the secret key shares $sk_1, \cdots, sk_n$ or the private inputs $\mu_1, \cdots, \mu_l$ will be leaked by partial decryptions $\{p_i\}_{i \in S}$, it requires each decryptor to add independent smudging noise to the partial decryption before broadcasting it. However, in our t-out-of-n $TFHE.FinDec$ procedure, these noise values will be multiplied by Lagrange coefficients, blown up by $\mathcal{O}((n!)^2)$. To solve this issue, we make use of the idea in [18]: let each party P_i secret share some small noise e_i into $(e_i^1, \cdots, e_i^n)$ and send the shares the other parties through private point-to-point channel (assuming PKI). Then each decryptor P_i locally adds $\sum_{j \in [n]} e_j^i$ to its partial decryption. By the linearity of the Shamir secret sharing scheme, this is equivalent to add $e_1 + \cdots + e_n$ to the original reconstructed output value. By using the above approach, we significantly decrease the noise of evaluated ciphertexts, and further reduce the computation costs and ciphertext size of our TFHE constructions.

To conclude, we improve both the efficiency of underlying general TFHE constructions, supporting t-out-of-n access structure, and the multiplicative depth of tree homomorphic evaluation circuit. Our multi-client private decision tree classification protocol is showed in the Fig. 6.

Protocol

1. On input $x_i \in Z^{k_i}$ from the client i, where $i \in [n-1]$, and $\mathcal{T}$ from the server, outputs $(pk, sk_1, \cdots, sk_n) \leftarrow TFHE.Setup(1^\lambda, 1^d, \mathbb{A})$.
2. All parties P_i for $i \in [n]$ runs $(e_i^1, \cdots, e_i^n) \leftarrow SS.Share(e_i, \mathbb{A})$. Each client P_i for $i \in [n-1]$ broadcasts $ct_i \leftarrow [TFHE.Enc(pk, x_i), \{TFHE.Enc(pk, r_{0,i}^\ell), TFHE.Enc(pk, r_{1,i}^\ell)\}_{\ell \in \mathcal{L}}]$, and the server broadcasts $ct_n \leftarrow [TFHE.Enc(pk, \mathcal{T}), \{TFHE.Enc(pk, r_{0,n}^\ell), TFHE.Enc(pk, r_{1,n}^\ell)\}_{\ell \in \mathcal{L}}]$.
3. The server homomorphically computes: $\{\mathsf{Enc}(cost_\ell), \mathsf{Enc}(result_\ell)\}_{\ell \in \mathcal{L}} \leftarrow TFHE.Eval(pk, Evaluation^*, ct_1, \cdots, ct_{n-1}, ct_n)$, in which $r_0^\ell = \sum_{j \in [n]} r_{0,j}^\ell, r_1^\ell = \sum_{j \in [n]} r_{1,j}^\ell$, then sends out the set of above evaluated ciphetext pairs in a random order, represented by ct_C.
4. Threshold number of online parties $\{P_j\}_{j \in S}$ broadcast their partial decryptions: $p_j \leftarrow TFHE.PartDec(pk, ct_C, sk_j)$ for $j \in S$, where we require the additional smudging noise used in each partial decryption p_j is $e_1^j + \cdots + e_n^j$, rather than an independently chosen random noise.
5. Each online party can recover: $\{(cost_\ell, result_\ell)\} \leftarrow TFHE.FinDec(pk, ct_C, \{p_j\}_{j \in S})$. Output the corresponding $result_\ell$ for the unique $cost_\ell$ equal to 0, as the classification label.

Fig. 6. Our multi-client private decision tree classification protocol

Lemma 1 (Correctness). *Assuming the evaluation correctness of the underlying TFHE scheme, and our Evaluation* algorithm, then the above construction is a multi-client private decision tree classification protocol, outputting the correct classification label.*

Proof Sketch. Based on the correctness of TFHE and *Evaluation**, the $cost_\ell$ is equal to 0 if and only if $\ell.cmp$ is equal to 0, then the corresponding result satisfies that $result_\ell = r_1^\ell \times 0 + \ell_{label} = \ell_{label}$.

Lemma 2 (Security). *Assuming both the semantic security and simulation security of the underlying TFHE scheme, with our Evaluation* algorithm, then the above construction is a mutli-client private decision tree classification protocol secure against "honest-but-lazy" adversaries.*

Proof Sketch. By the semantic security and simulation security of the underlying TFHE scheme, the only information that the adversary $\mathcal{A}$ can obtain from the protocol execution is $\{(cost_\ell, result_\ell)\}_{\ell \in \mathcal{L}}$, nothing more about other honest parties secret key shares or inputs. According to the *Evaluation** algorithm, each $(cost_\ell, result_\ell)$ is equal to $(r_0^\ell \times \ell.cmp, r_1^\ell \times \ell.cmp + \ell_{label})$, where r_0^ℓ and r_1^ℓ is fully unknown and uniformly random to each party. Then the only information that each party can derive from the set $\{(r_0^\ell \times \ell.cmp, r_1^\ell \times \ell.cmp + \ell_{label})\}$ is $(0, \ell_{label})$, namely the first component of which element is equal to 0 and the corresponding second component. Besides, since the encrypted ciphertext pairs $\{\mathsf{Enc}(cost_\ell), \mathsf{Enc}(result_\ell)\}_{\ell \in \mathcal{L}}$ are randomly shuffle by the server as required in line 3 in the Fig. 6, clients can not learn anything about the location of the output leaf node within the server's decision tree.

4   Conclusion

In this work, we provide a multi-client private decision tree classification protocol with the low communication and computation cost of clients, also the low interaction, which requires only a single round of participation from multiple clients supplying their inputs, and allows several weak clients to go offline after the first round if they are not interested in learning the classification output or lose connectivity caused by DDoS attacks. For the solution to be able to implement in practice, we improve both the multiplicative depth of tree evaluation circuit and the efficiency of underlying generic TFHE solutions. Especially, we use the idea that each participant in threshold decryption to add comparatively small smudging noise, thus significantly reducing the total computation cost and ciphertext size of TFHE. An interesting open problem is to show the concrete experiment results of our protocol or upgrade our protocol to actively secure avoiding the generic heavy NIZK tools.

Acknowledgment. The authors thank anonymous reviewers for valuable comments. Bo Pang and Mingsheng Wang are supported by National Key R&D Program of China-2020YFA0712303.

References

1. Asharov, G., Jain, A., López-Alt, A., Tromer, E., Vaikuntanathan, V., Wichs, D.: Multiparty computation with low communication, computation and interaction via threshold FHE. In: Pointcheval, D., Johansson, T. (eds.) EUROCRYPT 2012. LNCS, vol. 7237, pp. 483–501. Springer, Heidelberg (2012). https://doi.org/10.1007/978-3-642-29011-4_29
2. Badrinarayanan, S., Jain, A., Manohar, N., Sahai, A.: Secure MPC: laziness leads to GOD. In: Moriai, S., Wang, H. (eds.) ASIACRYPT 2020. LNCS, vol. 12493, pp. 120–150. Springer, Cham (2020). https://doi.org/10.1007/978-3-030-64840-4_5
3. Barni, M., Failla, P., Lazzeretti, R., Sadeghi, A.-R., Schneider, T.: Privacy-preserving ECG classification with branching programs and neural networks. IEEE Trans. Inf. Forensics Secur. **6**(2), 452–468 (2011)
4. Beaver, D.: Commodity-based cryptography. In: Proceedings of the Twenty-Ninth Annual ACM Symposium on Theory of Computing, pp. 446–455 (1997)

5. Boneh, D., Gennaro, R., Goldfeder, S., Jain, A., Kim, S., Rasmussen, P.M.R., Sahai, A.: Threshold cryptosystems from threshold fully homomorphic encryption. In: Shacham, H., Boldyreva, A. (eds.) CRYPTO 2018, Part I. LNCS, vol. 10991, pp. 565–596. Springer, Cham (2018). https://doi.org/10.1007/978-3-319-96884-1_19

6. Bost, R., Popa, R.A., Tu, S., Goldwasser, S.: Machine learning classification over encrypted data. Cryptology ePrint Archive (2014)

7. Brakerski, Z., Gentry, C., Vaikuntanathan, V.: (Leveled) fully homomorphic encryption without bootstrapping. ACM Trans. Comput. Theory (TOCT) $6(3)$, 1–36 (2014)

8. Brakerski, Z., Perlman, R.: Lattice-based fully dynamic multi-key FHE with short ciphertexts. In: Robshaw, M., Katz, J. (eds.) CRYPTO 2016. LNCS, vol. 9814, pp. 190–213. Springer, Heidelberg (2016). https://doi.org/10.1007/978-3-662-53018-4_8

9. Brickell, J., Porter, D.E., Shmatikov, V., Witchel, E.: Privacy-preserving remote diagnostics. In: Proceedings of the 14th ACM Conference on Computer and Communications Security, pp. 498–507 (2007)

10. Chen, H., Chillotti, I., Song, Y.: Multi-key homomorphic encryption from TFHE. In: Galbraith, S.D., Moriai, S. (eds.) ASIACRYPT 2019. LNCS, vol. 11922, pp. 446–472. Springer, Cham (2019). https://doi.org/10.1007/978-3-030-34621-8_16

11. Chen, L., Zhang, Z., Wang, X.: Batched multi-hop multi-key FHE from ring-LWE with compact ciphertext extension. In: Kalai, Y., Reyzin, L. (eds.) TCC 2017. LNCS, vol. 10678, pp. 597–627. Springer, Cham (2017). https://doi.org/10.1007/978-3-319-70503-3_20

12. Cheon, J.H., Kim, M., Kim, M.: Optimized search-and-compute circuits and their application to query evaluation on encrypted data. IEEE Trans. Inf. Forensics Secur. $11(1)$, 188–199 (2015)

13. Clear, M., McGoldrick, C.: Multi-identity and multi-key leveled FHE from learning with errors. In: Gennaro, R., Robshaw, M. (eds.) CRYPTO 2015. LNCS, vol. 9216, pp. 630–656. Springer, Heidelberg (2015). https://doi.org/10.1007/978-3-662-48000-7_31

14. Cramer, R., Damgård, I., Escudero, D., Scholl, P., Xing, C.: SPDZ$_{2^k}$: efficient MPC mod 2^k for dishonest majority. In: Shacham, H., Boldyreva, A. (eds.) CRYPTO 2018, Part II. LNCS, vol. 10992, pp. 769–798. Springer, Cham (2018). https://doi.org/10.1007/978-3-319-96881-0_26

15. Damgård, I., Escudero, D., Frederiksen, T., Keller, M., Scholl, P., Volgushev, N.: New primitives for actively-secure MPC over rings with applications to private machine learning. In: 2019 IEEE Symposium on Security and Privacy (SP), pp. 1102–1120. IEEE (2019)

16. De Cock, M., et al.: Efficient and private scoring of decision trees, support vector machines and logistic regression models based on pre-computation. IEEE Trans. Dependable Secure Comput. $16(2)$, 217–230 (2017)

17. Fredrikson, M., Jha, S., Ristenpart, T.: Model inversion attacks that exploit confidence information and basic countermeasures. In: Proceedings of the 22nd ACM SIGSAC Conference on Computer and Communications Security, pp. 1322–1333 (2015)

18. Dov Gordon, S., Liu, F.-H., Shi, E.: Constant-round MPC with fairness and guarantee of output delivery. In: Gennaro, R., Robshaw, M. (eds.) CRYPTO 2015. LNCS, vol. 9216, pp. 63–82. Springer, Heidelberg (2015). https://doi.org/10.1007/978-3-662-48000-7_4

19. Joye, M., Salehi, F.: Private yet efficient decision tree evaluation. In: Kerschbaum, F., Paraboschi, S. (eds.) DBSec 2018. LNCS, vol. 10980, pp. 243–259. Springer, Cham (2018). https://doi.org/10.1007/978-3-319-95729-6_16

20. Kiss, Á., Naderpour, M., Liu, J., Asokan, N., Schneider, T.: SoK: modular and efficient private decision tree evaluation. Proc. Priv. Enhanc. Technol. **2019**(2), 187–208 (2019)

21. López-Alt, A., Tromer, E., Vaikuntanathan, V.: On-the-fly multiparty computation on the cloud via multikey fully homomorphic encryption. In: Proceedings of the Forty-Fourth Annual ACM Symposium on Theory of Computing, pp. 1219–1234 (2012)

22. Mukherjee, P., Wichs, D.: Two round multiparty computation via multi-key FHE. In: Fischlin, M., Coron, J.-S. (eds.) EUROCRYPT 2016, Part II. LNCS, vol. 9666, pp. 735–763. Springer, Heidelberg (2016). https://doi.org/10.1007/978-3-662-49896-5_26

23. Peikert, C., Shiehian, S.: Multi-key FHE from LWE, revisited. In: Hirt, M., Smith, A. (eds.) TCC 2016. LNCS, vol. 9986, pp. 217–238. Springer, Heidelberg (2016). https://doi.org/10.1007/978-3-662-53644-5_9

24. Tai, R.K.H., Ma, J.P.K., Zhao, Y., Chow, S.S.M.: Privacy-preserving decision trees evaluation via linear functions. In: Foley, S.N., Gollmann, D., Snekkenes, E. (eds.) ESORICS 2017. LNCS, vol. 10493, pp. 494–512. Springer, Cham (2017). https://doi.org/10.1007/978-3-319-66399-9_27

25. Tueno, A., Boev, Y., Kerschbaum, F.: Non-interactive private decision tree evaluation. In: Singhal, A., Vaidya, J. (eds.) DBSec 2020. LNCS, vol. 12122, pp. 174–194. Springer, Cham (2020). https://doi.org/10.1007/978-3-030-49669-2_10

26. Tueno, A., Kerschbaum, F., Katzenbeisser, S.: Private evaluation of decision trees using sublinear cost. Proc. Priv. Enhanc. Technol. **2019**(1), 266–286 (2019)

27. Wu, D.J., Feng, T., Naehrig, M., Lauter, K.: Privately evaluating decision trees and random forests. Cryptology ePrint Archive (2015)

Advances in Adversarial Attacks and Defenses in Intrusion Detection System: A Survey

Mariama Mbow[1(✉)], Kouichi Sakurai[1], and Hiroshi Koide[2]

[1] Department of Informatics Graduate School of Information Science and Electrical Engineering, Kyushu University, Fukuoka, Japan
mbow.mariama.076@s.kyushu-u.ac.jp, sakurai@inf.kyushu-u.ac.jp
[2] Research Institute for Information Technology Cyber Security Center, Kyushu University, Fukuoka, Japan
koide@cc.kyushu-u.ac.jp

Abstract. Machine learning is one of the predominant methods used in computer science and has been widely and successfully applied in many areas such as computer vision, pattern recognition, natural language processing, cyber security etc. In cyber security, the application of machine learning algorithms for network intrusion detection system (NIDS) has seen promising results for anomaly detection mostly with the adoption of deep learning and is still growing. However, machine learning algorithms are vulnerable to adversarial attacks resulting in significant performance degradation. Adversarial attacks are security threats that aim to deceive the learning algorithm by manipulating its predictions, and Adversarial machine learning is a research area that studies both the generation and defense of such attacks. Researchers have extensively worked on the adversarial machine learning in computer vision but not many works in Intrusion detection system. However, failure in this critical Intrusion detection area could compromise the security of an entire system, and need much attention. This paper provides a review of the advancement in adversarial machine learning based intrusion detection and explores the various defense techniques applied against. Finally discuss their limitations for future research direction in this emerging area.

Keywords: Adversarial attack · Cyber security · Intrusion detection · Machine learning · Deep learning · Poisoning attack · Evasion attack

Network Intrusion Detection System (NIDS) [1,2] are playing an important role in cybersecurity for detecting malicious network traffic. NIDS uses signature or anomaly based detection to identify cyber-attacks. However with the growth of network traffic and attacks diversity [3], signature detection which can only detect existing attacks by using their signatures are being replaced by anomaly based detection which have potentially the capabilities to detect existing attacks as well as novel attacks. Among the various techniques applied to implement

C. Su and K. Sakurai (Eds.): SciSec 2022 Workshops, CCIS 1680, pp. 196–212, 2022.
https://doi.org/10.1007/978-981-19-7769-5_15

NIDS, Machine Learning (ML) based have been the predominant method and have seen a fast adoption due to their abilities to discriminate between abnormal and normal pattern over a data set. In the last decades there has been a wide research that apply machine learning (including deep learning) in NIDS settings [4,23,24]. However, serious security issues are now emerging with the discovery of the vulnerability of these algorithms [8].

Researchers [5–8] have shown that machine learning can be easily fooled when adding some perturbation during its training or prediction phase. These perturbations are called adversarial samples and they are specially crafted inputs that cause the learning model to wrongly classify/predict an input. For instance attackers can exploit the vulnerability of voice control system and influence the model to make wrong decision on recognizing voice command. In autonomous vehicles based machine learning the attacker can trick the model to make wrong decision on recognizing the traffic signs [10]. In intrusion detection the attacker might influence the classifiers to misclassify the attack traffic as benign and then bypass the security system. Failure in this critical cybersecurity area could compromise the security of an entire system. Then it is actually the security-critical area that face the biggest challenges from these threats [11].

Considering the limited reviews targeting the adversarial attacks against network intrusion detection system and the numerous papers being published recently, in this survey we aims to provide a comprehensive overview of the evolution of the works provided in this area with the following contributions:

1. We summarize and analyze the recent advance on adversarial machine learning applied to NIDS
2. By analyzing and comparing the different works proposed, we discuss open issues that can help as future direction in this evolving area.

The remainder of this paper is organized as follow: In Sect. 1 we discuss previous related works. Section 2 we discuss the background of basic concept on machine learning and adversarial attack taxonomy. In Sect. 3 we discuss the adversarial attack applied in NIDS. Section 4 discusses the adversarial defenses. Finally we propose some future direction in Sect. 5 and conclude in Sect. 6.

1   Related Work

Related works have been presented in [11,12]. In [12], authors worked on a review of adversarial machine learning in intrusion and malware detection. However they provided limited review on researches related to NIDS and mainly focused on the evasion attack and in white box scenario. Moisejevs et al. [11] provided an overview of adversarial attacks and defenses in intrusion detection. They attempted to focus on evasion and poisoning attacks in white box and black box scenario. However similar to [12], limited papers were reviewed and the most recent was in 2018. Recently there has been an increasing number of publications in adversarial machine learning [13] including applied in NIDS. The literature survey we provide differ from the previous in many ways. We include the more recent works. In addition we review all adversarial machine learning scenario in NIDS including black box and white box and applied during training time (poisoning attack) or during test time (evasion attack). More details of these techniques will be discussed in Sect. 2.

To prepare this survey, studies are selected on multiple databases such as Springer and Elsevier, IEEE, Research Gate and Science Direct using keywords "Intrusion detection", "Adversarial Machine learning", "Adversarial Deep Learning". We survey a total of 29 papers that works on adversarial attacks or defense technique.

2   Background

In this section, we discuss the basic concept of machine learning and adversarial attack.

2.1   Machine Learning in NIDS

Machine learning is a part of artificial intelligence (AI) with a multidisciplinary research area that spans several fields. These fields include probability and statistics, computer science, algorithms, psychology and brain science. There are four (4) approaches used in Machine learning such as Supervised learning, Unsupervised learning, Semi-supervised learning, and Reinforcement learning. However Supervised and unsupervised learning are the most common type used in NIDS [14]. Machine learning models are mainly divided into shallow or traditional model and deep learning model. The most common traditional ML models applied in IDS include support vector machine (SVM), decision tree (DT), random forest (RF), k-means, artificial neural network (ANN), and ensemble method [1,14]. Recently Deep learning (DL) methods have greatly improved NIDS by overcoming the difficulty of feature selection and representation. The number of published works on DL based NIDS has rapidly increased [4,14]. The common DL models applies in NIDS include recurrent neural networks (RNNs), long short-term memory (LSTM) networks, convolutional neural network (CNN), AutoEncoder (AE), Deep neural network (DNN), Deep belief network (DBN).

2.2   Adversarial Machine Learning

Adversarial attacks represent a major limitation for the adoption of machine learning in many area. These attacks against the machine learning algorithms are security threats that aim to trick the learning model by purposely adding tiny perturbations to the data to easily subvert their predictions. This phenomenon has been explored for more than a decade in the traditional machine learning [25]. However the discovery of these adversarial examples against neural networks, by Szegedy et al. [8] and in subsequently [5,26,27], has renewed interest in the AI community [25].

These perturbations against the learning algorithms can be performed in mainly during the training time or test time. In the training time also called poisoning attack [28] the attacker alter the input data to induce wrong model prediction. This technique is performed with data manipulation, data injection or logic corruption [29]. In test-time called evasion attack [30], the attacker aims to evade the trained model by tricking the input data.

2.3 Modeling the Attack Scenario

Huang et al. classified these threats on the basis of three (3) axes: *the influence on the classifiers, specificity and security violation (or impact)*. This taxonomy has been further studied by Biggio et al. [15], to model the attack scenario for a comprehensive understanding of the attacker strategy. According to [15], the attack scenario can be modeled based on the attacker's goal, knowledge, capability and strategy.

Adversary's Goal: This goal defines which security violation (Integrity, Availability and Privacy), the attacker aims to target and its specificity which mean if the attack is targeted or untargeted. It can be categorized in 3 types:

- *Integrity violation* that occurs when the adversary attempts to evade the detector. For instance, the attacker may aim to misclassify malicious sample as benign and result in an increase of false negative.
- *Avaibility violation* which leads to a useless system by creating many misclassifications. Thus increasing the false negative and false positive rate.
- *Privacy violation* in which the attacker try to get information from the learner.

In term of deep learning, papernot et al. [35] define the integrity violation as primary adversary's goal.

Adversary's Knowledge: This describes how well the attacker knows his target. Depending on the type of information there are three types of knowledge: white box, gray box and black box.

- White box: It assumes the adversary has complete information related to the network model: training data, features, learning algorithm, as well as trained model.
- Grey box: It assumes the attacker has partial knowledge about the target. This is also called the semi-white box.
- Black box: It assumes the attacker has zero or limited knowledge about the target. The attacker only knows the output of the model

Adversary's Capability: It assumes the types of influence the adversary can perform against the target.

Adversary's Strategy: It determines the workflow pursued by the adversary to launch the attack. The attack can be performed during the training time (poisoning attack) or during the test time (evasion attack).

3   Adversarial Attack Against NIDS

In this section, we review different studies that applied the adversarial machine learning in network intrusion detection system (NIDS) domain. As mentioned in Sect. 2 the attack can be performed during the training time called Poisoning attack or during test time called Evasion. We will review both evasion and poisoning attack and note down if the attack is performed in black box of white box scenario where possible.

3.1   Poisoning Attacks

Data Manipulation: Ali et al. [37] performed poisoning attack on DNN based IDS for a SDN-compliant heterogeneous wireless communication network. Launched in a white box using relabeling techniques in which malicious traffic is labeled as benign and normal traffic as malicious. Results show that the proposed poisoning attack decrease significantly the DNN classifier performance.

Papadopoulos et al. [33] Performed a label flipping attack in a white box to attack a SVM based NIDS for IoT environment. The method significantly degrade the model performance.

Data Injection: Nguyen et al. [61] propose a backdoor against federated learning based IoT NIDS. The adversary inject gradually on the compromised devices small amount of malicious data in the normal traffic during the training model. As a result they successfully reduce the model accuracy.

3.2   Evasion Attack

(a) *Adversarial Deep Learning Against Intrusion Detection Classifiers*: Rigaki et al. [40] investigate a targeted and untargeted gray box attack against RF, SVM, DT and their Majority ensemble voting. They generated adversarial sample with FGSM and JSMA on a multilayer perceptron (MLP) model and then transferred [19]. All classifier were affected, with the SVM being the most vulnerable and RF being the most robust. They analyzed the effect of the FGSM and JSMA. Concluded FGSM modified all features whereas JSMA alter only 6% of the feature. This make the JSMA more realistic.

(b) *Deep Learning-Based Intrusion Detection With Adversaries*: Wang et al. [20] performed a white box attack against MLP assessed on NSLKDD dataset. They generated adversarial examples with JSMA, FGSM, DEEPFOOL and CW. All attacks successfully degrade the performance of the MLP classifier, with the CW less devastating. They noticed that JSMA attack can achieve 100% probability of fooling the model with very less features.

(c) *Adversarial Attack against LSTM-based DDoS Intrusion Detection System*: Huang et al. [16] propose the first study on adversarial LSTM-based DDoS detection under black box setting. They utilized genetic Algorithm (GA) and Probability Weighted Packet Saliency Attack (PWPSA), to generate adversarial samples. In their experiment Both methods can fool the detector with high success rates.

(d) *Adversarial Machine Learning in Network Intrusion Detection Systems*: Alhajjar et al. [9] generate adversarial examples to evade 11 machine learning models (SVM, DT, NB, KNN, RF, MLP, GB, LR, LDA, QDA, BAG). They Explore the use of GAN, and evolutionary algorithms: particle swarm optimization (PSO) and genetic Algorithm (GA) as adversarial examples. Use the Monte Carlo (MC) simulation as baseline and transfer the attacks. The authors consider the constrained nature of the feature space in NIDS and design these algorithms to perturb the inputs without modifying the malicious functionality of the networks. The experiment results show these perturbations were able to fool all models with a high misclassification rate. SVM and DT were the most vulnerable.

(e) *Adversarial Attacks Against NIDS in IoT Systems*: Qiu et al. [21] propose a realistic and efficient novel adversarial attack method against DNN model in NIDS for IoT in a black box environment. Their proposed approach uses the model extraction technique to reproduce target model for crafting adversarial examples and with a small portion of the original train data to achieve a high efficiency. Subsequently, to identify the most significant feature that influence the detector with the least modifications, a saliency maps [22] is used. Then generate perturbations using the FGSM adversarial sample. The method is applied to target Kitsune, a NIDS for IoT. The experimental results show the attacker can successfully compromise the detection system with an average success rate of 94.31%.

(f) *Launching Adversarial Attacks against Network Intrusion Detection Systems for IoT*: Papadopoulos et al. [33] Performed a white box adversarial attack against both traditional machine learning and deep learning model to evaluate their robustness in NIDS for IoT. In their methodology, they studied both poisoning and evasion attack. The evasion is performed with the FGSM against an ANN based IDS implemented with Bot-IoT dataset. The experiment result show a significant performance degradation. Moreover, authors mentioned traditional machine learning are more vulnerable during training time. Therefore the poisoning attack is performed on SVM model with the label flipping method.

(g) *Adversarial Attacks to bypass a GAN based classifier trained to detect Network intrusion*: Piplai et al. [31] studied the effectiveness of adversarial attacks against adversarial training. They revealed that even training the model with an adversarial training method, the attacker can still fool the model. Adversarial training is a defense technique that aims to increase the robustness of the model against adversarial attacks.

(h) *Black-Box Attack Method against Machine-Learning-Based Anomaly Network Flow Detection Models*: Similarly to [9], Guo et al. [32] analyzed the constrained domain on adversarial attacks against NIDS. They performed a black box attack with limited number of query. An extension of BIM adversarial sample is used to craft adversarial sample in a substitute MLP model in a white box setting. Then used the transferability to achieve the black box attack. The method is evaluated on KDD99 and CICIDS2018 dataset. On KDD99, they targeted SVM, MLP, KNN, and CNN. Subsequently three model were targeted on CICIDS2018: Resnet, CNN and MLP. The experimental results show the proposed black box method can bypass the detector with high probability.

(i) *Adversarial Attack Against DoS Intrusion Detection: An Improved Boundary-Based Method*: Peng et al. [34] studied the robustness of ANN-based DoS IDS in a black box environment. They proposed an improved boundary based method to generate the adversarial samples. The presented approach optimizes a Mahalanobis distance by influencing the feature of both continuous and discrete DoS samples. The experimental results revealed that with limited queries, their proposed method can craft adversarial DoS examples and bypass the detection model.

(j) *A Brute-Force Black-Box Method to Attack Machine Learning-Based Systems in Cybersecurity*: Zhang et al. [36] propose a brute-force attack method (BFAM) to generate adversarial examples. The BFAM overcome some limit of GAN such as the unstable training [7]. They targeted LR, DT, MLP, naive Bayes (NB) and RF. Experimental results show that the proposed BFAM method is computational efficient and outperforms adversarial attack method based on GAN. However, RF has been the most resilient classifier to the generated adversarial example.

(k) *Generative adversarial attacks against intrusion detection systems using active learning*: Shu et al. [41] propose GAN active learning (Gen-AAL) to compromise the ML based NIDS in a black box with limited training data. In the GAN model the Variational AutoEncoder (VAE) is proposed as the generator and the discriminator is a MLP to implement a substitute model which approximate the target model. The active learning is used to decrease the number of required label to train the model. The experimental results show the proposed method achieve an evasion success rate of 98% by only using 25 labels instance during the training.

(l) *Evading a Machine Learning-based Intrusion Detection System through Adversarial Perturbations*: Fladby et al. [42] investigate an evasion attack against stratosphere linux ips (Slips) in a gray box setting. Slips is a ML-based Network Behavioral Analysis (NBA) which use the Markov chains algorithms. In the proposed method, authors use a custom attack to target the property network flow periodicity. The simultaneous perturbation stochastic approximation (SPSA) optimization method is used to perturb the network flows with minimal magnitude. Experimental results show the proposed method was able to evade the detector.

(m) *Evaluating Deep Learning Based Network Intrusion Detection System in Adversarial Environment*: Peng et al. [48] evaluate the robustness of four ML based NIDS under adversarial attack: RF, Logistic regression, SVM, and DNN respectively. The attack are performed with four adversarial samples: Projected Gradient Descent attack (PGD), Momentum Iterative FGSM (MI-FGSM), L-BFGS attack, and Simultaneous Perturbation Stochastic

Approximation (SPSA). All models performance sharply decrease and with the MI-FGSM attack achieving the highest attack success rate.

(n) *Analyzing Adversarial Attacks against Deep Learning for Intrusion Detection in IoT Networks*: Ibitoye et al. [49] investigate a white box attack against NIDS in IoT network. Two deep learning models have been first used to implement the NIDS; Feedforward Neural Networks (FNN) and its variant Self-normalizing Neural Network (SNN). Then the models resilience are evaluated. The adversarial samples are generated with FGSM and two of its variant: BIM and PGD. Both model performance degraded, however the SNN has been more resilient than the FNN. Moreover, authors found that feature normalization make the model vulnerable to adversarial sample.

(o) *Evaluating Deep Learning-based NIDS in Adversarial Settings*: Mohammadian et al. [50] investigated the effect of features and their vulnerability in a white box evasion attack. The approach targets an IDS implemented with DNN and utilizes a FGSM to generate attack. The attack was assessed on two datasets: CICIDS2017 and CIC-DDoS2019. To evaluated the most suitable feature for generating adversarial sample, they group features into different categories based on their nature. Then they craft adversarial sample in different feature set. The experiments show there are no general conclusion regarding the most vulnerable feature in both dataset.

(p) *NIDSGAN*: Zolbayar et al. [51] studied the effectiveness of GAN against ML based NIDS. They introduce NIDSGAN, an attack algorithm that generate adversarial network traffic to fool the IDS in a white-box, black-box and restricted black box evasion attacks. The approach take into account the domain constraints in network traffic to develop a realistic attack. In the proposed method, GAN is associates with active learning. The active learning method is used to decrease the training data size and enhance the attack success rate and GAN generates the attack. The attack is evaluated in two DNN models: AlertNet [52] and DeepNet [53]. The experimental results show the proposed method can evade the detector with a success rate of 99% in white box, 85% in black box and 70% in restricted black box.

(q) *A Comparative Study on Contemporary Intrusion Detection Datasets*: Pacheco et al. [18] evaluate the effectiveness of adversarial examples against the UNSB-NB15 and Bot-IoT datasets. Four NIDS target model were implemented using MLP, DT, RF and SVM. The attacks are performed in a white box with three adversarial sample generations: JSMA, FGSM and CW. The findings results demonstrate all models performance were degraded with RF beign the most resilient and SVM being the most vulnerable. And the JSMA attack has been the least effective in both datasets.

(r) *Black Box Attacks on Deep Anomaly Detectors*: Kuppa et al. [54] propose a realistic black box attack with limited queries to evade the detector. In the proposed approach, the Mani fold Approximation Algorithm is applied to the target model and is used to minimize the query. Then adversarial samples are generated with the spherical local subspaces. They evaluate the approach on 7 NIDS model: Isolation Forests (IF), Adversarially Learned Anomaly Detection (ALAD), One Class Support Vector Machines

(OC-SVM), Deep Autoencoding Gaussian Mixture Model (DAGMM), Deep Support Vector Data Description (DSVDD), AnoGAN and AutoEncoder (AE). The experiments show an attack success rate over 70%. However the proposed approach is more suitable for case where normal and attack boundaries are not well defined and when the NIDS is threshold based decision.

Table 1 summarizes the attacks method explored in this section.

Table 1. Summary of contributions in adversarial attacks against NIDS

Ref	Year	Environment	Dataset	Strategy	Knowledge	Target model	Attack Algorithm	Result
[20]	2016	Traditional	NSL-KDD	evasion	white box	MLP	JSMA, FGSM, DEEPFOOL, CW	CW attack less effective with AUC=0.80, FGSM most effective with AUC=0.44
[42]	2019	Traditional	CTU-13 dataset	evasion, poisoning	black box	RF, MLP, KNN	custom attack	MLP the most vulnerable one in evasion attack(68% attack severity), KNN is the most vulnerable model in poisoning attack(72% attack success rate)
[9]	2021	Traditional	NSL-KDD, UNSW-NB15	evasion	white box	SVM, DT, NB, KNN, RF, MLP, GB, LR, LDA, QDA, BAG	MC, PSO, GA, GAN	- DT and SVM the most vulnerable models(>90% evasion rate) In attack success, evolutionary computation methods (PSO and GA) achieved the best attack evasion rate on both datasets
[43]	2017	Traditional	NSL KDD	evasion	gray box	RF, SVM, DT based on CART, Majority ensemble voting	JSMA	SVM most vulnerable (97% accuracy drop), RF most resilient(10% accuracy drop)
[38]	2021	IoT	Bot-IoT	evasion, Poisoning	white box	ANN, SVM	FGSM, label poisoning	significant accuracy drop on untargeted and targeted poisoning attack(55% and 58% accuracy drop respectively), Significant accuracy drop on untargeted evasion attack(31% accuracy drop)
[21]	2021	IoT	Kitsune	evasion	black box	DNN	IFGSM, Substitute Model, Saliency Maps	94.31% attack success rate
[18]	2020	Traditional	CICIDS2017	evasion	black box	LSTM	FWPSA	High attack success rate on both methods(>69%)
[34]	2019	Traditional	KDDcup99, CICIDS2017	evasion	black box	ANN	Improved boundary-based method	Performance drop of true class confidence from 81% to 40%
[31]	2020	Traditional	Less bigdata 2019 cup	evasion	black box	GAN	FGSM	At least 41% success rate with some significant features
[45]	2020	Traditional	CTU-109-1 dataset	evasion	gray box	Stratosphere Linux IPS	custom attack, SPSA	Attack method were able to effectively confuse the NIDS
[32]	2020	Traditional	KDDcup99, CICIDS2018	evasion	black box	SVM, MLP, KNN,CNN, Resnet	Substitute BIM	All models achieved a high recall rate in baseline Significant drop of model performance under adversarial attack. In KDD99 with MLP, more than 94.3% adversarial DoS evade the detector , KNN was the most resilient model. In CICID2018 with MLP an average of 72.3% of evasion rate
[37]	2020	Traditional	NSL-KDD	evasion	black box	LR, DT, MLP,NB,RF	BPAM, GAN	BPAM outperforms GAN in most cases and decreases significantly the detection rate of target classifiers Best classifier under adversarial attack was RF(
[39]	2020	SDN	NSL-KDD	Poisoning	white box	DNN	relabelling	The accuracy rate decreases by about 13%-17%
[44]	2020	Traditional	CICIDS2017	evasion	gray box	Gradient boosted DT	Gen-AAL	achieve 98.86% attack success rate
[51]	2019	Traditional	NSL-KDD	evasion	white box	DNN, SVM, RF, LR	FGSM, MI-FGSM, L-BPGS, SPSA	MI-FGSM was the most effective attack with an attack success rate of: 31% on DNN, 20% on SVM, 31% on RF and 21% on LR
[53]	2022	Traditional	CICIDS2017, CIC-IDoS2019	evasion	black box	DNN	FGSM	Difficult to conclude the most suitable features for generating adversarial examples. features are dependent and related to each other
[52]	2019	IoT	Bot-IoT	evasion	white box	FNN, SNN	FGSM, BIM, PGD	Both model performance were significantly degraded but SNN demonstrate better resilience than FNN BIM was the most effective attack with an accuracy drop from 98.1% to 18% on FNN
[54]	2022	Traditional	NSKKDD, CICIDS2017	evasion	white box, gray box, black box	LR, SVM, DT,KNN, DNN	GAN	Attack success on average 90%, 85%, and 70% on white box, gray box and black box respectively
[16]	2021	IoT	UNSB-NB15, Bot-IoT	evasion	white box	MLP, DT, RF, SVM	JSMA, FGSM, CW	All attacks were able to effectively degrade the overall classifiers, CW was most efficient attack on the UNSWNB15 (decrease in accuracy by 42%) JSMA was the least efficient on both datasets RF was shown as the most resilient classifier SVM the least robust
[37]	2019	Traditional	CICIDS2018	evasion	black box	DAGMM ,AE, AnoGAN, ALAD, DSVDD, one-class SVM, IF	MAA, spherical local subspaces	methods can evade NIDS with high success rate (attack success rate > 70%)

4   Defending Against Adversarial Attacks

In this session we summarize existing works that propose a defense method against these adversarial machine on NIDS.

4.1   Defense Against Poisoning Attack

Data Transformation: Poisoning attacks are generally injecting during retraining phase of the target system. Therefore, Apruzzese et al. [39] propose a data transformation which consist of inverting the training data before storing to the database. Therefore the poisoned data will not have much effect during retraining.

Pruning and Fine-Tuning: Bachl et al. [58] Investigated the defense against backdoor attacks in ML based NIDS. RF and MLP models have been used to implements de NIDS in UNSW- NB15 and CIC-IDS-2017. They proposed a pruning and fine-tuning as defense method to decrease the backdoor efficacity.

In their findings, authors reveal the proposed methods are efficient for random forest but not for neural network. Also they suggested Partial Dependence Plots (PDPs) and Accumulated Local Effects (ALE) plots as an efficient method to visualize backdoor attack.

4.2 Defense Against Evasion Attack

Adversarial Retraining

(a) *Adversarial Training for Deep Learning-based Intrusion Detection Systems*: Debicha et al. [38] propose adversarial training as a defense method. The experimental findings show the adversarial training improve the robustness of the IDS against attacks. Moreover the performance of the NIDS was compared to the baseline NIDS implemented without adversarial training. However, the results finding show the adversarial training decrease the performance of the IDS accuracy in free adversarial.

(b) *Evaluation of Adversarial Training on Different Types of Neural Networks in Deep Learning-based IDSs*: Khamis et al. [17] propose adversarial training based on min-max optimization as a defense technique againts adversarial attacks. To validate the method, they first evaluated three deep learning classifiers: DNN, ANN, RNN in an adversarial setting with five attack algorithms: FGSM, BIM, PGD, CW and deepfool. Assessed on NSLKDD and UNSW-NB15 datasets. All classifiers were affected in both datasets with a significant decrease of the accuracy compared to the baseline models. However the adversarial trained has significantly improved the model resilience.

(c) *GAN For Launching and Thwarting Adversarial Attacks on NIDS*: Usama et al. [55] propose GAN based adversarial training. They first utilize GAN to compromise the NIDS performance in a black box setting while maintaining the functional behavior. The method was evaluated on DNN, LR, SVM, KNN, naïve Bayes (NB), RF, DT, and gradient boosting (GB) using the KDD99 dataset as benchmark. The experimental results showed the GAN successfully evade the detector with a decrease of all performance metric. As Defense method, authors proposed GAN based adversarial training. The adversarial training has enhanced the performance.

(d) *Adversarial Attacks Against Deep Learning-Based NIDS and Defense Mechanisms*: Zhang et al. [60] propose TIKI-TAKA, a framework to evaluate the robustness of deep learning based NIDS. In their approach, MLP, LSTM and CNN model based NIDS are first evaluated under adversarial attack in a black box built with five adversarial samples: Natural Evolution Strategies (NES) [43], Pointwise Attack [44], Boundary Atttack [45], OPT-Attack [46] and HopSkipJumpAttack [47]. Experiments show all models were vulnerable with an evasion success rates up to 37%. Then Three Defense methods have been proposed model voting ensembling, ensembling adversarial training, and query detection. These methods can be used jointly or separately and have been effective to decrease the success rate of evasion attacks.

Ensemble Model: Debicha et al. [56] investigated the ensemble model and adversarial training as defense method. They first studied the adversarial transferability method on network traffic between Neural network and multiple traditional machine learning based NIDS and trained with two different training sets. In a white box setting using FGSM and PGD attacks. The generated adversarial samples are transferred to five traditional ML based NIDS target: SVM, LR, DT, RF, Linear Discriminant Analysis (LDA), and their ensemble model. The experimental results show the attack transferred from DNN to traditional ML can successfully decrease the accuracy of the models with the DT and RF being more resilient. As defense method, the ensemble model and adversarial training have been applied. However the ensemble model did not improve the model robustness. In contrast, the adversarial training has improved the models resilience.

Defensive Distillation: Apruzzese et al. [57] introduce a variant of defensive distillation technique with RF against adversarial attack. In their approach, authors propose the use of probability labels to train the model instead of class labels applied in previous models. The experiments demonstrate the proposed method can decrease the impact of adversarial attack.

Feature Removal: Apruzzese et al. [39] investigated feature removal and adversarial training. They first performed an integrity violation attack on three machine learning algorithms: MLP, RF and KNN. The attack was assessed over the CTU-13 dataset. The experiment was performed in a black box attack. In the adversarial setting scenario, a custom adversarial attack is implemented. All classifiers were severely affected. Then authors propose two defense methods against the evasion attack: the adversarial retraining and feature removal. Both defense mitigated the attack severity.

Graph-Structured Data: Pujol-Perich et al. [59] propose a Graph Neural Network (GNN) based NIDS to improve the NIDS performance and its robustness against adversarial attack. The proposed GNN has been first evaluated in adversarial free and with state-of-the-art ML model based NIDS: MLP, RF, Ada-boost and decision tree ID3. The GNN model achieve a F score of 99% and is comparable to state of the art models. For the adversarial setup, two custom attacks were implemented. The first attack is implemented by increasing the packet size of attack flow. The second attack is performed by incrementing the inter-arrival time attack flow. In both attacks the GNN model has been robust as the accuracy keep the same level as in adversarial free. In contrast to the state-of -the art model which were vulnerable with a performance degradation up to 50%. Authors argue that the GNN can not only capture relevant pattern on each feature but can also seize the important structural flow pattern of attack. This ability make the GNN resilient against adversarial attack.

Table 2. Summary of contributions in adversarial defense against NIDS

Ref	Year	Environment	Dataset	Strategy	Knowledge	Target model	Attack Algorithm	defense
[17]	2020	Traditional	NSL-KDD, UNSW-NB15	evasion	white box	ANN, CNN, RNN	FGSM, BIM, PGD, CW, Deepfool	Min-Max
[40]	2021	Traditional	NSL-KDD	evasion	white box	DNN	FGSM, BIM, PGD, CW, Deepfool	Adversarial training
[63]	2022	Traditional	CICIDS2018	evasion	black box	MLP, CNN, LSTM	NES, BOUNDARY, HOPSKIPJUMPATTACK, POINTWISE, OPT	model voting ensembling, ensembling adversarial training, query detection.
[58]	2019	Traditional	KDD99	evasion	black box	DNN, LR, SVM, KNN, NB, RF, DT, GB	GAN	Adversarial training
[59]	2021	Traditional	NSL-KDD	evasion	black box	DNN, SVM, DT, LR, RF, LDA, ensemble model	FGSM, PGD	Ensemble model, Adversarial training
[60]	2020	Traditional	CTU-13	evasion	white box	RF	custom attack	Defensive distillation with RF
[61]	2019	Traditional	UNSW- NB15, CIC-IDS-2017	Poisoning	black box	MLP, RF	custom	pruning, fine-tuning
[62]	2021	Traditional	CICIDS2017	evasion	white box	GNN, MLP, RF, Ada-boost, ID3	custom attack	Graph Neural Network
[42]	2019	Traditional	CTU-13 dataset	evasion, poisoning	black box	RF, MLP, KNN	custom attack	Adversarial retraining feature removal against evasion Data transformation

5   Discussion

In the previous sessions, we explored several works that studied the adversarial machine learning in NIDS and their defenses. We can notice a yearly increase of papers, that demonstrate a growing interest on the impact of adversarial machine learning in network intrusion detection. Based on the surveyed studies, some important observations can be drawn:

– The majority of the papers fall into a white box attack assuming the adversary has full capability and knowledge. In intrusion detection domain this assumption is not realistic. It is unlikely that an adversary get power on the model internal configuration. However, white box attack can be useful to improve the NIDS model robustness from the algorithm designer or defender's point of view.

– Very few papers have addressed the constraint in network traffic. Contrary to image classification and object recognition which belong to unconstrained domain, network security application belongs to constrained domain [9,32]. The adversarial situation in network traffic is therefore quite different due to the three characteristics that we might have in the data: (1) we can have in a single feature different value (binary, categorical, continuous). (2) features in a dataset can be correlated. (3) some feature are key features and cannot be controlled by adversaries, in other word their modification might lead to a lost of critical information and therefore weaken the attack. However due to the constrained domain some feature modification might break the functionality of the network traffic. Therefore adversarial machine learning that perform well in other applications have limited success in network [9,21]. More research is needed in this area to understand the feasability of these attacks.

- There are not many studies on the defenses technique in NIDS. Most of studies propose an adversarial training, however adversarial training has certain limitation. They cannot detect attacks that differ from the ones in the training dataset.
- Most of the studies focused on traditional networks. Fewer investigated these attack in IoT networks. More research is needed in IoT area. They are emerging in various contexts (e.g. federated learning), and need protection against adversaries.

6   Conclusion

Adversarial machine learning is a challenging and growing research area. Several approaches in NIDS has been presented recently. This confirm that despite the high performance of ML and DL applied in NIDSs, they are vulnerable to adversarial perturbation. This survey presents a comprehensive view of the different methodology of adversarial attacks applied against ML-based NIDS. It also discusses the different defense techniques proposed (summarized in Table 2). Furthermore, this survey addresses the limitations of the reviewed literature and outlines some directions for future work.

Acknowledgments. This research is supported by the Ministry of Education, Culture, Sports, Science and Technology (MEXT). This research is also supported by JSPS KAKENHI Grant Number 21K11888 and Hitachi Systems, Ltd. The last author, Kouichi SAKURAI, is grateful to The Telecommunications Advancement Foundation (TAF) for their academic support on this research.

References

1. Thakkar, A., Lohiya, R.: A review of the advancement in intrusion detection datasets. Procedia Comput. Sci. **167**, 636–645 (2020)
2. Lazarevic, A., Kumar, V., Srivastava, J.: Intrusion detection: a survey. In: Kumar, V., Srivastava, J., Lazarevic, A. (eds) Managing Cyber Threats. Massive Computing, vol. 5, pp. 19–78. Springer, Boston (2005). https://doi.org/10.1007/0-387-24230-9_2
3. Hindy, H., et al.: A taxonomy of network threats and the effect of current datasets on intrusion detection systems. IEEE Access **8**, 104650–104675 (2020)
4. Ahmad, Z., Shahid Khan, A., Wai Shiang, C., Abdullah, J., Ahmad, F.: Network intrusion detection system: a systematic study of machine learning and deep learning approaches. Trans. Emerg. Telecommun. Technol. **32**(1), e4150 (2021)
5. Goodfellow, I.J., Shlens, J., Szegedy, C.: Explaining and harnessing adversarial examples. arXiv preprint arXiv:1412.6572 (2014)

6. Huang, L., Joseph, A.D., Nelson, B., Rubinstein, B.I., Tygar, J.D.: Adversarial machine learning. In: Proceedings of the 4th ACM Workshop on Security and Artificial Intelligence, pp. 43–58 (2011)

7. Goodfellow, I., et al.: Generative adversarial nets. In: Proceedings of the 27th International Conference on Neural Information Processing Systems, vol. 2, pp. 2672–2680 (NIPS 2014). MIT Press, Cambridge (2014)

8. Szegedy, C., et al.: Intriguing properties of neural networks. arXiv preprint arXiv:1312.6199 (2014)

9. Alhajjar, E., Maxwell, P., Bastian, N.: Adversarial machine learning in network intrusion detection systems. Expert Syst. Appl. **186**, 115782 (2021)

10. Liu, Q., Li, P., Zhao, W., Cai, W., Yu, S., Leung, V.C.: A survey on security threats and defensive techniques of machine learning: a data driven view. IEEE Access **6**, 12103–12117 (2018)

11. Moisejevs, I.: Adversarial attacks and defenses in intrusion detection systems: a survey. Int. J. Artif. Intell. Expert Syst. **8**(3), 44–62 (2019)

12. Martins, N., Cruz, J.M., Cruz, T., Abreu, P.H.: Adversarial machine learning applied to intrusion and malware scenarios: a systematic review. IEEE Access **8**, 35403–35419 (2020)

13. Carlini, N.: A complete list of all (arXiv) adversarial example papers. https://nicholas.carlini.com/writing/2019/all-adversarial-example-papers.html. Accessed 30 Oct 2021

14. Liu, H., Lang, B.: Machine learning and deep learning methods for intrusion detection systems: a survey. Appl. Sci. **9**(20), 4396 (2019)

15. Biggio, B., Fumera, G., Roli, F.: Security evaluation of pattern classifiers under attack. IEEE Trans. Knowl. Data Eng. **26**(4), 984–996 (2013)

16. Huang, W., Peng, X., Shi, Z., Ma, Y.: Adversarial attack against LSTM-based DDoS intrusion detection system. In: 2020 IEEE 32nd International Conference on Tools with Artificial Intelligence (ICTAI), pp. 686–693. IEEE (2020)

17. Abou Khamis, R., Matrawy, A.: Evaluation of adversarial training on different types of neural networks in deep learning-based IDSs. In: 2020 International Symposium on Networks, Computers and Communications (ISNCC), pp. 1–6. IEEE (2020)

18. Pacheco, Y., Sun, W.: Adversarial machine learning: a comparative study on contemporary intrusion detection datasets. In: ICISSP, pp. 160–171 (2021)

19. Papernot, N., McDaniel, P., Goodfellow, I.: Transferability in machine learning: from phenomena to black-box attacks using adversarial samples. arXiv preprint arXiv:1605.07277 (2016)

20. Wang, Z.: Deep learning-based intrusion detection with adversaries. IEEE Access **6**, 38367–38384 (2018)

21. Qiu, H., Dong, T., Zhang, T., Lu, J., Memmi, G., Qiu, M.: Adversarial attacks against network intrusion detection in IoT systems. IEEE Internet Things J. **8**(13), 10327–10335 (2020)

22. Simonyan, K., Vedaldi, A., Zisserman, A.: Deep inside convolutional networks: visualising image classification models and saliency maps. arXiv preprint arXiv:1312.6034 (2013)

23. Berman, D.S., Buczak, A.L., Chavis, J.S., Corbett, C.L.: A survey of deep learning methods for cyber security. Information **10**(4), 122 (2019)

24. Buczak, A.L., Guven, E.: A survey of data mining and machine learning methods for cyber security intrusion detection. IEEE Commun. Surv. Tutor. **18**, 1153–1176 (2016)

25. Biggio, B., Roli, F.: Wild patterns: ten years after the rise of adversarial machine learning. Pattern Recogn. **84**, 317–331 (2018)
26. Nguyen, A., Yosinski, J., Clune, J.: Deep neural networks are easily fooled: high confidence predictions for unrecognizable images. In: Proceedings of the IEEE Conference on Computer Vision and Pattern Recognition, pp. 427–436 (2015)
27. Moosavi-Dezfooli, S.M., Fawzi, A., Frossard, P.: DeepFool: a simple and accurate method to fool deep neural networks. In: Proceedings of the IEEE Conference on Computer Vision and Pattern Recognition, pp. 2574–2582 (2016)
28. Muñoz-González, L., et al.: Towards poisoning of deep learning algorithms with back-gradient optimization. In: Proceedings of the 10th ACM Workshop on Artificial Intelligence and Security, pp. 27–38 (2017)
29. Tabassi, E., Burns, K.J., Hadjimichael, M., Molina-Markham, A.D., Sexton, J.T.: A taxonomy and terminology of adversarial machine learning. In: NIST IR, pp. 1–29 (2019)
30. Biggio, B., et al.: Evasion attacks against machine learning at test time. In: Blockeel, H., Kersting, K., Nijssen, S., Železný, F. (eds.) ECML PKDD 2013. LNCS (LNAI), vol. 8190, pp. 387–402. Springer, Heidelberg (2013). https://doi.org/10.1007/978-3-642-40994-3_25
31. Piplai, A., Chukkapalli, S.S.L., Joshi, A.: NAttack! adversarial attacks to bypass a GAN based classifier trained to detect Network intrusion. In: 2020 IEEE 6th Intl Conference on Big Data Security on Cloud (BigDataSecurity), IEEE Intl Conference on High Performance and Smart Computing (HPSC) and IEEE Intl Conference on Intelligent Data and Security (IDS), pp. 49–54. IEEE (2020)
32. Guo, S., et al.: A black-box attack method against machine-learning-based anomaly network flow detection models. Secur. Commun. Netw. **2021**, 1–13 (2021)
33. Papadopoulos, P., Thornewill von Essen, O., Pitropakis, N., Chrysoulas, C., Mylonas, A., Buchanan, W.J.: Launching adversarial attacks against network intrusion detection systems for IoT. J. Cybersecur. Priv. **1**(2), 252–273 (2021)
34. Peng, X., Huang, W., Shi, Z.: Adversarial attack against DoS intrusion detection: an improved boundary-based method. In: 2019 IEEE 31st International Conference on Tools with Artificial Intelligence (ICTAI), pp. 1288–1295. IEEE (2019)
35. Papernot, N., McDaniel, P., Jha, S., Fredrikson, M., Celik, Z.B., Swami, A.: The limitations of deep learning in adversarial settings. In: 2016 IEEE European Symposium on Security And Privacy (EuroS&P), pp. 372–387. IEEE (2016)
36. Zhang, S., Xie, X., Xu, Y.: A brute-force black-box method to attack machine learning-based systems in cybersecurity. IEEE Access **8**, 128250–128263 (2020)
37. Ali, M., Hu, Y.F., Luong, D.K., Oguntala, G., Li, J.P., Abdo, K.: Adversarial attacks on AI based intrusion detection system for heterogeneous wireless communications networks. In: 2020 AIAA/IEEE 39th Digital Avionics Systems Conference (DASC), pp. 1–6. IEEE (2020)
38. Debicha, I., Debatty, T., Dricot, J.M., Mees, W.: Adversarial training for deep learning-based intrusion detection systems. arXiv preprint arXiv:2104.09852 (2021)
39. Apruzzese, G., Colajanni, M., Ferretti, L., Marchetti, M.: Addressing adversarial attacks against security systems based on machine learning. In: 2019 11th International Conference on Cyber Conflict (CyCon), vol. 900, pp. 1–18. IEEE (2019)
40. Rigaki, M.: Adversarial deep learning against intrusion detection classifiers (2017)
41. Shu, D., Leslie, N.O., Kamhoua, C.A., Tucker, C.S.: Generative adversarial attacks against intrusion detection systems using active learning. In: Proceedings of the 2nd ACM Workshop on Wireless Security and Machine Learning, pp. 1–6 (2020)

42. Fladby, T., Haugerud, H., Nichele, S., Begnum, K., Yazidi, A.: Evading a machine learning-based intrusion detection system through adversarial perturbations. In: Proceedings of the International Conference on Research in Adaptive and Convergent Systems, pp. 161–166 (2020)
43. Ilyas, A., Engstrom, L., Athalye, A., Lin, J.: Black-box adversarial attacks with limited queries and information. In: International Conference on Machine Learning, pp. 2137–2146. PMLR (2018)
44. Schott, L., Rauber, J., Bethge, M., Brendel, W.: Towards the first adversarially robust neural network model on MNIST. arXiv preprint arXiv:1805.09190 (2018)
45. Brendel, W., Rauber, J., Bethge, M.: Decision-based adversarial attacks: reliable attacks against black-box machine learning models. arXiv preprint arXiv:1712.04248 (2017)
46. Liu, S., Sun, J., Li, J.: Query-efficient hard-label black-box attacks using biased sampling. In: 2020 Chinese Automation Congress (CAC), pp. 3872–3877. IEEE (2020)
47. Chen, J., Jordan, M.I.: HopSkipJumpAttack: a query-efficient decision-based attack. IEEE Secur. Priv. **2020**, 1277–1294 (2020)
48. Peng, Y., Su, J., Shi, X., Zhao, B.: Evaluating deep learning based network intrusion detection system in adversarial environment. In: 2019 IEEE 9th International Conference on Electronics Information and Emergency Communication (ICEIEC), pp. 61–66. IEEE (2019)
49. Ibitoye, O., Shafiq, O., Matrawy, A.: Analyzing adversarial attacks against deep learning for intrusion detection in IoT networks. In: 2019 IEEE Global Communications Conference (GLOBECOM), pp. 1–6. IEEE (2019)
50. Mohammadian, H., Lashkari, A.H., Ghorbani, A.A.: Evaluating deep learning-based NIDS in adversarial settings. In: ICISSP, pp. 435–444 (2022)
51. Zolbayar, B.E., et al.: Generating practical adversarial network traffic flows using NIDSGAN. arXiv preprint arXiv:2203.06694 (2022)
52. Vinayakumar, R., et al.: Deep learning approach for intelligent intrusion detection system. IEEE Access **7**, 41525–41550 (2019)
53. Gao, M., Ma, L., Liu, H., Zhang, Z., Ning, Z., Xu, J.: Malicious network traffic detection based on deep neural networks and association analysis. Sensors **20**(5), 1452 (2020)
54. Kuppa, A., Grzonkowski, S., Asghar, M.R., Le-Khac, N.A.: Black box attacks on deep anomaly detectors. In: Proceedings of the 14th International Conference on Availability, Reliability and Security, pp. 1–10 (2019)
55. Usama, M., Asim, M., Latif, S., Qadir, J.: Generative adversarial networks for launching and thwarting adversarial attacks on network intrusion detection systems. In: 2019 15th International Wireless Communications & Mobile Computing Conference (IWCMC), pp. 78–83. IEEE (2019)
56. Debicha, I., Debatty, T., Dricot, J.-M., Mees, W., Kenaza, T.: Detect & reject for transferability of black-box adversarial attacks against network intrusion detection systems. In: Abdullah, N., Manickam, S., Anbar, M. (eds.) ACeS 2021. CCIS, vol. 1487, pp. 329–339. Springer, Singapore (2021). https://doi.org/10.1007/978-981-16-8059-5_20
57. Apruzzese, G., Andreolini, M., Colajanni, M., Marchetti, M.: Hardening random forest cyber detectors against adversarial attacks. IEEE Trans. Emerg. Top. Comput. Intell. **4**(4), 427–439 (2020)

58. Bachl, M., Hartl, A., Fabini, J., Zseby, T.: Walling up backdoors in intrusion detection systems. In: Proceedings of the 3rd ACM CoNEXT Workshop on Big Data, Machine Learning and Artificial Intelligence for Data Communication Networks, pp. 8–13 (2019)
59. Pujol-Perich, D., Suárez-Varela, J., Cabellos-Aparicio, A., Barlet-Ros, P.: Unveiling the potential of graph neural networks for robust intrusion detection. ACM SIGMETRICS Perform. Eval. Rev. **49**(4), 111–117 (2022)
60. Zhang, C., Costa-Pérez, X., Patras, P.: Adversarial attacks against deep learning-based network intrusion detection systems and defense mechanisms. IEEE/ACM Trans. Netw. **30**, 1294–1311 (2022)
61. Nguyen, T.D., Rieger, P., Miettinen, M., Sadeghi, A.R.: Poisoning attacks on federated learning-based IoT intrusion detection system. In: Proc. Workshop Decentralized IoT Syst. Secur. (DISS), pp. 1–7 (2020)

Posters

POSTER: Zero-Touch Provisioned Device Lifecycle and Its Security in IoT

Danu Dwi Sanjoyo[1]([⊠]) and Masahiro Mambo[2]

[1] Graduate School of Natural Science and Technology, Kanazawa University,
Kanazawa, Japan
sanjoyodd@stu.kanazawa-u.ac.jp
[2] Institute of Science and Engineering, Kanazawa University, Kanazawa, Japan
mambo@ec.t.kanazawa-u.ac.jp

Abstract. Due to the rapid deployment of zero-touch provisioned devices, the Internet of Things (IoT) has become a complex network. The increased number of connected devices improves network accessibility, but it also results in an expanded attack surface. The security of the device's lifecycle needs careful attention. We discuss a lifecycle of zero-touch provisioned devices and its security in the IoT networks. The adoption of zero-touch provisioned devices stimulates the evolution of new types of security attacks. Based on the typical security properties, we consider the best practice to ensure the security of a zero-touch provisioned device's lifecycle. Ensuring identification management is one of the crucial aspects of achieving security properties. It deals with the identity construction of each device, authenticating the authorized devices, and detecting malicious activities. We confirm that our security design of zero-touch provisioned device lifecycle can satisfy the fundamental security properties.

Keywords: Internet of Things · Zero-touch provisioning · Device's lifecycle security · Mutual authentication · Impersonation attack

1 Introduction

The emergence of the zero-touch operation on the Internet of Things (IoT) service society changes the threat approach to device lifecycle. A device can automatically detect, connect to, and gather service from an online provider by employing zero-touch provisioning. The device must securely provide safe service and act appropriately since established at a designated location. When the device is close to the end of the operation, the precise handling should assure that no other entity will illegally extend the activity of the obsolete devices. Practically, no one is required to physically contact the device since departing the manufacturer along the zero-touch device lifecycle. In terms of service provisioning, the zero-touch operation offers effortless, costless, and time-saving.

On the other hand, the security of the zero-touch-based device lifecycle in the IoT network needs extra attention. Distinguishing the threat of a zero-touch

© The Author(s), under exclusive license to Springer Nature Singapore Pte Ltd. 2022
C. Su and K. Sakurai (Eds.): SciSec 2022 Workshops, CCIS 1680, pp. 215–218, 2022.
https://doi.org/10.1007/978-981-19-7769-5

provisioned device in IoT is essential before constructing the device's lifecycle security. A zero-touch-based device has a distinct typical feature to an attended IoT device. Since the term zero-touch requires no physical contact after leaving the manufacturer, confidential data and arbitrary configuration should occur online. Therefore, the device must own the necessary identity-based security credentials within assembling by the manufacturer.

Investigating the security of the device lifecycle should consider the IoT lifecycle stages. Heer et al. [1] divided the IoT device lifecycle into bootstrapping, operational, and maintenance and re-bootstrapping. The re-bootstrapping phase indicates that the authors prepared the device re-ownership mechanism. While S. Wellsandt [2] classified the lifecycle into three stages: Beginning of Life (BoL), Middle of Life (MoL), and End of Life (EoL). N. Yousefnezhad et al. [3] used the IoT product lifecycle of BoL, MoL, and EoL to investigate the attack surfaces and security solutions. For a zero-touch provisioned device, it is necessary to classify the lifecycle based on the location of its presence to investigate the possible threats.

We examine to combine the approaches for the device lifecycle analysis with the emerging zero-touch provisioning techniques and propose a future research direction for securing a zero-touch provisioned device lifecycle in the IoT network. We assume that external adversaries can take over the network by eavesdropping, modifying, and inserting fraudulent messages aiming to steal the secrets or get connection privilege. In the first part of the Discussion section, we present the zero-touch provisioned device lifecycle by classifying the zero-touch device lifecycle into three stages: in-manufacturing, in-service, and in-distribution and the possible threats of each stage. In the second part, we point out which fundamental security properties become more critical in the zero-touch provisioned device lifecycle.

2   Related Work

Several works, including proposed solutions and surveys, exist to strengthen the security of the device lifecycle in IoT networks. S. Boire et al. [4] proposed an extended design of Extensible Authentication Protocol (EAP) that combines the network connectivity, identity and certificate provisioning, and application-layer connectivity to authenticate, provision, and configure new devices. This protocol relies on authentication, integrity, and confidentiality on IoT device post-installation certificates. Likewise, Z. He et al. [5] designed an enrollment protocol to automatically certify the digital identity of a resource-constrain device at the beginning of deployment. By employing trusted CA(s), J. Hoglund et al. [6] developed PKI-based automated certificate enrollment for highly constrained devices before deployment. However, this scheme lacks security against physical access to the device and is vulnerable to compromised attacks. S. Maksuti et al. [7] presented an automated and secure onboarding with three credential options: a local cloud certificate, manufacturer certificate, or pre-shared key. This protocol provides mutual authentication for diverse IoT devices by relying on the chain of trust model between the end node and the cloud server. However, this proposal lacks in discussing device lifecycle and internet-based connection security. On the contrary, A. Pandey et al. [8] proposed an "AutoAdd" IoT secure bootstrapping mechanism as a commissioning step in the device lifecycle by involving the device buyer as a digital certificate holder and becomes the root of the trust anchor of the device certificate. However, the authors missed the physical attack countermeasure and the buyer's information protection. M. Liyanage et al. [9] discussed the possible threats and the device lifecycle on Zero-touch networks and Service Management (ZSM) separately. Even though N. Yousefnezhad et al. [3] presented the potential security issues and solutions based on the IoT product lifecycle, the utilization of zero-touch provisioned devices is absent in this survey. Many proposed solutions exist to overcome the security problems in IoT networks. However, none of those papers explicitly discusses the security aspects corresponding to the zero-touch device lifecycle.

3   Discussion

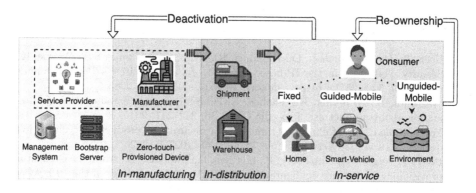

Fig. 1. Zero-touch provisioned device lifecycle

The zero-touch provisioned device lifecycle consists of the in-manufacturing, in-distribution, and in-service stages. Figure 1 illustrates the zero-touch provisioned device lifecycle. After leaving the manufacturer, it moves to the consumer's designated location via direct shipment or convenient warehouses. The consumer can settle the IoT device at a fixed place (e.g., home, office, roadside), guided-mobile site (e.g., vehicle, drone), or unguided-mobile (e.g., sea, river, wild animal). The service provider arranges the application-related load through its bootstrap server and management system. A new consumer can take over the IoT device by performing a re-ownership mechanism. When finished exploiting the device, it is crucial to complete deactivation.

Each stage of the zero-touch device lifecycle is at risk of a different attack. In the in-manufacturing phase, adversaries may intrude by stealing the secret information and replacing the credentials with forgery. In the in-service step, adversaries may hack the working device to disclose confidential information or launch an active attack to seize the connection privilege. While in the in-distribution phase, adversaries may physically grab the device to obtain sensitive information or inject malware inside the device.

Authentication, integrity, non-repudiation, confidentiality, and access control are the fundamental properties in the zero-touch provisioned device's lifecycle. The client device and server should have mutual authentication in each communication. Adversaries may try to get the secret by performing an impersonation attack during the authentication process. Regarding data integrity, verifying the owner of each exchanged information among parties is essential. Tampering attack is dangerous to data integrity due to the initiation of the impersonation. Therefore, non-repudiation property is critical to identify the maliciousness in the network. Establishing an objective logging or auditing protocol can avoid the repudiation threat. In terms of privacy preservation, there is no doubt that confidential information must be encrypted. However, the security designer should provide an efficient and secure key distribution. Finally, proper access control on the zero-touch device can prevent resources and data exploitation attacks.

References

1. Heer, T., Garcia-Morchon, O., Hummen, R., Keoh, S.L., Kumar, S.S., Wehrle, K.: Security challenges in the IP-based internet of things. Wireless Pers. Commun. **61**(3), 527–542 (2011). https://doi.org/10.1007/s11277-011-0385-5
2. Wellsandt, S., Hribernik, K., Thoben, K.-D.: Sources and characteristics of information about product use. Procedia CIRP **36**, 242–247 (2015)
3. Yousefnezhad, N., Malhi, A., Främling, K.: Security in product lifecycle of IoT devices: a survey. J. Netw. Comput. Appl. **171**, 102779 (2020)
4. Boire, S., Akgün, T., Ginzboorg, P., Laitinen, P., Tamrakar, S., Aura, T.: Credential provisioning and device configuration with EAP. In: Proceedings of the 19th ACM International Symposium on Mobility Management and Wireless Access, pp. 87–96 (2021)
5. He, Z., Furuhed, M., Raza, S.: Indraj: digital certificate enrollment for battery-powered wireless devices. In: Proceedings of the 12th Conference on Security and Privacy in Wireless and Mobile Networks, pp. 117–127 (2019)
6. Höglund, J., Lindemer, S., Furuhed, M., Raza, S.: PKi4iot: towards public key infrastructure for the internet of things. Comput. Secur. **89**, 101658 (2020)
7. Maksuti, S., et al.: Automated and secure onboarding for system of systems. IEEE Access **9**, 111095–111113 (2021)
8. Pandey, A.K., Rajendran, B., Roshni, V.: AutoAdd: automated bootstrapping of an IoT device on a network. SN Comput. Sci. **1**(1), 1–5 (2020)
9. Liyanage, M., et al.: A survey on zero touch network and service (ZSM) management for 5G and beyond networks. J. Network Comput. Appl. 103362 (2022)

POSTER: Separation of Activation Code Delivery on V2X Pseudonym Certificate Revocation

Jan Wantoro[1]([✉]) and Masahiro Mambo[2]

[1] Division of Electrical Engineering and Computer Science, Graduate School of Natural Science and Technology, Kanazawa University, Ishikawa 920-1192, Japan
jan@ums.ac.id, jan@stu.kanazawa-u.ac.jp
[2] Institute of Science and Engineering, Kanazawa University, Ishikawa 920-1192, Japan
mambo@ec.t.kanazawa-u.ac.jp

Abstract. The automotive industry constantly tries to improve driving safety and efficiency by applying various cutting-edge technologies, one of which is vehicle to everything (V2X) technology. However, V2X technology still leaves problems concerning communication security between vehicles. For example short-term pseudonym certificates of V2X retains a revocation problem arised from public key infrastructure (PKI), which is not easy to manage. Many studies are trying to solve it, and one of the most promising techniques is activation code for pseudonym certificate (ACPC). The ACPC implements an activation code to prevent revoked vehicles from using their pseudonym certificate. Even so, the delivery cost of ACPC activation codes is higher than the security credential management system (SCMS) certificate revocation lists (CRL) for a low number of revoked vehicles. We propose to divide activation codes of ACPC into different groups of delivery time by introducing an activation period offset. Our method achieves a smaller broadcast size of activation codes for each delivery time.

Keywords: V2X · Certificate Revocation · Pseudonym Certificate

1 Introduction

The application of V2X technology allows vehicles to communicate with other vehicles or roadside devices in real-time. They communicate wirelessly, generally based on dedicated short range communications (DSRC) and cellular technology (4G or 5G). Vehicles send messages to other vehicles about their position, direction, speed, and other relevant information so that each vehicle understands the situation of other vehicles around it. The message received by the vehicle must be ascertained for authenticity, lest someone sends a fake message for his benefit and interferes with the driving safety application. The standards organizations in Europe and the US use digital certificates to maintain message security of V2X.

© The Author(s), under exclusive license to Springer Nature Singapore Pte Ltd. 2022
C. Su and K. Sakurai (Eds.): SciSec 2022 Workshops, CCIS 1680, pp. 219–222, 2022.
https://doi.org/10.1007/978-981-19-7769-5

To manage digital certificates of the V2X, they use PKI with some adaptation mainly to meet four privacy key attributes: anonymity, pseudonymity, unlinkability, and unobservability [2]. In both standards car's pseudonym certificates are used interchangeably over a short period. So that it is hard to trace the vehicle's path using the pseudonym certificates.

The different pseudonym certificates over this short range cause some side effects. In addition to the increasingly complex structure of the PKI, the pseudonym certificate revocation becomes challenging to handle. Misbehaving vehicles must be removed from the V2X system to avoid damage and road accidents. For example, vehicles that spread inappropriate messages cause a wrong decision. The certificate authority must revoke such a vehicle's certificate so that other vehicles are ignoring the messages spread by misbehaving vehicles.

Revoking the pseudonym certificate on a misbehaving vehicle is generally done using CRL. After the certificate authority gets information about the misbehaving vehicle, it identify the misbehaving vehicle. Then it inserts the certificate identity in the CRL to known by the end entities. However, there were many obstacles to delivering CRL to the vehicle timely, mainly due to the limited resources and dynamic network characteristics of V2X. One promising way to solve this certificate revocation problem is to apply the certificate activation techniques such as in ACPC [4] and issue first activate later (IFAL) [5].

Certificate activation is a technique in which encrypted certificates assigned to each period are given to the vehicle during registration. Then the vehicle needs a key/code of each period to decrypt/activate the certificate to use it. The certificate authority periodically sends the activation codes to the unrevoked vehicles, while not to revoked vehicles. As a result, the revoked vehicles can no longer use their certificates in the next period. This certificate activation technique has several advantages, including lower costs on network resources and the message verification process compared to standard CRLs.

The certificate activation strategy still needs an improvement in the size of the activation codes when the number of revoked vehicles is small. That is, the size of the delivered activation codes is larger than the size of the CRL for a small number of revoked vehicles. Another problem is that all unrevoked vehicles must receive activation codes in the same period. It causes an additional network burden due to repeated broadcasts or simultaneous requests of the activation codes.

2 Contributions

We should fine out a new strategy for delivering activation certificates to solve the problems. This study evaluates the simultaneous delivery of activation codes for unrevoked vehicles in V2X communication. To reduce the size of sending activation codes, we divide the activation codes into several groups. Each group is sent at different periods to spare the network load. To do so, we introduce an activation period offset to facilitate the shift of the certificate activation period as shown in Fig. 1. Even if the entire vehicle has an activation code from the same tree root, vehicles have different certificate activation periods.

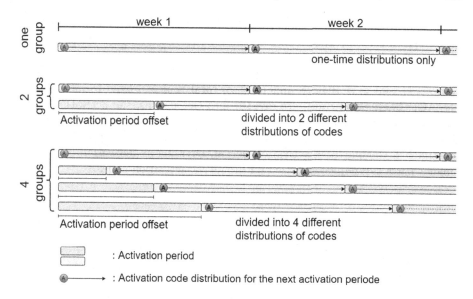

Fig. 1. Activation code delivery with different activation period offset

3   Related Work

The delivery technique of activation codes has not yet been discussed in previous studies. The IFAL does not use a binary tree, so the delivery of the activation codes depends on the policy file created at the beginning of registration. Suppose that the policy file is applied differently to the group of vehicles. The activation codes can be sent at different times. However, the authors show a scenario of simultaneously broadcasting to all unrevoked vehicles, causing a gigabyte of delivery activation codes.

The ACPC has a better privacy protection than the IFAL. Like binary hash tree based certificate access management (BCAM) [3], ACPC broadcasts the activation codes to all unrevoked vehicles. However, it must send the activation codes simultaneously for all vehicles. Further research in uACPC has tried to exploit the ACPC property which allows the vehicle to fetch a sufficiently small activation codes via a unicast mechanism [1]. However, it also lacks in a mechanism to split the activation codes distribution at different times.

4   Preliminary Results

According to the recommendation from SCMS, the validity of pseudonym certificates is one week. Suppose the activation codes are distributed within one week before the certificate starts to be used. In that case, the ACPC must broadcast the activation codes once a week to unrevoked vehicles. Meanwhile, our scheme can arrange two or more different distributions time within that period.

The provisional results show that dividing the activation codes at different times allows the activation codes broadcast size to be smaller than the original ACPC. The original ACPC also sends all activation codes once a week. In Fig. 2, assume that total vehicle in the system is 1,048,576 unit, and number of unrevoked vehicle is 104,858 unit (10% of total vehicles) fixed to all period. If the ACPC activation codes are divided into two groups, the activation code's total size is half the original one because the delivery is done on two different days. That way, the network load at the delivery time is divided into two different times in the one-week activation period. Dividing an activation period into smaller parts can reduce the size of a broadcast activation codes.

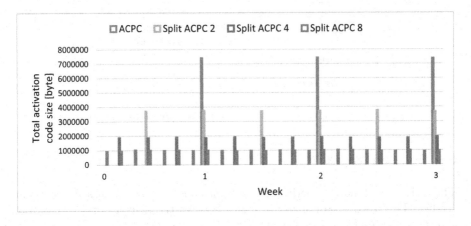

Fig. 2. Activation code distribution size

References

1. Cunha, H., Luther, T., Ricardini, J., Ogawa, H., Simplicio, M., Patil, H.K.: uACPC: client-initiated privacy-preserving activation codes for pseudonym certificates model. SAE Int. J. Transp. Cybersecurity Priv. **3**(11–03-01-0004), 57–77 (2020)
2. ETSI, T.: 102 941 intelligent transport systems (its); security; trust and privacy management v1.4.1. Technical Specification (2021)
3. Kumar, V., Petit, J., Whyte, W.: Binary hash tree based certificate access management for connected vehicles. In: Proceedings of the 10th ACM Conference on Security and Privacy in Wireless and Mobile Networks, pp. 145–155 (2017)
4. Simplicio, M.A., Jr., Cominetti, E.L., Patil, H.K., Ricardini, J.E., Silva, M.V.M.: ACPC: efficient revocation of pseudonym certificates using activation codes. Ad Hoc Netw. **90**, 101708 (2019)
5. Verheul, E., Hicks, C., Garcia, F.D.: IFAL: issue first activate later certificates for V2X. In: 2019 IEEE European Symposium on Security and Privacy (EuroS&P), pp. 279–293. IEEE (2019)

POSTER: Privacy-preserving Federated Active Learning

Hendra Kurniawan[1(✉)] and Masahiro Mambo[2]

[1] Graduate School of Natural Science and Technology, Kanazawa University,
Kanazawa, Japan
hendra@umrah.ac.id
[2] Institute of Science and Engineering, Kanazawa University, Kanazawa, Japan
mambo@ec.t.kanazawa-u.ac.jp

Abstract. Active learning is a technique for investigating a way to maximize performance with minimal labeling effort and let the machine automatically and adaptively selects the most informative data for labeling. Since the labels on records may contain sensitive information, a privacy-preserving active learning scheme was proposed by applying differential privacy. Another type of privacy-preserving machine learning as federated learning should be considered, which is a distributed machine learning framework providing the protection of client data. We propose an encryption-based Federated Learning approach to protect privacy in Active Learning. The experimental result shows a homomorphic encryption-based federated learning scheme can preserve privacy in active learning while keeping accuracy.

Keywords: Privacy-preserving · Federated learning · Active learning

1 Introduction

The rapid expansion of big data has propelled the development of machine learning. This tendency has presented conventional machine learning with substantial hurdles. Because large data are typically held on distributed devices by different firms, it is becoming increasingly difficult to learn a global model while resolving its associated privacy problems.

Obtaining sufficient labeled data for modeling purposes is one of the most challenging aspects of a wide variety of learning tasks since acquiring labeled data is typically costly and requires human effort [1]. In many fields, there is an abundance of unlabeled data, and labels can be attached to such data which requires an expensive cost by the expert during the labeling process. It is possible to obtain labels in these instances, but it will be prohibitively expensive for the consumer. As far as labels are concerned, it's crucial to note that not all records are created equal.

Active learning is a technique for investigating a way to maximize performance with minimal labeling effort. In particular, it seeks to minimize labeling

C. Su and K. Sakurai (Eds.): SciSec 2022 Workshops, CCIS 1680, pp. 223–226, 2022.
https://doi.org/10.1007/978-981-19-7769-5

costs without sacrificing performance by selecting the most informative samples from an unlabeled dataset and submitting them to an oracle, e.g., a human annotator for labeling [1].

In many cases, however, the labels on records may contain sensitive information and accessing them may incur a high query cost, e.g., obtaining permission from the relevant entity. Since traditional methods of active learning are failing to keep up with the times, privacy-preserving active learning has been hailed as a promising new technique [3].

This paper studies and analyze the privacy-preserving of active learning. We present an encryption-based federated learning method for active learning. To the best of our knowledge, this is the first study to investigate privacy preservation in machine learning from this perspective. In summary, the main contributions of this paper are as follows:

1. A homomorphic encryption-based federated learning scheme is proposed to protect the confidentiality of the sensitive data.
2. A multi-party computation protocol is proposed to protect the machine learning models from the adversaries.

2   Related Work

A study in privacy-preserving active learning has been proposed by feyisetan et al. [3]. They describe a method for implementing active learning with quantitative assurances that protects privacy. The authors suggested a framework for active learning that ensures the confidentiality of queries made to an external oracle. They use random probabilistic techniques to estimate if a query meets k-anonymity requirements. Then after a query is assumed to satisfy k-anonymity, only one of k queries is forwarded to n external annotators to prevent the accumulation of privacy losses. In addition, a differential privacy technique is used in the active learning environment to pick a subset of training samples to send for annotation.

In the scope of our federated learning scheme, a server holds labeled data and the client has a huge amount of unlabeled data to performs active learning queries. To prevent privacy leakages no client data is sent to the server for annotation.

3   Proposed Method and Preliminary Result

The proposed privacy-preserving federated active learning has two phases:

1. Server executes model training based on labeled data and model update using client encrypted model.
2. Client performs active learning queries to predict unlabeled instance using decrypted server model.

At server, a model from labeled data training will be encrypted using a public key ecryption function Enc_{pub_key} then the encrypted model will be shared to the client. Client will decrypt the server model by using Dec_{priv_key} and predict unlabeled instances for annotation, then run the active learning query for a certain stop criteria. If the query meets the stop criteria, client will finalize the model. The final model will be encrypted using public key ecryption function Enc_{pub_key}, then share to the server. Server will receive encrypted model from client, then server updates its model using average function of additive homomorphic encryption operation and multiplicative homomorphic encryption operation. Figure 1 shows the propose scheme of encryption-based federated active learning.

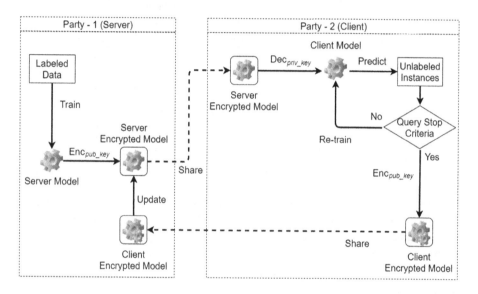

Fig. 1. Propose Scheme of Encryption-based Federated Active Learning

A Python based ModAL framework [2] is used to provide active learning strategy, and for Somewhat Homomorphic Encryption (SHE) computation we use Pyfhel libraries [5]. The library offers standard SHE operations such as encoding, key generation, encryption, decryption, addition, multiplication, and relinearization.

We implement Entropy-based sampling [6] and BALD [4] strategy for active learning. The 60,000 samples of MNIST handwritten dataset is used during simulation, and employed Multi-Layer Perceptron (MLP) neural network architecture. The dataset is divided into two parts: 10,000 samples is labeled dataset for model training in the server, and 50,000 samples used by client. Client will run 10 query rounds to predict a batch of 500 unlabeled instances and re-train the model. 1,000 samples of labeled data is used for model testing.

Table 1. Accuracy and Execution Time of Federated Active Learning. (AL: Active Learning, FL: Federated Learning, FL-Enc: FL with encrypted data)

Query Round	Entropy Sampling Accuracy		BALD Accuracy	
	AL with FL	AL with FL-Enc	AL with FL	AL with FL-Enc
Query - 1	0.7361	0.7328	0.8406	0.8364
Query - 2	0.7962	0.7934	0.8590	0.8556
Query - 3	0.8208	0.8175	0.8632	0.8598
Query - 4	0.8560	0.8521	0.8875	0.8845
Query - 5	0.8627	0.8577	0.9004	0.8965
Query - 6	0.8745	0.8704	0.9087	0.9046
Query - 7	0.8792	0.8758	0.9123	0.9093
Query - 8	0.8890	0.8857	0.9184	0.9140
Query - 9	0.8975	0.8930	0.9264	0.9220
Query - 10	0.9082	0.9033	0.9320	0.9282
Execution Time (second)	403,072	3,030,203	1,320,671	9,510,541

Table 1 shows accuracy and execution time (second) of Entropy based sampling and BALD sampling federated active learning strategy. With client using both encrypted data (AL with FL-Enc) and unencrypted data (AL with FL), the classification accuracy exceeds 80%, indicating that somewhat homomorphic encryption does not degrade model performance. On the other hand, there is significantly difference in execution time for encrypted and unencrypted data.

The benefit we get from our proposed scheme are: (1) The server can update its model based on the encrypted model of the client, (2) Ensure there is no privacy breach, the final active learning model is encrypted before being shared with the server.

References

1. Aggarwal, C.C., Philip, S.Y.: A survey of uncertain data algorithms and applications. IEEE Trans. Knowl. Data Eng. **21**(5), 609–623 (2008)
2. Danka, T., Horvath, P.: modAL: a modular active learning framework for Python. https://github.com/modAL-python/modAL. arXiv at arxiv.org/abs/1805.00979
3. Feyisetan, O., Drake, T., Balle, B., Diethe, T.: Privacy-preserving active learning on sensitive data for user intent classification. arXiv preprint arXiv:1903.11112 (2019)
4. Gal, Y., Islam, R., Ghahramani, Z.: Deep Bayesian active learning with image data. In: International Conference on Machine Learning, pp. 1183–1192. PMLR (2017)
5. Ibarrondo, A., Viand, A.: Pyfhel: python for homomorphic encryption libraries. In: Proceedings of the 9th on Workshop on Encrypted Computing and Applied Homomorphic Cryptography, pp. 11–16 (2021)
6. Wang, D., Shang, Y.: A new active labeling method for deep learning. In: 2014 International joint conference on neural networks (IJCNN), pp. 112–119. IEEE (2014)

Author Index

Printed in the United States
by Baker & Taylor Publisher Services